FUTURE IN SIGHT

FUTURE IN SIGHT

100 Trends, Implications & Predictions

THAT WILL MOST IMPACT BUSINESSES AND THE WORLD
ECONOMY INTO THE 21ST CENTURY

·

BARRY HOWARD MINKIN

LEARNING
RESOURCES
CENTRE

MACMILLAN • USA

MACMILLAN
A Simon & Schuster Macmillan Company
1633 Broadway
New York, NY 10019

Library of Congress Cataloging-in-Publication Data
Minkin, Barry Howard.
      Future In Sight: 100 trends, implications and predictions that will most impact businesses and the world economy into the 21st century / Barry Howard Minkin.
          p. cm.
      Includes index.
          ISBN 0-02-585055-5 (cloth)
1.   Business forecasting   2.   Twenty-first century—Forecasts.
3.   Economic history—1990-   I.   Title.
HD30.27.M56 1995
658.4'0355—dc20   95–18221   CIP

10   9   8   7   6   5   4   3   2   1

Printed in the United States of America

FOR MISS REBA, BRETT, MELISSA AND KIRK

and in loving memory of Isadore "Joe" Minkin and Dr. Theodore "Ted" Abe

ACKNOWLEDGMENTS

As I look up from the computer terminal and realize how quickly two years of my life have been spent writing about the future, I'm again reminded about how we must not waste the present and how important are aware and caring people to our personal lives and to the future of this planet. I want to acknowledge a few of the many caring people in my life.

Thanks first to Lou Platt, Jack Welch, Tom Peters, Ken Colmen, Roger Kilburn, Tony Finizza, Charles Sanford, Jr., Bernard Fleitman, Davis Masten, Mitch Gooze, Steven Fowkes, Richard Carlson, David Palmer, Willis Harman, Bernard Schwartz, Constance Bagley, Hewitt Crane, Vic Para, Charles Turk, Tom Mandel and Patricia Singer, who were major contributors to the trends in the book.

Special thanks to Marilyn Kaplan for her support in editing and helping me remember to think about my own future; thank you, Jenifer Leland of Stanford, for sharing your computer and personal wisdom and for your special caring; thanks to John Cardis for his editorial insights and friendship.

At the risk of sounding like an Academy Award winner let me not forget my editor, John Michel, and my agent, Susan Golomb, for their fine counsel; Dudley Andersen for providing material; and the Jackson Library at Stanford University as well as the other Bay Area libraries for their research assistance.

Finally thanks to Rina, Avril, M.L., Jan, Maureen, Steve, Carl, Judy, David, D.J., Rachael, Betti, Joel, Sheila, Victor, Zach, Marsha, Earl, Lisbeth, Blythe, Karen, Saul, Allan, Lori, Susan, Beth, Tom, Catherine; Roger, Theresa, Dennis and their great aerobic classes; and the Minkin, Weiss, Nagel, Shayne, Kaplan, Eydus and Abe families whose support and love sustain me.

CONTENTS

PREFACE

We live in the shadow of the third millennium.
Turning the corner on a new century always invites an assessment of where mankind has been and what our future will be. But balancing on the cusp of a new millennium makes this pressing focus an imperative. Naturally, we ask ourselves whether it will be a time of unprecedented disaster, remarkable fulfillment or business as usual?

Perhaps, however, a more important question is how do we look at the future? Will it be the same game with the same rules? Or the same game with new rules? Or a new game entirely. For certain, the future will involve transformation of global society at all levels. In *Future In Sight,* I sought to identify and describe which global trends will transform business as we know it, the implications of these trends and how and when the transformation will occur.

These Are Confusing Times
Indeed, the world we live in is confusing because an epic transformation of our world has already begun. By 2005, we will be in the middle of a number of transitions of which the outcomes are highly uncertain. The gap between old and young, rich and poor, north and south and other salient dichotomies will spark increased conflicts among different cultures. Political and economic restructuring will mean short-term dislocations before we can reap their promised long-term benefits. The emergence of information economies raises fundamental questions about economic activity, growth and wealth. Environmental concerns will intensify well into the next century.

How do we even know what *is* happening, much less what will happen? The "news" describes today's accelerating changes by round-the-clock firing of a barrage of random facts; people and events, catapulted into print and onto radio and television, assault us daily. Lacking a structure into which to fit this data, we experience it as random sound bites. *However, the changes we are experiencing are neither random nor independent of one another.* This important observation is the underlying theme of *Future In Sight.* Indeed, *this book intends to identify the clear patterns underneath the confusion so that we can chart a course through the future; not some distant future to be blissfully ignored but an imminent future—a future in sight.*

Only the Lead Dog Sees the Landscape—Old Eskimo Proverb

As we accelerate into the next century, sharp eyes and quick reflexes are needed to navigate the turns in the road. Bereft of a crystal ball, how are we even to look at the future? Life is complex now; it will become more complex. To contemporary eyes, how can the future be anything but a blur? But for those who know where—and how—to look, the future begins to emerge, becoming clearer every day.

My gaze is directed to the future as it has been for 30 years as a global business analyst for scores of organizations of all sizes and within most industry classifications. As the faint outline of a pencil sketch hints at the picture that will clearly emerge after the artist has added color and definition, clients such as Pepsico, Bank of America, ARCO and Mitsubishi employ me to draw outlines of what is to come from early, numerous, distant, weak and often confusing trends.

A glimpse of the future is possible if we can discern which trend lines to analze and carefully extend into the future. Of course, those who see the trends, understand the implications and can predict the direction *enjoy an important strategic advantage over others* who fail to determine the proper direction. This observation is true for businesses, individuals or governments.

The TIP Format

Just as it is important to glean the proper information, it is also important to make sense of it once in hand. Today, most of us devour an excess of information, yet we are starved for knowledge. Many executives assaulted by the media barrage insist on having key points presented in only a few pages in what's called "executive summary" format. I have chosen to use a similar format to summarize the wealth of information and insights acquired in writing this book. My approach is to summarize a major trend, highlight its implications and predict how and when the trend is likely to develop. The first letters in trends *(T)*, implications *(I)* and specific predictions *(P)* spell out the acronym *TIP.* The TIP approach is my attempt at making this book practical, clear, concise and easy to read.

I can't promise to provide the big picture in precise detail—it would take volumes—there are simply too may trends to consider. However, I believe that examining the most important global trends that will affect our lives during the first decade of the next century and considering their implications enable us to predict when and how significant changes will occur.

A Growing Need for Forecasting

As the twenty-first century looms, futurology becomes more prevalent. Businesses, individuals and government want to be ready for whatever will confront them in the years to come. They must plan, and planning is arguably more difficult in this period of great confusion than ever before. Indeed, strategic planning that exists in the predict-and-prepare mode has been under attack recently. Good planning requires accurate forecasting, and too often, the art of forecasting is left to "quants"— people who are seduced into analyzing only what they can measure or "quantify"—while ignoring the shrewd "guess" of experts in relevant fields.

Looking at the Future That's in Sight

Anticipating the longer term is especially compelling today, considering the speed at which the world is changing; but there is the future that seems just around the corner, and there is the far future. By the standards of science fiction writers, who often roam centuries ahead, the time span of this book is modest—predictions jump between now and 2030, a range of about 35 years, which is far enough away to allow trends to develop yet near enough to be useful for long-range planning.

Applying predictions to the next few decades also makes firmer forecasts possible because much of the research basic to the developments expected as we cross into the millennium is already well along. The new ceramic turbines that will power our cars and provide our electricity are being tested in laboratories today, theoretical work has been done to provide anti-aging drugs and "particle" finance is beginning to solve important and practical financial problems, ranging from limiting an airline's exposure to fuel price increases to helping a company hedge the value of a pending acquisition.

I consider 100 global trends and list hundreds of predictions that will play key parts in shaping the next decade. This "workbook" also includes my Econo-2000 forecasting model and "Demon Question" to help personalize the trends and techniques presented. For example, what products or services do you or could you develop for a growing immigrant market?

Pick those predictions that apply to you. My hope is that these predictions add up to a real strategic advantage. Even if you don't agree with all the trends and predictions, this compact book will provide some valuable TIPS about the shape of the future.

Chapter 1

FUTUROLOGY: ANOTHER OF THE WORLD'S OLDEST PROFESSIONS

•

There are two times in a man's life when he should not speculate—when he can't afford it, and when he can.

MARK TWAIN

[Our purpose is] to learn not to hide our uncertainties, but to structure them.

YEHEZKEL DROR

•

Is it really possible to predict the future?

Given past performance, why should we bother? Fortune-tellers, mystics, astrologers, psychics, priests, princes, prophets and other soothsayers have traditionally had the corner on forecasting. Even today, these seers and would-be seers have by far the greatest influence of all those who deal with the future, affecting as they do the expectations and actions of hundreds of millions of people daily. Though millions of people around the world will continue to rely on this "black art," past evidence suggests that we are not successful at predicting the future. There have been a few exceptions (Jules Verne for one, who predicted submarines and trips to the moon), but by and large, our record has been dismal. This is especially true in the business world and, in particular, in predicting which of today's technological advances will be tomorrow's commodity. For example, in 1878, the young American inventor Thomas A. Edison tried to develop an electric light. The British Parliament set up a committee to decide if the undertaking held any promise. The committee's conclusion, based on the testimony of experts, was that Edison's ideas on electric illumination were "unworthy of the attention of practical or scientific men." Later, when the telephone was patented, one prominent Englishman asked, "What is the need for the telephone when there are plenty of messenger boys in London?" A somewhat more forward-thinking American forecaster predicted that we would need one telephone in every town. And of course, there is more than one example of learned men who proved conclusively that the airplane would never fly.

Making forecasting more scientific has been going on since the end of World War II, when the atomic bomb caught most people completely unaware. To avoid such "surprises," a whole new discipline of futurism was born.

The future is the only part of our lives that we can change by what we do or don't do. If we are to grow and progess in our careers, we obviously must equip ourselves with the skills and knowledge needed to be proactive to the threats and opportunities of the future. Our very survival and well-being depend on our ability to anticipate and cope with future problems and threats, to perceive, evaluate and control the effects of our actions in order to imagine and create more desirable futures.

This chapter describes how to improve our ability to pursue these goals. First, however, let's look at how the invalidated but nevertheless accepted theories of economic history have blinded today's leaders still charting their course by inadequate measures and outdated techniques.

Keep the Con in Economics

Like the con men in Hans Christian Andersen's classic *The Emperor's New Clothes,* who sell the Emperor a suit made of invisible cloth that only the "pure of mind" can see, economists have long been selling us business forecasts based on invisible, untested and unverifiable econobabble theories. Economists love to appear on programs like *MacNeil-Lehrer* and debate ferociously over the potential impact of proposals like a hike in the discount rate by the Federal Reserve. One economist says the increase will stimulate us right back to the happiest of economic times; while the other will smirk and suggest that his adversary has no understanding of anything even remotely resembling economic forecasting.

The casual viewer might think these people have few beliefs and theories in common. Yet almost all leading economists share one unifying belief: They make their living predicting how tomorrow will be like yesterday. Because they are forever looking in the rearview mirror of the past, they do not see—indeed, cannot see—the road ahead.

Straight-Line Projections Were for the "Happy Days" Decades

Economists look for past trends that can be projected to predict future economic events. This method works quite well when the economy is moving relatively slowly with few variables or when the variables are behaving in a reasonably predictable manner. In the "Happy Days" of the 1950s and 1960s, for instance, economists looked good because the trends consistently headed upward, so it was quite easy to project straight-line growth. It didn't take skilled economists to produce accurate forecasts—most businesspeople I know were able to handle the job. About then, forecasting became a growth industry. The business schools began churning out MBAs who were trained in building econometric models that based their estimates on past correlations.

In the 1970s, however, we entered a completely new era—one without historic precedent. This era of unprecedented global competition, consolidation, insane government growth, overcapacity, unbridled consumer debt, bank mistakes, layoffs and corporate stagnation dramatically changed our economy and forever ended the days of straight-line projections.

Making Waves by Recycling Business Cycles

In the business world, we seem to follow a cycle that alternates between boom and bust, rarely achieving a balanced state where prices are stable, and we're all employed. Economists believe they can predict the path of these cycles. In fact, mainstream economists and stockbrokers rely so much on business cycle theory for their thinking that they no longer question its value as a predictor of economic events or, indeed, its existence. The economic monthly indicators published by the federal government are supposed to forecast the cyclical ups and downs. For example, a three-month downturn in these "leading economic indicators" such as money supply and housing starts is supposed to indicate that a recession will be upon us in six months.

The notion of business cycles is not new. Wavelike expansions and contractions in business can be traced to the founding of the United States. Economists and stockbrokers have continually seen cyclical movements in employment, factory output, interest rates, bank credit as well as in such far-removed phenomena as marriage, birth and divorce rates. By studying many economic time series, The National Bureau of Economic Research (NBER) believed it identified 30 complete business cycles between 1834 and 1958 that had an average length of just over four years. Cycles of three to five years are called the Kitchin Cycle, named for Joseph Kitchin, who first wrote about them. The Kitchin Cycle, which the government and the mass media most often cite, tracks inventories, wholesale prices, interest rates and bank clearings. Over 130 years ago, a Frenchman named Juglar wrote about business cycles averaging 8–11 years; while a Russian named Kondratieff found statistical evidence for cycles of even longer duration. Kondratieff Cycles are purported to average between 40 and 50 years.

But Do These Cycles Really Exist? Many prominent experts seriously doubt the existence or applicability of business cycles. W. Allen Wallis, former professor of statistics and economics at the University of Chicago, has wisely pointed out that "almost any series if stared at long and hopefully enough begins to shape up into patterns and cycles." Even Arthur Burns and Wesley Mitchell, former experts with the NBER group that studied and identified the short cycle, warned "that when we speak of observing business cycles, we use figurative language. . . . Business cycles can only be seen in the mind's eye."

Howard Barger, former professor of money and banking at Columbia University, noted that no two cycles are exactly alike in duration, amplitude or even in the area of the economy principally affected. Even no two Kitchin Cycles, which average only four years, are exactly alike. Their peaks and valleys vary considerably, and some peaks were followed by severe financial collapse; while others were succeeded by declines so gradual that nobody even recognized the decline until many months latter. Barger asked the obvious question: "If individual business cycles display so many differences from each other, how can we say anything useful about business cycles in general?"

There Isn't Much Substance in "Big Macromeasures." Most of what we hear in the media these days consists of economists' discussing such indicators as gross national product (GNP), the federal discount rate, changes in money aggregates and so on. Supposedly, these measures tell us about the health and direction of the economy. But these measures are so "aggregated" that observing them produces little knowledge of what's going on in the real world. The more we understand how these measures are derived, the more cautious we are, and the less value we place on the data. Yet economists, futurists, government officials and other pundits in the "E-con" game use these numbers to predict our future.

Over the past century and a half, what is seen in these macromeasures such as GNP is not the purported uniform rising and falling of economic activities in unison but changed readings taken from many recording instruments of varying reliability. These readings have to be disassembled for our purposes and the components reassembled in a new way.

The whole procedure is far removed from what happens in the real world.

For example, someone tending an open-hearth furnace has a close-up view of steel production. But what that person sees, hears and smells is only a tiny fragment of a vast process. By working at one furnace, that person cannot see the hundreds of other furnaces operating in the rest of the country. And smelting is only one stage in a process that includes mining and transporting iron, limestone and coal; raising capital; hiring and training workers; making and selling goods that create the demand for steel; and price setting.

No one can watch all these activities. Yet people dependent on the steel industry need an overall view of what is happening. To get it, the complex steel-making process is reduced to a column of numbers showing the number of tons of ingots turned out in a given area during successive days or weeks.

We can readily see that tonnage reports from the complex steel operation have little connection with the complex real world. Moreover, "the" business cycle and measures such as GNP are the cumulative result of the combined effect of the underlying supply and demand variables from many businesses as diverse as steel and beef. Price fluctuations and their effects on the supply and demand for beef and the time it takes to breed and bring cattle to market throughout the country are only a few of the complexities in the cow business.

Think of the scores of other industries each with their own complex variables combined together to provide a simple statistic of growth or decline. Yet economists and other pundits who never left the biosphere covering Washington and their universities use these numbers to predict business trends. In all fairness, however, I must admit that some are expert about the product of the back end of the cow business.

Keeping Stock of Stockbrokers

Brokers, like their economist kin, also look to the past to predict the future. This after-the-fact method of prediction tends to fit what has transpired into convenient correlatives and produces such diverse fancies as the "random walk theory" and stock market analysis based on the movement of the stars. At the other extreme are analysts who get too close to the problem and tend to forecast events based on today's news, often occasioned by a press release from one government office to another. Thus, TV anchor people can report quite seriously, "Stocks moved lower today on news that subway workers in New York may go on strike."

We've already seen what is wrong with analyzing the past. Despite centuries of research, no one has produced a model or approach that works. The problem with getting too close to the present is that stockmarket trends, moves and activities are hyper-responsive and seldom linked to specific environments or industries. (Would people really sell Boeing because New York's subway workers might strike?) Most stockbrokers and economists don't have any true understanding of what makes companies, sectors and industries tick. Looking at sales results and financial statements is at best not enough and is often altogether misleading. You can't develop a real understanding of a business through statements any more than a doctor can diagnose a patient by looking at a wallet-sized photo of that person.

Tough Times for Futurists

Business forcasting books have been groundbreaking number one national best-sellers. However, the credibility of Naisbitt, Kiplinger and other best-selling authors, economists and "experts" who have predicted a "global economic boom" in the 1990s is being questioned because too many global businesses find themselves wearing sackcloth and ashes while groping for ways out of their present economic quagmire.

Indeed, global business predictions have been so off-base this year that you wonder what license qualifies these people to operate their crystal ball. All too often, their sound bites are overhyped and general, purporting to identify trends in some vaguely urgent manner. Whether calling for action or vigilance, these breathless proclamations often have little grip on reality. Why? Because, like economists', most futurists' lives are sheltered from the world of commerce or else have touched it only tangentially.

HOW I DO MY THING

My goal in this book has been to minimize as much as possible idle speculation about the future and to substitute what I believe to be the most reliable and comprehensive approach now available for business forecasting.

I honed my insights by working 30 years as a global management consultant for scores of international companies in a wide variety of sizes and classifications. I believe that "you have to get into it to understand it." You can't expect to sit in Washington, stand on Wall Street, be at the top of a ski slope in the Rockies or among the eucalyptus at Stanford University and talk about global business based on what you've read, analyzed or viewed in the latest statistics.

To select the trends in this book, I used a three-part approach: (1) The Econo-2000 model (see below) to determine important company success indicators, identify those trends that will most change those company specific indicators and make some predictions about the interaction of trends and indicators; (2) I scoured thousands of published global trends and predictions; and (3) I consulted and interviewed experts in business, lifestyles, science, technology and other disciplines to learn about additional trends and predictions. The balance of this chapter provides further details, issues and concerns about this three-part approach.

PART 1—ECONO-2000

Overview

The Econo-2000 model has three specific objectives: First, to determine the most important indicators (determinants) for business, investment or career success. Second, to identify those trends that will most change those indicators. Third, to make predictions by feeding the indicators and trends into a model that includes alternative economic scenarios.

The output from step 3 is specific predictions that are relevant to individual business, investment or career decisions. Moreover, the model can help determine which trends you should track in depth and which you should scan occasionally in the business media, in reading this book or in sifting through the barrage of information you receive daily.

Background Lessons Learned in the Real World

While leading a large Stanford Research Institute (SRI International) intra-industry project for a major Midwest utility client, I first became aware of the dissonance between my real-world observations and traditional forecasting techniques. The utility companies, like the banks, predicted growth in energy demand by developing formulas that connected energy growth to macroeconomic parameters such as GNP, population and employment. Projections about energy needs of a particular industry were viewed as a multiple of GNP growth. For example, food industry growth might be 0.4 times the growth of GNP and chemicals 1.5 times the growth rate.

From my fieldwork, however, I observed that such historical extrapolation and macroeconomic and megatrend predictions are no longer accurate. The assumption that the future will be like the past is clearly not true. In the early 1900s, a forecaster might have predicted that New York City traffic would cease because of the increase in the amount of horse-drawn vehicles and that the volume of horse manure would cause serious pollution problems. Extrapolation from the past missed the traffic and economic lifestyle changes, not to mention the environmental threats introduced by the advent of motor vehicles.

I also learned firsthand that companies are as individual as people. The reasons affecting the success or failure of companies even in the same industry can be different. I also observed that most of the determinants of a company's direction were not the type of general data collected or analyzed by economists, futurists and others charged with determining our direction. Table 1-1 lists some of the reasons that determine success at the company level. (The trends selected for this book address different aspects of all the reasons listed plus others.)

Based on what I learned in the field, I developed a simple and logical approach to forecasting that I call the *Econo-2000 model.* The model allowed me to be the first person in the world to predict that the manufacturing sector in the United States had peaked and would never equal its 1979 share of GNP (15 years later, my prediction is still correct). In my management consulting practice, I use the Econo-2000 technique along with my 30-year real-world knowledge of global business, seasoned with a generous dash of instinct, to develop market and economic forecasts for my clients. As my reputation for accurate forecasting grew, I was asked to publish my forecasts in the *Corporate Times* in Silicon Valley. My regular monthly column, "Future In Sight," contained dozens of specific and accurate predictions, ranging from high tech to high touch.

Most entrepreneurs and small-business operators who can't afford to hire strategic marketing consultants or a staff of strategic planners would benefit from some future exploration using the Econo-2000 model. Individuals trying to determine what occupations will yield the greatest success in the next decade and investors and banks looking for a logical hook for identifying threats and opportunities facing various companies may also benefit from using the model. I recommend using three alternative economic scenarios, though I believe that the pessimistic or status quo scenarios are the most useful. My credo is plan for the worst, hope for the best. A major reason businesses fail is because of lack of vision; therefore, regardless of which economic scenario you choose, develop a plan.

Econo-2000 Model: Six-Step Method

1. Identify the company-specific indicators that determine how a company will fare. In my oversimplified example, I use only two or three. There may, however, be many indicators that affect the future direction of a business and throw all attempts at forecasting into disarray. My experience suggests, however, that only a few indicators have a major impact on a business's success or failure.

2. Determine how those indicators will be affected by a future economic scenario. (I chose a declining growth example.)
3. Make predictions based on the interaction between the indicators and the scenario.
4. Analyze the ripple effects on other companies, industries and trends.
5. Repeat the process and estimate the impact on all companies and countries in your sample.
6. Aggregate company results.

A prediction about the future of a particular industry would be the summation of the outlook for companies within an industry sample. An aggregate of industry forecasts would provide a country specific economic forecast.

Let's Look at an Example

Table 1-1. Factors That Determine Economic Success at the Company Level

Key Indicator Legend		Key Indicator Legend	
01	New Products/Services	17	Experience
02	New Markets	18	Cost of Operations
03	% Distribution Controlled	19	Control of Production
04	Market Share	20	Quality Concerns
05	Market Maturity	21	Time Utilization
06	Sales Volume	22	Union Problems
07	Competition	23	Turnover
08	Customer Demographics	24	R&D Productivity
09	Customer Psychographics	25	Environmental Factors
10	Perceived Value of Product or Service	26	Maintenance
11	Service or Product Necessity	27	Distribution/Handling Costs
12	Availability of Used Equipment	28	Government Protection
13	Sense of Urgency	29	Social Pressure
14	Strategic Responsiveness	30	Liability Problems
15	Structural Responsiveness	31	Political Clout
16	Flexibility	32	Government Stability
		33	Political Unrest

Table 1-2. Econo-2000: Simplified Example

Company/ Division	Key Indicators	Effect of Econo-2000 Assumption	Prediction	Ripple Effect
BMW	Perception of quality, status	Fewer car sales; more business failures; fewer high-end purchases	Increased sales through 1985; larger share of declining market from 1986	Negative for machinery segments, fabricated metals, primary metals
Cadillac	Perception of quality, status	Fewer car sales; more business failures; fewer high-end purchases	Steady decline from 1983	Negative for regional services sectors
Volkswagen	Perception of quality, labor relations	Fewer car sales; more business failures; fewer high-end purchases	Decline from 1983	European and U.S. auto, machinery, fabricated metals and primary metals suffer

Table 1-2 presents my 1975 prediction about 1985 sales trends for BMW, Cadillac and Volkswagen to show the first four steps of the Econo-2000 technique.

Step 1.—The key indicators for BMW (See Table 1-2, column 2) were the perception of status, perception of quality and demographics.

For Cadillac, the indicators of success or failure were the same. The key difference was that the perceptions of car quality and status were positive for BMW and negative for Cadillac. In the 1980s, the 25–44 age group was the largest growing segment of the population and also bought the most cars. The BMW was becoming a status symbol for the yuppies, while the Cadillac was considered an older person's car. Moreover, German car quality was perceived as excellent, while doubts existed about the inferior fit and finish of U.S. cars.

The key Volkswagen indicators were perception of quality and labor relations. The aging Beetle needed to be replaced by a new family of vehicles. Volkswagen's decision to open a plant in the United States, using members of the United Auto Workers Union (UAW), gave rise to public concern that Volkswagen's quality would suffer. Among the indicators of Volkwagen's success or failure were the difficulties it experienced with the UAW. Again, *such major indicators of corporate success or failure were not and are still not tracked by futurists and economists.*

Step 2.—Table 1-2, column 3 shows the effect of a Econo-2000 scenario that envisions a shrinking industrial base, more unemployment and less discretionary income. The effects on all carmakers are a sales decline, the production of smaller and less expensive cars, more competition and failing or merging automakers.

Step 3.—Therefore, I correctly predicted (see Table 1-2, column 4) that BMW would get a larger share of the declining high-end market, that Cadillac's sales would continue to decline as its regular customers died off without replacements and that Volkswagen's sales would continue to decline because of increased domestic and offshore competition.

Step 4.—Table 1-2, column 5 shows the ripple effect of these predictions on other sectors of the economy.

A Current Automobile Prediction

Currently, I am predicting the sales of Mercedes-Benz will steadily decline (1995–2005) in the United States, will have major growth in China and will have flat sales in Western Europe. Let's walk through the steps together.

> •
>
> DO YOU WANT TO KNOW "WHAT'S IN IT FOR ME?" THEN RUN THROUGH THE ECONO-2000 STEPS FOR YOUR BUSINESS.
>
> •

Step 1.—The key indicators for the success of Mercedes-Benz are that the perception of quality is excellent and that the car bestows a high degree of status on the owner. The amount of money people have to spend after paying fixed monthly bills (discretionary income) is a third indicator of Mercedes' future.

Step 2.—From three possible economic scenarios—optimistic: the economy will improve; status quo: the economy will stay as is; or pessimistic: the economy will deteriorate—we selected the pessimistic scenario based on analyzing many global companies and trends.[1]

This scenario envisions a shrinking industrial base and less discretionary income in most regions of the world (except for China, some Southeast Asian countries, the Middle East, Western Europe, Washington, D.C., and California).

Besides the economic scenarios, certain trends will change key Mercedes' indicators: Quality is taken for granted in high-priced cars,

[1]Barry H. Minkin, *Econoquake: How to Survive & Prosper in the Coming Global Depression* (New York: Simon & Schuster, 1993)

diluting a major Mercedes selling point; Mercedes is planning to build cars in the United States, diluting the mystique of German quality and workmanship (as happened with Volkswagen); fewer people will be able to afford high-priced cars and service in the United States as executive positions are lost because of mergers, acquisitions, increased bankruptcies and cost cutting in health care and the legal system; competiton will rise for upscale vehicles as well as for which luxury items to buy. Moreover, luxury is being redefined as usefulness and meeting individual lifestyles; for example, the growth of luxury four-wheel-drive, off-road vehicles rather than diamonds and Mercedeses; and because people hate to drive behind a car that spews diesel exhaust, there will be government efforts to protect people and the environment. A positive trend is the Asians' continued love of luxury, brand-name products.

Step 3.—Based on steps 1 and 2, I predict a steady decline in sales from 1995 levels of Mercedes in the United States; an increase in sales to successful Asian baby boomers in California; increased car sales and construction of a Mercedes plant in China; flat sales (no major increase or decrease) in Switzerland and the Middle East; and declining sales in other European countries.

Step 4.—The ripple effect will be a downturn in the German economy, giving rise to shorter work weeks, innovative job creation programs and higher unemployment, leading to a decline in the admission of foreign workers.

PART 2—THE FUTURE DIRECTION OF PRESENT TRENDS

Today, there are countless trends that will constitute the world history of tomorrow. Clearly, some trends will contribute to the look of tomorrow; others will dissipate and disappear. So one big problem is deciding which current trends will be long lasting and which won't.

No one can stand up and announce: "This trend is over and a new one has begun." But change is happening, and the principal trends rooted in the 1990s are growing into the realities businesses will face at the end of the next decade. Trends are not always easy to understand and isolate; they overlap, merge and sometimes cancel out one another. So the trends presented in this book should not be thought of as completely separate but rather as dominant threads in a coat of many colors.

I scanned thousands of studies, articles, books and experts' predictions from around the world, choosing to include only those trends that fit my perspective about the emerging shape of the future. These trends range from broad to very specific. Some of the megatrends transforming our business landscape are well established, lend themselves to quantitative description and are easily tracked. These include such demographic and economic trends as world population growth, scarcity of resources and immigration.

Other trends that often have a greater impact on the future of business and the global economy are more subtle and easily lost in the roar of the daily media barrage. Examples of these less visible but important trends include technology trends such as anti-aging, smart drugs and ceramic electric turbines that will provide clean, abundant energy; marketing trends such as the "sensory assist," which will replace current market research techniques; customization; MTV in Asia; and such lifestyle trends as the new youth culture and family fragmentation.

Trends Are Not Trendy

There is a difference between a trend and a fad. A trend is long term, makes basic sense and has sustaining value, while a fad has a short life, and when it's out of fashion, it's really out.

Yin and Yang and Megathemes

For many trends, a counter trend (yin and yang) exists in tandem. For example, in the year 2010 the pecentage of poulation over 65 years old will be the highest ever in the United States, Japan, West Germany and the United Kingdom. In Latin America however, only 3percent of the population will be over 65.

Indeed, what I take away from all this analysis is a better sense of the underlying contradictions. The global village is continually shaken by the collision of opposing realities. As I introduce various trends, I highlight megathemes, including several yin and yang contradictions underlying the trends such as big-small, together-fragmented, rich-poor, forward-backward, young-old. The other megathemes that weave through all the trends in the book are dramatic change, sowing the seeds of future problems, revaluing resources, shifting focus and sophisticated competition.

I'm Not Wild about "Wild Cards"

The unexpected "wild card trends" that no one ever dreamed of often throw predictions off target. "The random event, the maniac, the prophet and the genius" have been the pitfalls of prophecy, said Robert A. Nisbet in *Commentary*. So a few wild cards such as the breakup of China are included and noted as wild cards throughout the book.

Trends can be like icebergs on the move— only partly visible, enormously powerful and capable of changing or destroying all that's in their paths. People who deal in the business world know that the art of anticipating trends is difficult at best. But they also realize that not trying is tantamount to accepting the most unlikely scenario of all: no change.

> ASK YOURSELF WHAT SIX TRENDS WILL MOST CHANGE YOUR ORGANIZATION, CAREER CHOICE OR INVESTMENT DECISIONS. HOW WELL DO YOU UNDERSTAND THESE TRENDS? WHERE CAN YOU LEARN MORE ABOUT THESE TRENDS?

PART 3—INPUT FROM THE GLOBAL NETWORK OF EXPERTS (DELPHI TECHNIQUE)

I've never suffered from "hardening of the categories," having consulted globally with companies in most all the standard industrial classifications. Filtering my "real-world experience" through the Econo-2000 model has allowed me to identify which areas and trends will have an important impact on business. However, former CEO of Grumman Corporation Jake Swebal said, "The person doing the job knows more about it than anyone else." So it is with trends: People working on the cutting edge are more likely than bystanders to be following a trend closely and to be aware of its implications. Consequently, I've interviewed leaders in the 10 key

> IT IS PROBABLY WORTH ASKING SIMILAR QUESTIONS ABOUT YOUR BUSINESS AND INDUSTRY: WHO IS MOST KNOWLEDGEABLE ABOUT THE TRENDS MOST IMPORTANT TO YOU? HOW WOULD YOU REACH THESE PEOPLE? WHAT THREE QUESTIONS WOULD YOU ASK THEM?

areas I examine in this book. I asked them to identify and discuss the most important trends that will change their spheres of interest over the next decade and to comment on the predictions of other experts.

These contributors are a diverse group from many disciplines and cultures and include such luminaries as Tom Peters; Lou Platt, CEO of Hewlett Packard; Tony Finizza, chief economist of ARCO; Jack Welch, CEO of GE; Charles Sanford, CEO of Bankers Trust; Willis Harman, futurist; and Bernard Schwartz, CEO of Loral Corporation. To achieve some consistency in approach and coverage, I started with the same question: What one or two trends do you think will have the greatest impact on business worldwide 10 years out? The responses, taken together, provide a surprisingly consistent perspective on the future.

Chapter 2

NEW MARKETING TRENDS GET THE RESULTS YOU WANT

•

I am captivated more by dreams of the future than by the history of the past.

THOMAS JEFFERSON

The urge to know has evolved from an instinct into a profession.

HARLOW SHAPLEY

•

Marketing must operate both short and long range, both on the line and at the strategic hub of the company. Marketing has not only strategic responsibilities, but also very specific tactics. Marketing above all is an art and a craft. It has a long way to go before it can become a science if indeed it ever can, despite what some practitioners claim grandiloquently in their best-sellers. There is a simple and important reason for this conclusion: Doing research about customer preferences, no matter how skillfully done, can only tell a company what the customer thinks he likes or would like, but it can never take the additional leap of creating a new product concept.

Several years ago, one of the world's largest breweries decided to create a surefire brew for market consumption. The company engaged in elaborate research—asking customers what size bottle, color of beer, size of head and degree of strength they preferred, and even asking them what colors would be attractive on the label.

The product was launched with great fanfare and millions of dollars. It was a total disaster—and predictably so. The marketing group had asked the customers to do the creative work for them. If customers could tell you precisely what they wanted in a new beer, then they would be the braumeisters and the heads of the marketing groups. Who would need any technicians?

Any time you hear marketing people tell you they can't devise a program until they have the strategic research results, you know they're being driven by numbers instead of creativity. Let's be clear about this because it's an important point for the coming decade: *Marketing people propose, customers dispose.*

In other words, marketing people direct, customers react. A marketing group must look at the marketplace, intuit a series of ideas that espouses a new way of getting to the customer, put the ideas into some rough schematic and get customer acceptance or nonacceptance. The customer can never take the burden off the marketing group—but the consumer can confirm or deny the product's acceptability to whatever customer segment is under review. Much market research must be done before a marketing person can develop ideas that need market testing.

Here are some customer factors, found throughout this book, that need to be explored before any specific marketing concept can be developed:

- Demographics: Who are the buyers and how many?
- Geographies: Where are the buyers and what trends for change do their habitat customs show?
- Economics: How much do the buyers make and on what do they spend?
- Lifestyles: How do the buyers live or want to live?
- Psychographies: What intangibles drive the buyers to do what they do, display, wear, think, yearn, despise and secretly value?

Along with the strategic management group, the marketing group keeps a steady eye on changing marketing trends such as those described in this chapter.

TREND

SAY GOOD-BYE TO HOW WE BUY—CHANNELS OF DISTRIBUTION ARE GOING TO CHANGE DRAMATICALLY

Contributor—Lou Platt, CEO, Hewlett Packard

I have always been impressed and, frankly, puzzled about why Hewlett Packard Corporation (HP) in tough economic times has done well. After my interview with Lou Platt, HP's CEO, I'm less confused. I left with the impression that this company truly understands the importance of the "forward end of the business"—in other words, HP is strategically responsive to the opportunities and threats that the future presents. Lou Platt in the first trend introduces us to "dramatic change," one of the 10 megathemes that encompass all the business trends in this book.

We've seen major changes in how we buy things in the late 1980s and early 1990s: witness the emergence of large discount chains and the evolution of telemarketing from the telephone to the television set. Expect to see more dramatic changes in the way business and consumers buy products in the decade ahead as *interactive* telemarketing becomes a reality.

IMPLICATIONS

Think back—just to the early 1980s. If you wanted to buy something, you went to the store to buy it, consulted with a salesperson and had a fairly normal salesperson-customer exchange; or if you wanted a more professional product, the salesperson came to you at your place of business. But as consumers become more educated, they will make their choices outside this traditional buying environment.

How will you buy a car at the end of this decade?

Today everyone buys a car in essentially the same way. You go around to a bunch of dealers, drive the cars and get insulted by the salespeople. It's really a terrible process.

Imagine instead, sitting in front of your TV 10 years from now, accessing all the information about cars, including independent studies about quality and price. All the information is on-line, and you can access it from your TV and print the information on your printer. You decide to test drive two cars with particular model numbers and input a request over the network for dealers to bring the cars to your home for a test drive. You drive them and then send a bid request over the network asking the dealers for their best prices for each car, delivered to your home. The transaction is completed without your ever visiting the dealers' showrooms.

PREDICTIONS

Retailers will continue the trend toward less frills, more warehouse stores and less face-to-face sales interactions in the future. When you made a purchase in the last six months, how many times have you had a knowledgeable sales-person? As the quality of salespeople continues to decline, consumers will do some independent study to make a wise choice and then go to a no-frills, low-overhead supplier to get a good price for the same quality goods. Costco and other warehouse stores will do better than traditional retailers.

Major opportunities will abound for companies to supply products and services that help the consumer to make better educated product decisions. As selling becomes less personal, consumers will be relying more on outside sources to educate them about product features, benefits and performance. More independent organizations like J. D. Powers and Associates and *Consumer Reports* will do testing and evaluation. Consumers will rely more on expert sources such as *Photography Magazine* for an evaluation of cameras that they'll buy via mail order or TV.

There will be growth opportunities for both independent and corporate service centers that can provide a highly reliable service channel for maintenance, repair and product replacement. Companies will find it harder to distinguish themselves for quality or service and to make these their primary selling advantages. Companies are going to be less willing to give free technical support and trouble-shooting services in the future as they move to this low-cost, no-frills environment. People will expect and get less free service with bargain prices. But if consumers are paying for technical support and service, they should expect high-quality help. (If you're going to pay $15 for an answer about a laser printer's problem, the answer better be right!) New service channels will emerge to take care of products that are bought through interactive TV or warehouse stores that do not provide repair service.

TREND

IN ASIA, IT HELPS TO *ROCK* FOR A BUSINESS TO *ROLL*

The good news: A magnet is pulling the fragmented youth of the world together into a huge global consumer market. The bad news: We again may be sowing the seeds for future problems as the younger generation revolts against traditional values and dances to their own tune.

Music Television (MTV) will have a megaton impact on lifestyles throughout Asia in the 1990s. Teenagers across Asia are being bombarded by a nonstop barrage of Western pop culture. The buying decisions of millions of Asian youths (teens through 35) will be most influenced by this trend.

MTV Asia is beamed into more than 11 million homes in 47 countries. In China, 4.8 million people watch. In India, MTV claims 3.3 million TV watchers. Competition between cable companies has brought the subscription price down to under three dollars a month. MTV is much more than music TV program: it's a lifestyle channel.

IMPLICATIONS

MTV fashions, foods, beverages and records will become big sellers no matter whose label is on them. Before MTV, people relied on retailers to tell them what fashions, records and products were current and best. Now and in the future, Asian youth will know what they want.

Advertising on MTV has lifted many obscure brands and performers to stardom. A little-known heavy metal band, Tang Dynasty, sold more than half a million copies in China alone after an MTV appearance. Polo, Gucci, Lacoste? Not in China—the labels of choice are

Silverlion, Goldlion and Van Garie, the brand names of Goldlion Holdings of Hong Kong. Before the company was allowed to sell any products in China, Goldlion's chairman, Tsang Hin Chi, used TV ads to develop name recognition and an image that Goldlion was a top international brand.

While most TV programing is passive, MTV in Asia will become increasingly interactive. For the first time, Asian youth will be asked what they think about issues ranging from safe sex to the environment as well as what type of programming they want. But more than likely, MTV will shape young Asian minds, not vice versa.

The on-air environment of MTV clashes with the culture of many Asian countries. Programs are unpredictable, irreverent and often blatantly sexual. Controlled Asian governments will continue to restrict ownership of satellite dishes and to censor broadcasts. They know the media can be a dangerous weapon against their regimes.

PREDICTIONS

Major advertisers from all over the world will use MTV to imprint their brands on the youth of Asia. MTV will continue to grow and be very profitable.

As satellite receivers become too small for governments to effectively control their importation, good information and rapid economic expansion will hasten a trend toward greater openness in closed Asian societies.

Competition in the news and entertainment fields will increase as new players enter the market. Expect the number of channels to double in the next few years when two new satellites begin service.

Cable TV channels such as CNN, STAR, ESPN, FOX, TBS and HBO will try to be perceived as less United States–centered broadcasters and will become more globally oriented. Tailoring programs to regional tastes will be very important.

Asian businesses and politicians will want their share of the entertainment explosion. Expect local cable companies to be given competitive advantages over foreign organizations.

TREND

SENSORY ASSIST (SA): WHAT IT FEELS LIKE
TO BE THE CUSTOMER

Contributor—Davis Masten, CEO, Cheskin and Masten

Davis Masten is a popular consultant and futurist to many Fortune 500 companies. We met to share future insights with a mutual client, and I hope we will continue to collaborate. Davis has that rare ability to see the outer edge of future trends while providing practical insights to his clients about how to prepare today for tomorrow. What follows are his views about a trend I call sensory assist (SA), which will lead to dramatic changes in the way market research is conducted.

Senior management will continue to be frustrated with the traditional marketing approaches that are not able to name or deliver the functional benefits of products that really address customers' needs. The problem is obvious: 80 percent to 90 percent of the input we receive and send is nonverbal, and yet all the market research except for behavioral store techniques is verbal. But how do we verbalize the feelings of love, hope, pain and pleasure? In addition to the verbal input, we're going to get *sensory assistance* (SA) in the decision-making process.

There are a variety of techniques that will become accepted ways to get an in-depth, never-before-possible understanding of customers. Right now, marketing deals with tools like demographics and psychographies that lead us to believe that we understand the customer. Though somewhat useful, these techniques are seen as "the" answer to the question of how to identify and understand a customer segment. Current techniques give logical, rational explanations about where the customer fits in but do not explain how the customer *feels*.

Technologies such as virtual reality (VR) take video and add 3-D and enhanced sound. Ten years from now, those techniques will be routine in business for point of sales applications. When ethnology and other social science techniques used by anthropologists and others to study people at work or play are combined with the new technologies of immersion (such as VR), a powerful set of marketing tools we call sensory assist (SA) is achieved.

IMPLICATIONS

The Five Components of SA

Improved observational techniques: The first step will be to get out from behind the desk, get into the market and observe the customer. For decades, the Japanese advertising agencies have enhanced and enlarged techniques to observe the consumer, using such methods as the "K.J." approach, adapted from the work of a Japanese anthropologist, to systematically observe and record data about consumer behavior.

Ethnology: Ethnology is the study of how culture influences socioeconomic systems. Ethnology techniques are more than language and thoughts: They are ways of immersing people deeply and rapidly into a culture so they will be able to make better decisions for their companies. Such techniques will become popular in the United States as the business community becomes aware that white men from the suburban upper class will not be representative of the consumer in the next decade; therefore, businesses must learn what it is like to be Hispanic or Asian.

Market Immersion: Companies must immerse themselves in select markets, looking for new opportunities to achieve a competitive edge.

Virtual reality is just an easy way to talk about an early component of SA. I do a lot of work in virtual reality and generally, it's more hype than reality, just another visual technique more often than not. I already know that if I sit down with a group and show them 10 photos, it will give them a better feel for what I'm talking about than if I just talk for an hour. That's no great news. But what if I had video cameras and observers in the homes of people using a product I watched them buy. I also might have people in the target-market segments, people taking pictures of each other throughout work and play. I would then have an enriched source of nonverbal inputs into various market segments.

Pictures and video are just part of SA. There's smell and the other senses that marketers just don't pay any attention to. Of course, the perfume people pay attention to smell and are concerned about packaging. But very few people see marketing holistically. I believe that a holistic look at the senses is going to be the standard in 10 years. Now it's just "stuff" at the edge, and a lot of people scratch their heads and say "isn't this sweet or curious."

By using all the senses, you enhance a person's ability to learn more rapidly and intuitively. VR is solely about being able to control the environment, to control sight and sound and building smell into it. We can help people to understand what a new environment feels like in a safe way. Like a fighter pilot simulation, SA will help the executive to learn how to maneuver in a unfamiliar setting. Ten years out, for example, we'll put on enhanced 3-D glasses to experience the Japanese consumer market. We'll not only be able to see and hear what is happening in the stores our Japanese customers shop in, but also be able to observe how and where and who they meet as well as know their behavior at home.

Whereas once Barry took Rod Bell, former VP of Pepsico to The Whole Foods Market, ten years from now, we'll be able to sit in a room anywhere in the world and know how it feels to be a new customer in that market. You might run this in Japan, learning what shopping in Whole Foods in Japan would be like. You will be able to experiment in markets more effectively and globalize products faster because the ammunition is the senses—something that everyone shares.

Improvisation: Market research will include role play. For example, to understand beer drinking in a bar, we will not only observe it, but also role-play drinking beer and improvise miniacts to understand the part beer plays in various settings.

Visualization: Most of us can't visualize the future. It's too abstract. To make the future tangible, we create a visual representation that other people can react to. For example, it's hard for people to imagine a new computerized spreadsheet program, so we design a visual representation that people can see and respond to.

SA will provide new market segmentation, models and metaphors that contribute to our "Educated Gut," allowing for faster and more accurate marketing decisions.

PREDICTIONS

Traditional market research will continue on a downward trend, not only because of the poor economy but also because of major leaps forward in SA. People will realize the verbal "stuff," although not totally worn out, is limiting. The claims about what market research can do are much larger than what is delivered.

SA techniques are going to be resisted by middle managers who need numbers to justify their existence and to cover their backsides. SA will happen on the edges of the business world and be used by visionary businesspeople who will bring these concepts forth, followed by some middle managers, then move slowly to the decision makers, who will recognize the benefits. The CEO will say "this is the direction we're going," but it will take three to five years for this approach to be acculturated by most companies.

The trend will move faster if championed by the retailers, who can put pressure on the manufacturer by insisting that if the manufacturer wants to be in their stores, products must be viewed though the SA process. Retailers will ask the manufacturers for help in understanding how the customer is going to feel when walking into their store and what can they do to influence the customer's senses in that context.

The SA techniques will be used worldwide because SA won't be expensive to implement. More likely, SA will develop outside the United States. Japanese companies such as Matsushita and Sharp have consumer research labs and are years ahead of the United States in helping their people to understand and track consumers. Matsushita tracks over a hundred families in a multiyear longitudinal anthropological study about how the families interface with TV. Sharp has a lab where they bring designers to "feel" who the customer is. I don't think the Japanese are where SA will be 10 years from now, but I think they're leading the way.

Fifty years from now, we may have chip implantation that helps us to understand feelings and actually share pain, pleasure and other sensations.

TREND

SENGOKU JIDAI—NEW SOCIETAL MARKET WARS

Ever greater and more "sophisticated competition" is the megatheme introduced by the next trend. Survival of the fittest will require some sharp edge to use on some very tough competition.

America's trading competitors are increasingly becoming more competent and sophisticated. Most have mounted aggressive campaigns that amount to a new form of societal competition in which a nation's full economic, social, political and marketing resources are marshaled in a global economic sweepstakes.

IMPLICATIONS

Japan, Korea, Taiwan, Brazil, France, West Germany and other industrial and developing nations have created national economic combines of government, business and labor. They select a few industries that will be favored, reduce investment risks in these enterprises and facilitate large-scale economies of research, development and production. Moreover, prices, specifications and standards are jointly determined and aggressive export drives are launched when the industry achieves world-class competitiveness.

As trading competitors violate trade agreements, introduce protectionist trade measures and pursue rapacious export programs, other countries follow, increasing the trade squabbles into global market wars that threaten the well-being of all nations, industries, workers and consumers. A major item on the world business agenda is defining the word competition, a seemingly simple task that's rife with potential pitfalls. Some fear that to endow the word with a definition—promoting free trade— no holds barred—may give up the store. On the other hand, to restrict key industries could be to choke development in the country or region.

PREDICTIONS

Before the year 2000, new microprocessors will be produced that enable video game machines to double as cable TV controllers, E-mail boxes and all-around ramps to the information highway. That prospect underlies a market battle the Japanese call "Sengoku Jidai" after the Period of Warring States that proceeded Japan's seventeenth-century unification.

Telecommunications services and equipment are also rapidly becoming strategic battle areas, and as international competition intensifies in services, equipment development escalates and trade patterns change. Three approaches to competition in telecom services are evolving worldwide: (1) Monopoly modernization, either where profits are plowed back into the network as in Singapore or where profits accompany privatization and foreign investment, as in South America; (2) The affiliate system, favored in most European countries, where the telecom monopolies rely on outside product companies (e.g., mobile communications) to attract users to the network; and (3) Full competition—as seen in the United States, United Kingdom, Japan, Australia, New Zealand and Sweden where voice, data and switching are open to competition.

In Europe, ambiguity in policy and regulatory impediments will be used to limit non–European Community satellite providers from competing directly in the telecommunications environment without having to form alliances with the local country telecommunications monopolies.

Europe's chemical industry will face serious decline as it loses in the global market wars. Europe, home to 18 of the world's top 30 chemical companies, accounts for almost half of global chemical sales, making chemicals the single biggest contributor to Europe's ailing trade balance. But the chemical trade surplus is shrinking fast, and the long-term picture for Europe is frightening: The total trade deficit has grown to $70 billion; EC world export share has dropped from 21 percent in 1980 to 16 percent; and 20 million Europeans were unemployed in 1994. Besides global competition, the causes for the continuing decline are domestic recession, overcapacity and energy costs, which can represent 15 percent to 50 percent of manufacturing costs for chemicals.

TREND

BACK TO THE FUTURE

Contributor—Mitch Gooze, CEO, OMT Group

The yin and yang theme of forward-backward is delightfully illustrated by Mitch Gooze. Mitch is a well-seasoned management consultant and former high-tech senior executive whom I've collaborated with over the years and use as a sounding board for my ideas. Mitch, like many of the others I've chosen to include in this book, has the ability to take a different perspective when he looks at the forest in which we're all lost.

The most important trend is *recycling* how business is conducted. If you think back, pre–Industrial Revolution merchants and craftsmen were successful in their communities based on their ability to do a good job for the customer. Unless you were the only business in town, your success was predicated on giving customers what they wanted. So pre–Industrial Revolution, the customer was king. Craftsmen and merchants were more customer focused.

After the Industrial Revolution, companies in businesses such as shoes were able to mass merchandise products. For example, the U.S. Shoe Company could offer a pair of shoes for 25 cents that had once cost a dollar. But the shoes really weren't as good as the ones the craftsman had custom designed. However, weighing the extra income now available to buy other things against the lower quality and happiness quotient, people chose to trade 75 percent of their money for slightly inferior shoes. We tricked ourselves into believing there was a mass market. We believed that we could sell most products from shoes to autos through this mass market. In truth, there never was a mass market. If I make you an offer you can't refuse, you will forgo some of the things you would like to have in exchange for lower price and other considerations.

The world has moved on. In the last 20 years, our ability to manufacture in small batches or on a small scale has dramatically improved. In most industries, large manufacturers don't really have an advantage over small ones in what used to be called "economies of scale." Of course, you can't be a small 747 manufacturer, and few capital intensive industries exist today. The steel industry used to think it was a mass producer, but it doesn't anymore. In fact, a large steel company is a loser. And the day might come when being a big semiconductor manufacturer or airplane manufacturer might be a loser.

So with rare exceptions, the small company is not at a manufacturing disadvantage compared with how it used to be. Therefore, it can tailor goods and services to what the customer always wanted, without the customer paying a premium or only a slightly higher premium for a custom-made product. What's shocking a lot of people is the belief that the mass market disappeared. My response is that there never was a mass market; we used to buy people into submission.

IMPLICATIONS

The emerging *mass customization* strategy promises to unleash a wave of changes and has far reaching implications for today's marketers. In brief, mass customization is based on tying computer-based information systems together with new modes of operation such as flexible manufacturing and just-in-time production, then linking those systems to provide each customer with attractive, tailor-made benefits like those of the pre-industrial craft era at the low cost made possible by modern mass production. Early examples that are beginning to appear include Motorola Inc.

Along with a lower manufacturing cost for small companies is the concurrent trend of lower cost distribution (*see* "Say Good-bye to How We Buy" p. 19). As a moderately sized manufacturer, if I can get my goods where I want with pinpoint accuracy and don't have a major disadvantage because of size, I can tailor my offerings to a category of customers. If I'm a larger manufacturer, I simply tailor multiple offerings to multiple categories of customers whom I think I understand. (*see* SA p. 23).

With mass customization, marketing communications must become a two-way process. In addition to needing improved customer-to-supplier information flow, a mass customization strategy will also have an impact on traditional supplier-to-customer marketing communications.

The trick in the future is to go back to the past. The whole concept is to get back to the original customer. The important insight is to realize *there never was a mass market,* and the real need is to find as many of the *right* customers as possible.

PREDICTIONS

The earliest impact of mass customization will be in sectors involving feature-rich, information-intensive products and services. Network TV will still reach lots of consumers but with a continually shrinking share of viewers. With 500-channel TV competing for viewers, there will be less bang for the 30-second advertising spot.

Technology and economics will rapidly provide the ability to deliver individualized advertising. Whether we reach the precise point where we could deliver an ad to Barry Minkin's television set and not his neighbor's is irrelevant. The point is I can deliver to categories of people and can do that today with selected buying. Hughes launched a DBS satellite (a broadcast TV satellite) that has a capability of broadcasting to individual homes any information a supplier wants to send. It's called "direct TV" and includes a direct TV box in each subscriber's home. Each receiver is coded, so if Barry Minkin is a subscriber to the Hughes DBS satellite, an ad can be targeted and sent solely to him. Today the economics of sending such an ad doesn't make sense. But targeting to a group (e.g., middle-aged economists with great future vision) may be feasible.

Ten years from today, if a supplier doesn't know who its current and potential customers are based on some set of characteristics that are meaningful in its market, the supplier will be incapable of economically communicating with the marketplace. Suppliers cannot afford to pay for mass advertising without receiving commensurate benefits. The competitor who figures out who his customers are and should be— selects how to communicate only with those people—will profit.

TREND

RETAIL REVOLUTION

Sophisticated competition and dramatic change will characterize retail businesses in the coming decades.
In a fragmented market, one place to reach the consumer is at the retail level. Retailers face a set of uncertainties as they look ahead to the year 2000 and beyond. They do not know who the players will be, how the rules will change or what the playing field will look like. The only certainty is change.

By the year 2000, the retailing environment will be global. Competition will be very sophisticated in the store, and a prime reason for the extinction of many retail giants will be failure to adapt to a changing marketplace. The next decade will be noted for superior design in products, private label, decor and a refined look.

In 2010, technology will be inexpensive and available to everyone. We'll see more high-tech advertising such as video screens on shopping carts and video catalogs to help find the product. Electronic home shopping will become relatively commonplace by 2010 due to the impending fusion of fiber-optic technology with computer and video technology.

IMPLICATIONS

To survive the tough economy ahead, retailers must keep expenses down, stop building, develop a clear, compelling reason for being, restore pricing integrity, seek out unique products and create a professional sales force.

U.S. suppliers will increasingly feel the effects of the vast consolidation trend underway in retailing. In numerous categories, giant power retailers are using sophisticated inventory management, finely tuned selections and competitive pricing to crowd out weaker players. Too many new products are entering the pipeline, putting pressure on suppliers to sell them and on the retailers who don't have the space to display them.

Vendors will continue to be assaulted by an unceasing barrage of demand from retailers, who want everything from discounts for new store openings to payments of fines for shipment errors. One benefit for the consumers is that the super-retailers' focus on efficiency forces suppliers to eliminate excess cost.

The competitive edge will go to the retailer who can best use technology and who can bridge the gap between high tech and high touch. In 2010, retailers must have a quick-response program. Agility is important, too, and means balancing two opposing objectives: (1) providing personalized service to consumers, and (2) maintaining massive volume that creates economies of scale and competitive prices.

There should be opportunities for U.S. retailers to expand abroad, particularly into Japan. However, despite the worship of American products, there are differences in Japan that limit opportunities for U.S. retailers. Some Japanese department stores are three to four times the size of U.S. stores, allowing more space for the presentation of merchandise. The Japanese distribution system is also different. It is a three-legged system consisting of the retailer, the wholesaler and the manufacturer. But arrangements may vary, for example, the wholesaler may own the merchandise and negotiate with the retailer for space to operate the department.

Foreign retailers have spotted the shopping potential of Asia's emerging middle class. The market is still tough to break into. Retailers are hoping for a surge in consumer demand in Asia because of a phenomenon called "magic moments," the point when a large part of the population crosses an income threshold beyond which people buy entirely new categories of goods, whether they be packaged foods, television sets or mopeds. For example, in 1987 only 3 percent of Taiwanese bought groceries in a "modern" shop such as a supermarket. By 1993, the figure had risen to 50 percent. Last year, Vietnam's first supermarket opened and closed four days later. The problem? Overwhelming demand. With checkout queues over an hour long, the store had to close and rethink operations.

PREDICTIONS

Retailers that now account for half of all U.S. sales will disappear by the year 2000 because of bankruptcy, mergers and reorganizations. Discounters especially will be hard hit. Triumphing over them will be the superpowers such as Wal-Mart, Kmart, Target and Costco.

> •
> WHAT PRODUCT DOES YOUR BUSINESS PRODUCE THAT COULD BE SUPPLIED AS A PRIVATE-LABEL PRODUCT?
> •

Consumers are flocking to new retailing channels and will continue to patronize warehouse clubs and tightly focused "category killers," specialty retailers and factory stores that are taking over discount sales of products from toys to tires.

The warehouse club business, estimated at about one-fourth the size of the discount department store business, will continue to evolve throughout the 1990s and will have substantially transformed major segments of the retail and wholesale distribution industries by the year 2000.

Private label is no longer a phenomenon associated with the recession or the economy but has a loyal consumer base that continues to develop. Store brands, which now account for about 15 percent of scannable grocery product sales, will grow to 30 percent of sales by 2000. Perhaps most important is exactly how store brands are growing. Commodity items like milk and sugar have been dominated by private label for years. By the year 2000, expect double-digit increases in store-brand growth coming from high-margin categories traditionally dominated by megabrands, where the retail price can be 40 percent lower for a private label equivalent.

For most marketers the change means becoming a private-label supplier. Growth will be fueled by the increasing number of national brand marketers that will actually manufacture private-label products for retailers. The growing partnership between national brand marketeers and retailers' store-brand teams will yield new comarketing opportunities for both store-brand coupons on national brand product packaging and shared ad space between national brands and noncompeting private-label products.

In the United States and Canada, retailing will be in retrenchment. For the Far East and Latin America, rapid expansion will take place. China's retail market will be $600 billion a year by the year 2000. Early entrants in China's retail sector will be Hong Kong, Japanese and Southeast Asian companies. U.S. and European retailers will be slow to jump on the retailing bandwagon. Though getting into the China market early will enable some retailers to establish their names and earn good returns, foreign investors in the retail sector will face a number of hurdles. For instance, it can take a year just to get approval from the State Council.

Tougher competition and the magnified effects of the retailing recession will cause aggressive changes in inventory management. Retailers had been stocking stores with too many styles and overbuying within each style, creating too much competition within the store. Why have six colors of an item if four will do? The overstocking means too little space for hot-selling, high-profit items and depressed margins because less profitable merchandise was marked down. Expect less choice in style and color.

Computing power will continue to change retailing. Point of sale (POS) scanning systems will give many organizations a competitive edge in controlling their inventory costs and allowing them to respond quickly to sales trends. Many retail buying organizations are demanding that their suppliers' computer systems be linked to their systems for ordering and payment. In the late 1990s and toward the year 2000, these services will continue to be developed with the important goal of quantifiable measurement of marketing activity.

Other retail trends to follow: Malls will be different by 2010—they will be major entertainment centers. Airport retailing will emerge as a profit center. The average airport shopper has a household income 23 percent higher than the average shopping center customer.

TREND

LOW PRICES ARE HERE TO STAY

Do low prices forecast a bountiful harvest for business and the consumer or the seeds of future problems?
The next decade will be an age of disinflation—cost cutting and discounting will be standard business practice. Battered by worldwide overcapacity, high unemployment, slow economic growth and fierce global competition, companies won't be able to raise prices. In a low inflation landscape unfamiliar to most executives, companies will be forced to devise radically different pricing, manufacturing, marketing and compensation strategies to increase profits and market share.

Another evolving theme will be the change in our 1980s and early 1990s belief in self-actualization, self-interest and endless upward mobility. Now self-interest and upward mobility are evolving into family interest and a very unfortunate trend, downward mobility. Stagnant incomes bring frugality and savings back in fashion, but they also change consumer confidence and optimism into uncertainty and fear.

IMPLICATIONS
Advertisers adapt to this change by shifting the emphasis of product benefits. Products once sold as enhancements to personal style are repositioned to emphasize their practical benefits.

When prices were soaring, hiking revenues and reported profits were as simple as changing a price tag. But disinflation like inflation has a life of its own. A 1 percent drop in price will slash operating profits by 12.3 percent for the average Standard and Poor's 1000 company. Pricing pressures lead to more restructuring, which leads to more layoffs, which lead to consumers with less discretionary income, which reinforces the trend toward lower prices.

The pricing pressures are global—worldwide overcapacity plagues automobiles, chemicals, machine tools and computers. Since 1984, as prices for VCRs dropped more than 3 percent a year, Zenith Electronics Corporation estimated lost revenue from falling prices topped $2 billion. This is a nagging problem for U.S. consumer electronics companies like Zenith who moved manufacturing offshore to cut costs and improve profits.

The whole approach to pricing products will change and become a catalyst to streamline the corporation. In traditional pricing practice, a company decides on a selling price by adding all its costs, factoring in returns, overhead and standard profit margins. Such cost-driven pricing is a recipe for prices higher than the market will pay and allows an opening for lower cost competitors.

Instead, companies will reverse the equation by setting a target price for a new product or model change, which includes the price the marketing department believes consumers will pay as well as the profit-margin goals set by management. To achieve cost targets requires the use of a "matrix" organization design that assembles teams from engineering, research and development (R&D), marketing, finance and production. Such reengineering of corporations to meet target pricing will also promote faster new product development, simplify design and reorganize the work flow.

To survive in a low-inflation world, slash-and-burn cost-cutting will evolve into sophisticated strategies that will streamline and integrate business units. There will be an opportunity for new information technologies that help companies price better. Computer networks and databases will allow management to move away from traditional average-pricing techniques and instead closely track customer preferences. Sophisticated activity-based cost-accounting systems will allow managers to quantify in-depth production costs and highlight inefficiencies.

PREDICTIONS

LEARNING
RESOURCES
CENTRE

Factory stores, warehouse clubs, European hypermarkets and super-centers—all high-volume retailers that sell brand-name products at less-than-manufacturers'-suggested prices—will continue to transform major segments of the retail and wholesale distribution industries by the year 2000.

Selling quality and value will be the most difficult marketing challenge of the next decade. Consumers will expect low prices even on high-quality and value-added products. Customers will not accept premium pricing, without increased perceived benefits and strong advertising and merchandising campaigns. Many full-service and value-added products will be forced to strip down products and services customers don't value to compete in a low-cost, low-price environment. As the quality of generic products improves, brand loyalty will continue to wane. The fundamental question will be how much premium will consumers pay for a name brand versus a low-cost rival. It will be increasingly difficult to raise prices even on innovative products, thus further eroding R&D activities.

Japan and most of Europe will also experience deflation, causing more layoffs and disruption of traditional lifestyles. The lower prices, however, will be a boon for importers of European and Japanese products. The Japanese will buy less Louis Vuitton and more from The Gap.

Suppliers will be pressed to the breaking point to cut costs, and contracts will routinely be renegotiated. In the past, during an acquisition of a system or service, most of the time was spent determining requirements, preparing requests for proposals and evaluating responses. Joint teams for implementation included both the buyer and the seller. In the future, vendors will take a low-ball approach to pricing and plan on making up the loss in changes to complex systems.

Designs for new products will use fewer parts and reuse existing parts and designs. There will be greater cooperation and cost sharing with customers, and costly promotional spending will be slashed to help pay for price cuts.

TREND

THOSE WITH THE GOLD RULE—THE CHANGING CONSUMER

Rich-poor extremes will affect how we view tomorrow's consumer and is another trend that will sow the seeds of future problems.

The affluent markets earn over half the nation's income and have over two-thirds of all discretionary dollars. Indeed, the top 1 percent consists of families with incomes over $165,000. They will become the new mass market and will set the standard for the nation's consumption.

At the same time, if present trends continue, all but a small minority of consumers in the United States will soon be impoverished. The slow growing U.S. economy happens to be an increasingly fractured economy in which the top 20 percent as a whole is increasing its share of all income, and the remaining 80 percent has absorbed all the slow growth with a large fraction actually impoverished. The U.S. underclass, urban or rural, perhaps 6 percent of the population at most, already lives in full Third World conditions. The U.S. economic decline, even if it is only relative, can't remain only economic. Many American business, academic and cultural institutions are shrinking rather than growing.

IMPLICATIONS

Ken Colmen of SRI observed that while the overall standard of living on a global basis increases, it will go down for certain classes of consumers. We know in the United States that the next generation can't keep up with the past generation. This fact changes people's attitudes and opens different markets. Most of those people living in poverty aren't unemployed: They're working but not earning enough to afford life's necessities, not to mention luxuries. They're called the working poor.

What this trend means is that as people move in a downward economic direction they will become less materialistic, which will in turn negatively affect a lot of the world's consumer markets. If you look in the closets of the middle class and upper-middle class, you'll see they contain more clothes than the owners will wear for the rest of their lives. Do they need all of them? What are they going to be spending on and what are their options? We're coming to the end of the strongly acquisitive decade where consumers wanted and could afford to own more.

PREDICTIONS

The gap between the rich and the poor will widen worldwide. In the United States about 13 percent of households are upscale; while almost the same number are poised at the poverty line. The middle class will try desperately to hold on but nevertheless will shrink. There

> •
> WHAT STRATEGY DOES YOUR BUSINESS HAVE FOR MARKETING IN THE AGE OF SURPLUS?
> •

will be a movement toward both income poles with a smaller percentage moving toward upscale income levels.

The values of the industrialized world will shift from external values to inner values. We will become a lot more socially responsible and conscious though continually unable to cope with ever-increasing societal problems. Previously, people believed that what happened in Harlem was Harlem's problem as long as it didn't come downtown. But widening income inequality poses problems of resentment of the wealthy, which could reach a boiling point, leading to more riots like those in Los Angeles after the Rodney King verdict.

Because of these problems, Colmen thinks wealth must be redistributed. A professional group that thought it was entitled to wealth will have less wealth and more social responsibility. There will be more concern with the total population, particularly the poor. The thinking goes that if everyone is better off, the world is a better place. We see, for example, that cities in the United States are not safe places to live and work; after a while, you don't want to have to hide in safe zones.

TREND

TARGETED PERSONAL ADVERTISING (TPA)

Contributor—Mitch Gooze, CEO, OMT Group

Mitch Gooze predicts how the fragmentation part of the together-fragmentation megatheme will provide opportunities that will shift our advertising focus.

The mass media will figure out how to deliver individualized communication because if they don't, they won't survive. Magazines have already figured this out and many more specialty magazines exist. Video media will come up with similar capabilities.

Reaching fragmented markets is difficult and expensive, causing a consolidation of major media into fewer primary outlets.

More companies will be turning to data-based marketing to compete for market share and profits. Data-based marketing involves using computer software to keep detailed customer information for marketing. In 1990, more than half a million businesses in the United States alone were significantly relying on data-based marketing.

IMPLICATIONS

You and your business will receive more targeted product advertising as marketers rely on more sophisticated target marketing to find niches. Greater use of geodemographic and psychographic targeting will be required to reach your best prospects. Targeted media will increase as well as a dramatic increase in the number of cable channel viewers.

How advertising works today and how it might change in the retail tire industry.

In any town in America, if you open your newspaper, you'll find tire advertising. However, you never really see these tire ads until you're looking for tires. When you're looking for tires, there they are—but trust me, they're there all the time. If you work out the math about how long tires last and how many cars people typically have, you'll find that in any week about 2 percent of the population is looking for tires. So if

I'm a tire retailer who advertises in the weekly newspaper, I'm advertising to get to 2 percent of the population. The other 98 percent couldn't care less. Why do all the tire retailers do it? My response is that the entire industry (without realizing it) got together and decided to be equally wasteful with their money. As long as everyone agrees to advertise the same way, the playing field is level.

Now imagine, if you will, I sell you a set of tires. I know what tires you bought, what car you drive, how many miles you drive, where you live and who you are because I asked you all those questions when I sold you your last set. I know when you'll need new tires; indeed, I can narrow your next buy to a three-month window.

Why don't I have regular but staggered communications? Suppose you need new tires in three years—why don't I communicate with you twice a year? On your birthday and for the holiday season, I'll send you a greeting card, so you'll know that I remembered you. Then three months before you need tires, I'll call or write you. These targeted, personalized techniques will be less expensive and a magnitude more effective than the advertising industries' current newspaper ad campaigns to sell tires and many other products.

PREDICTIONS

During the 1980s and early 1990s, the consumer market was fragmented into segments by race, ethnic origin, household types and educational levels. Now fragmentation is evolving into "affinization," the proliferation of

> •
> WHICH AFFINITY GROUPS
> SHOULD YOUR BUSI-
> NESS BE TARGETING?
> •

groups organized around special interests. Affinization can be neighborhood-based or community-based as millions of baby boomers put down their roots. It can also be politically based as people organize around political agendas. Credit card companies are adapting to this trend by issuing "affinity cards" that offer small automatic donations to groups like the Sierra Club or the American Association of Retired People (AARP). Look for affinization to spread to other areas during the next decade.

A growing issue is how multinational companies should advertise their brands abroad. What are the merits of running the same ad around the globe versus turning over ad duties to the field in order to be sensitive to local culture. *"Be global, but local" will be the advertising motto for the next century.*

Against a background of cropped marketing budgets plus media price inflation and growth of private labels, clients will rethink how they spend their money. As advertising loses the ability to be a consumer magnet, we will see more companies ditching advertising and putting money into package design. Package design will become more critical.

Manufacturers will downsize packages to assure display space and make shipping around the globe more convenient. However, "giant-sized" units and portions from pizza to bottles of aspirin with 25 percent extra will be "in" with advertisers, while "mini" everything from sales of Ritz-Bits to promoting tiny donuts is "out."

Mid-sized companies will continue to lead in growth, filling the vacuums created by big business. Big advertising companies should anticipate continuing uncertainty and dislocation as organizations struggle to find the greater flexibility and longer range planning advantages of a mid-sized company. Custom publishing products are hot: 45 percent of advertisers said that their companies participated in such projects within the last three years. Moreover, 72 percent of the advertisers in a recent survey plan to make custom-publishing deals within the next year.

It's a commercial. No, it's a promo. No, it's a show—It's blur-mercial!

A variety of hybrid formats merging programming, promotion and advertising will flood the airwaves. These infomercials featuring commercials as programs that explain the how and why of exercise, food-making equipment as well as ways to become a millionaire through seminars, books and tapes have been shown to create significant consumer demand.

As major marketers arrive on the infomercial scene, the little guys who pioneered the material will get pushed out. And media availability, already at an all-time low because so many players have begun to flood the market will only worsen. Of course, that means marketers with pockets deep enough to pay premiums for time will put a squeeze on the others. By the year 2000, 80 percent of infomercial media purchases will be made by major marketers.

Though network share of prime-time programming is declining, network programming still accounts for the majority of prime-time viewing. Cable accounts for only about a 20 percent share, and Americans view only about a third of the channels available during the week.

Women 55 and over watch more TV than any other group, followed by men over 55.

Marketers are beginning to tap into women's growing "in-your-face" attitude by portraying men in the same negative ways in which women have been featured for decades. Some advertisements poke fun at mens' shortcomings; others use reverse sexism.

Almost one-third of adult TV viewers graze between channels due to boredom; that percentage will increase as the number of channels increase. News watching on TV will continue to decline. More women will watch sports, and men making under $30,000 will continue to constitute the largest segment for all sports viewing.

By 18, the American teen will have spent 17,000 hours watching TV, 11,000 hours in school and about 1,000 hours at the movies. By 11th grade, 39 percent of whites and 45 percent of Hispanics are watching television 3 hours or more daily as compared with more than 60 percent of blacks. Blacks will continue to watch more television throughout the day than others do. Major marketers will line up with video games using their logo's and characters.

Spanish language radio stations in the United States will continue to experience increases in Hispanic audiences. The larger audiences will continue to catch the attention of advertisers who are aware that Hispanics will become the largest ethnic minority group in the United States by 2010. Over 50 percent of Hispanics watch Spanish television exclusively.

As America becomes more ethnically diversified, so will its condiments (viva la salsa! adios ketchup).

By the year 2000, about 5 million Asians will be living in California. For the last two years, television advertising for the Chinese New Year's Parade in San Francisco has been sold out almost a year in advance. This endorsement epitomizes the growing awareness among advertisers that the Asian market is worth tapping. Asians coming to the United States are unfamiliar with all the American brand names.

Companies that get their foot in the door and create some strong brand presence will get the business.

Some additional predictions: A trend to reward the customer above and beyond the words "thanks for buying from me" will grow. States will continue trying to tax advertising and the media, though a federal tax is unlikely. Expect a shake out in home shopping by catalog and cable because of overextension and competition—fewer newspaper and book publishers, fewer sources of information and greater need for entertainment value in information to attract and hold users. The consumer will expect higher standards of service and choice in all aspects of life—whether it is the availability of cheese at the local supermarket or being able to choose what school a child attends.

TREND

IT PAYS TO BE NICE OR CAUSE MARKETING

Like knowledge, corporate consciousness and ethics will be perceived as valuable company resources.
Inspired by cause-marketing success stories such as Ben & Jerry's Ice Cream (which gives away 7 percent of pretax profits), many big name-brand companies are jumping on the bandwagon. Companies poured nearly a billion dollars into causes from the homeless to breast cancer (up 151 percent since 1990). Cause-marketing advocates say such campaigns can meet traditional marketing goals such as improving market share, motivating the sales force and improving a weak public image.

IMPLICATIONS

More corporate management and employees believe that corporations should be ethical entities—capable of reaping profits and, through stewardship, preserving the earth for future generations. Stewardship represents, in the broadest sense, the profound concern that all people should have for the earth and all its creatures and is much broader than environmentalism. The concern is that the growth of the world's economy, population, technological change and income inequality will combine to produce an unsustainable future. Therefore, attention to growth management must become part of every economic development strategy.

More than three-quarters of all Americans say their buying decisions are affected by a company's reputation about environmental issues. Yet, over 40 percent of all Americans believe business is doing a poor job in satisfactorily controlling pollution and over 90 percent of all Americans believe the public and private sector are doing an inadequate job to protect against pollution.

PREDICTIONS

Cause adverting will trumpet different issues in different global markets, for example, breast cancer in the United States and violence against women in Malaysia. Other issues such as animal welfare, will affect farming practices and land use, and environmental groups in the foreseeable future will curb the use of nuclear energy and the disposal of radioactive waste.

Green issues will continue to have a high profile. Many retailers and other sections of industry have recognized the advantage to emphasizing green aspects of their products—recycling of paper, glass and other products, while motor manufacturers looking for long-term recyclability of their products are using renewable resources as part of manufacturing.

Chapter 3

GROWTH BUSINESSES FOR THE YEAR 2000 AND BEYOND

•

You can never plan the future by the past.
EDMUND BURKE

If you do not think about the future, you cannot have one.
JOHN GALSWORTHY IN 1928

•

Rich or poor, it's nice to have money. One reason predicting the future is important is that we can profit by knowing it. Imagine for a moment that in 1970 you knew that small cars were going to replace the gas guzzlers coming out of Detroit and that Honda would move from selling almost no cars in the United States in 1970 to selling over 300,000 cars in 1982; or what if you knew that IBM would allow a couple of computer hackers to take the lead in the growing personal computer market with a startup called Apple; or what if you knew that houses would triple in value from their 1970 prices in the sunbelt states due to population migration and inflation. If you had known all these outcomes, you might have made a personal fortune.

Aren't there dozens of things about the next three decades you'd like to know? How about knowing what will happen to some of the growth businesses discussed in this chapter: Anti-aging drugs; telecommunications; entertainment; multimedia; infrastructure; liquid crystal displays;

and air transport. This chapter discusses how these businesses will affect your life.

TREND

ANTI-AGING DRUGS—SIX SCORE AND 10

Contributor—Steven William Fowkes, executive director,
Cognitive Enhancement Research Institute (CERI)

Young-old is obviously the megatheme for a wild card growth business that could make many people rich in the next decade.

A wild card trend that could have as profound effect as any scientific discovery in history is the pursuit of ways to prevent and cure aging. If some gerontology breakthroughs happen, today's young will keep their vigor well into their 80s, and today's seniors will feel they are growing younger. Gerontologists, neurologists, pharmacologists and other scientists will continue to chip away at the maxim that three score and 10 years constitutes a natural and acceptable human life span.

The oldest living humans live about 110 to 120 years. However, the average life span is only about 70 to 80 years. The maximum life span of rats is about 140 weeks or about three years. Substances such as vitamin E and BHT have been shown to extend the average life span in laboratory animals. Some scientists think these substances may also increase the odds of humans' reaching their maximum life span.

IMPLICATIONS

Deprenyl, recently recognized as a promising and safe drug for treating Alzheimer's disease, has dramatically extended the life span in rats by 40 percent. This increase would equal a human being living to 150! Because it corrects so many problems associated with aging (including decrease of sexual activity in men over 50), deprenyl can justifiably be called an anti-aging drug.

How Deprenyl Works

Deprenyl is the only drug known to selectively enhance the activity of a tiny region of the brain called the *substantia nigra*, which is exceptionally rich in dopamine-using neurons. Dopamine is the neurotransmitter that regulates such primitive functions as fine motor control, immune function, motivation and sex drive. Degeneration of neurons in the substantia nigra is implicated not only in the development of Parkinson's disease but also in the aging process. The steep decline of the Dopamine-containing neurons in the human brain after 45 is a universal characteristic of the aging process.

Deprenyl protects against the rapid age-related degeneration of the Dopamine-rich substantia nigeria.

Another promising anti-aging drug is melatonin, which regulates many neuroendocrine functions, including the ability to think clearly, remember facts and make sound decisions. This biological clock is disrupted by aging, stress and jet lag. The decrease in melatonin secretion with age is so reliable that it has been proposed as a measurement of biological age and may be the reason older people have trouble sleeping at night and are so fatigued during the day.

The FDA, in a battle about vitamins and nutritional supplement claims, will be in for a long fight because approximately half of all Americans take vitamin supplements, and about half of those take daily supplements. Moreover, a recent survey of 37,000 Americans established that 80 percent consumed less than the "recommended daily allowances" (RDAs) through their food. More ammunition for the pro-vitamin side—in stable chemicals, electrons almost always occur in pairs. In a species of chemical known as free radicals, however, one electron pair is stripped away, leaving the second desperate to find a mate. Free radicals attack proteins, DNA and other long molecules, causing a cross-linking reaction that harms the cells. By supplementing their diet with foods containing vitamins A, C and E that destroy "free radicals," the average life span of mice was extended by 75 percent.

PREDICTIONS

Deprenyl will be shown to slow aging in humans as it does in animals and will become a big moneymaker, while drugs such as melatonin will be used to treat age-associated memory impairment.

Though it must be considered that ultimately skin aging is unavoidable, breakthroughs in treating aged skin will yield good results and profits: Retin A will continue to be a sought-after wrinkle remover. Expect a dramatic increase in use of treatment creams containing free radical inhibiting vitamins A, C, E and an enzyme called Superoxide Dismutase, which eliminates superoxide radicals. Americans spend $3.3 billion on vitamins and nutrients every year, and the figure will grow.

Expect controversy from animal rights groups about the use of thymus extract obtained from young bovines that, when used with vitamin A palmitate, ascorbyl palmitate, vitamin E acetate and an extract of Sylibum marianum seeds has been shown to give good results in treating aging skin. Moreover anti-abortion rights advocates will object to anti-aging procedures using cell transplants from aborted fetuses.

TREND

TELECOMMUNICATIONS—SEE IT COMING

Dramatic change and smaller-faster characterize our next trend.

Expect explosive growth in the broad area of telecommunications, including the telephone, cordless phones, cellular phones, fax machines and fiber optics. Telephone information and entertainment services will grow dramatically throughout the next century.

Telecommunications is spelled I-S-D-N (Integrated Services Digital Network).

Recall the old, black rotary dial phone. I did recently as I helped a friend read through 40 pages of instruction on how to operate her new cordless phone. On the surface, besides portability, what the telephone does for us seems to have changed very little. But behind the telephones, out there in the networks, much has changed. Passage to international communications infrastructure is much easier than before. We are rarely out of sight of a telephone, and accessibility has dramatically increased with the promotion of portable and mobile telephones.

The telecommunications industry has been coming at portable communications both from the large and the small ends. The large method is cellular radio, with an investment in network infrastructure. At the other end are radio cells that shrank, compelled by traffic increase. As cells get even smaller, telecommunications will become so individualized that they will resemble Dick Tracy's wrist radio.

The economics of telephone communications today is controlled by the cost of providing local access. Technology presents greater economies of scale on the network level but few in the local loop providing access from the home to the local distribution point. Integrated Services Digital Network (ISDN) is end-to-end digital service, standardized throughout the world. ISDN could be thought of as a digital socket on the wall that transmits and accepts digital streams of data.

IMPLICATIONS

Telemarketing services will identify who is calling before the telephone even rings. All of the germane file information about the account of the caller will materialize on the screen as soon as the call is answered. Account clerks can convey data with their local computers or even with the computer of the caller on the same ISDN line and without a modem. ISDN links voice and data transmission on the same channel. No longer do the computer terminal and the phone on the same desk have to exist in different worlds.

High-fidelity systems will transmit more genuine sound, and we will realize how much has been missing with current telephone caliber speech—particularly tone and nuances of expression. High-fidelity music could also be carried over telephone lines. Another voice assistance that ISDN will make possible is speech that's encrypted for privacy. The market for guarded telephone service is variously estimated from inconsequential to a billion-dollar industry.

A messaging pattern that will have steady popular growth is the fax machine. You will be able to send someone a fax while you are speaking on the telephone. The fax will use one channel of ISDN while your voice uses another. The quality of fax reproduction will increase to the caliber of glossy-printed materials. Document retrieval and still images of high-quality black-and-white and reasonable-quality color pictures will be obtainable on our computers with ISDN.

Images will take an important role in telecommunications. The higher data rates in ISDN will accelerate the spread of image-based applications. The video phone was marketed by the Bell system beginning in 1971, but few customers were willing to pay the one hundred dollar a month service fee, so it was soon discontinued. Video-telephone service could be realized on ISDN through a plug-in board on a personal computer. Again, the attraction of ISDN is the logical combining of data streams, one of which would carry motion video.

PREDICTIONS

Video and audio text will be fast growth businesses during the early part of the year 2000 as consumers enjoy the novelty and advertisers experiment with innovative ways to communicate with new markets.

The evolution of cellular phones should enable complete mobility and obviate fixed wiring for home and office. Standards and systems are being designed to give each of us a personal telephone number that tracks us as we move. The network will keep you in touch with an old buddy by dialing his old telephone number or Social Security number; the network will know where he is. However, the tradeoff for accessibility is privacy.

Expect the use of 800 and 900 numbers to more than double by the year 2000 with more than two-thirds of 900 usage for entertainment. Videotext will also grow as the number of households with a modem attached to home computers increases dramatically (approximately one-sixth of the 25 million homes with PCs already have modems).

TREND

GAMBLING ON THE ENTERTAINMENT FUTURE

As gambling and entertainment explode in popularity, are we sowing the seeds of future problems?
Entertainment is the growth industry of the 1990s. In the United States alone, $340 billion was spent in finding ways to amuse ourselves from video rentals to theme parks to casinos. Moreover, the entertainment and recreation industry accounted for an amazing 12 percent of all new net employment in the United States. Though toys and sporting equipment are the largest area of consumer spending, the fastest growing segment of the entertainment industry is gambling.

IMPLICATIONS

Today, some form of gaming is legal in every state except in Hawaii and Utah. At the core of the increase in gambling are three influences: (1) the change of the public's view toward gaming as an acceptable form of entertainment; (2) the poor financial condition of most states; and (3) the bandwagon effect.

PREDICTIONS

The future prosperity of the entertainment industry depends on how much discretionary income people have after paying for essentials like rent, health care and food. If economic factors are positive in the next decade, people will spend heavily on entertainment; but even if they are negative, entertainment will do okay as the escape-from-depression remedy of choice worldwide.

Gaming will continue to spread across the country and will be a $48 billion industry by the year 2000, implying a growth rate of 7 percent or more for the decade. Slot machines have overtaken table games and will continue to be the single largest gaming attraction in the United States. The primary risks to rapid growth of the gaming industry are saturation and scandal. Existing gaming operations as well as newly opened territories are vulnerable to overbuilding. The shake out could speed up as industry giants move in with their slick marketing operations.

TREND

MULTIMEDIA MANIA

Smaller and faster interchangeable tools to overcome sophisticated competition are behind our next trend.
The way we work, play and live will be recast by an eruption of information services—a multimedia revolution. Fiber-optic networks will

permit us to answer our televisions and watch our phones. These networks will be the backbone of the so-called information highway. The new economic frontier is the knowledge economy—an economy so powerful that some 97 percent of all employment growth is coming from knowledge work. Wealth in the next decade will be generated predominantly by the value people add to products and services through new ideas. Information and the ability to share it will light the way into the next economy.

Providing nations with the information infrastructure to propel this knowledge work is the key concern of policy makers in America, Europe and Asia. The foundation concept in all these plans is the information highway—the computer-based high-speed network that creates a vast new cyberspace of linkages for entertainment, information and communications.

IMPLICATIONS

The fast lane of the information highway will continue to be hype without the local telephone network upgrades—the digital driveways that deliver multimedia to the home. Pressure will increase to introduce competition into the local telephone market (one of the last monopolies) to spur development of these digital driveways, driving down costs and making multimedia services more affordable.

Gigabit networks or data superhighways, as they are called, will be the prime competitive battleground of the next decade. Information infrastructure will become the economic weapon of tomorrow. In fact the battle has begun: growth in business and consumer spending on information and multimedia equipment as a share of U.S. gross domestic product (GDP) has more than tripled since 1989.

Multimedia is a new way of communicating. It will revolutionize human communication. Multimedia technology allows companies to create a symphony of text, graphics and audio with the user acting as conductor. For consumers, an assortment of services will spring up such as movies on demand, video training manuals and computerized travel guides. There will be many distinct kinds of multimedia and personal communications network (PCN) terminals—combining voice, data and image communications on-line.

Multimedia will be driven by whatever the customers want. In most multimedia markets, confusion still exists about what customers want and what they're willing to pay. There is agreement, however, that consumers want access to more technology. Indeed, 20 years ago there were only 50,000 computers; today the industry sells more than 50,000 computers in one day. One-third of all American homes have personal computers. The public network known as Internet now serves over 15 million people in 50 countries, and usage is growing at 15 percent per month.

As we telecommute from home we will have less traffic congestion and air pollution. It's true that such conferencing among people at a distance without the necessity for travel has long been an elusive goal for telecommunications. Today such conferencing is accomplished with speakerphones and to a much lesser extent with special video-conferencing facilities. Videoconferencing is expensive and can only be done from special locations. Neither is completely satisfactory in replacing face-to-face meetings. Although the next decade does not promise the total replacement of face-to-face meetings with electronic togetherness, new varieties of computer-mediated interactions among people will nevertheless increase.

As an illustration of multimedia conferencing, visualize my calling someone in another location. I could place the call directly from my computer workstation. When you answer the ring though your personal workstation, your computer screen becomes shared visual space. The same happens with another colleague. During our conference, I want to discuss a memo I have been writing. I summon it from a document database and the memo emerges on our respective computer screens. We edit the memo as we speak and concur on the new wording. You have a new product concept and call up a blackboard program from your computer and begin to draw the product. Our third associate who has been quiet during the memo writing thinks the product should be configured differently and changes it on the blackboard. You decide to have a side chat with me about not liking the alteration without insulting our co-worker—the system allows side and subconferences to be easily arranged.

Meanwhile, a marketing executive sitting at her desk reads the week's copy of the company "newspaper." From a graphics menu she clicks on "a state-of-the-company report," featuring a video of the CEO speaking about the company's strengths, weaknesses, opportunities and threats, followed by text and graphics displaying financial and sales information for the past four months. She than touches the menu button entitled "softball game highlights" and is treated to a chorus of baseball songs along with a photo montage of last month's company outing. She signs up on-line for the corporate consciousness meeting and then calls up a report of the status of client prospects that is updated daily by her assistant. Before signing off, she replies to a corporatewide survey on elder care concerns. Her response travels across the computer network and is added to her co-workers' answers in a database that crunches the numbers and delivers a report to the VP Human Relations by the end of the day.

The VP Human Relations uses the system to help communicate a new health insurance program that is more complex with employee choices. The company decides to install kiosks, much like automated teller machine stands, in the lunchrooms at each of its plants. After a short music video introduction, employees are invited to touch the screen and ask "what if" questions about how the plan would work, the costs and the benefit coverage available for their individual families. The training department has found that the ability to randomly access information makes multimedia a perfect medium for training and communication. Interactive programs are adapted to the individual employee's learning styles and needs. With interactive programs the trainers create simulations that allow users to review or skip information at their discretion and that can test and correct employee knowledge on the spot.

PREDICTIONS

Multimedia will be heavily used to create polished sales presentations, particularly by smaller companies that need to create the impression that they are more substantial.

New services will be available that will let parents away from home or at the office remotely monitor children; provide video-on-demand services, in America first and then globally; transform the way children learn and provide global access to multimedia classrooms. Most encyclopedic information is already on-line. But soon—with capabilities like video, audio and interactive multimedia— kids will be watching, listening and talking to their on-line encyclopedias. Distance learning—the use of videoconferencing to hold classes wherever students might be—will revolutionize higher education and present a cost-effective alternative to today's spiraling college costs.

By the early twenty-first century, U.S. research laboratories, universities, libraries, hospitals, businesses and eventually consumers will be hooked into a vast high-speed computing network able to ship billions of bits of digital information anywhere in the country with the blink of a cursor. The cost of such a network in the United States will be about $150 billion. With such a network, a doctor in a rural community could use advanced diagnostic equipment from a large research hospital in a distant city to analyze a patient's medical information.

Japan, France, Germany and Singapore will also develop data superhighways. Japan has vowed to spend $120 billion by 2005 to have a high-speed fiber-optic telecommunications system. European nations are backing a plan called the "European Nervous System" that will connect government institutions, labs and businesses in a continentwide computer network. Singapore has embarked on a multimillion dollar plan to create the most advanced information network in the world.

Mergers and acquisitions will be everywhere. I also see it happening in communications. We are seeing mergers right now among cable TV and entertainment companies and telephone companies. At the same time, production will become more decentralized. So instead of 20–500 blockbuster movies a year, we will have hundreds of mini-interactive movies. Customers will be able to select any one of a large number of movies from a list of box office hits and order these selections anytime.

TREND

THE BIG FIX—REPAIRING THE INFRASTRUCTURE

Rich and poor nations are becoming aware of the need to revalue their infrastructure resources.

In the chase for growth, Asian countries have run up a catalog of urban and infrastructure problems, apparently believing they can pick up the bill later.

Distracted by figures, pundits have overlooked the direct connection between economics and the urban environment. Indeed, many of Asia's cities are degrading faster than the region's robust economies are growing.

The flood of people pouring into Asia's cities is not about to stop. By 2020, a staggering 1.5 billion people will be added to the urban centers of Asia. As a result, Asia threatens to become a region of megacities, each with over 8 million inhabitants.

Radical solutions and innovations are needed in repairing and building infrastructure to meet this historical population and economic growth.

IMPLICATIONS

With the number of passengers worldwide expected to double to 2 billion annually by 2005, airport authorities around the world are rushing to build gigantic facilities. Denver International Airport, for example, opened with the ability to accommodate 34 million passengers annually. They now plan to accommodate 110 million by 2020.

In most countries of the world, repair of infrastructure is something that governments postpone for long periods. If you look at phone systems and other infrastructure in many developing countries, you'll consistently find that governments are paying lost opportunity costs rather than out of pocket infrastructure expenses. Ken Colmen shared the information that in Zambia, for example, the only roads, built by the British many years ago, are in a state of serious disrepair. The only road repair done is putting mud into the holes. The problem is that by not building the infrastructure, Zambians miss tremendous agriculture opportunities. Because they can't ship agriculture products and must sell them locally, Zambians don't earn as much. But since commerce doesn't come to a complete halt, they continue to forego repairs and replacement.

Bernard Schwartz, CEO of Loral Corporation, sees major opportunities for modernization of government systems infrastructure. Look, for example, at the Justice Department, the IRS and the air traffic control system in the United States. They're all 20 to 25 years old and don't incorporate modern technology, business practices and new systems such as bar coding. Upgrading these services and systems is going to be extensive. There is opportunity in both hardware and software applications, and there are few companies that service the market because of the high entry cost. In fact, Loral bought IBM Federal Systems, which is a leader in that area, to exploit that opportunity in what is expected to be a fast-expanding business sector in the next decade.

PREDICTIONS

China will spend as much as $200 billion by the year 2000 on infrastructure development. The Pearl River Delta will continue to drive the province of Guangdong's economic success. Despite rising costs in the Delta, foreign investors continue to come in droves. However, energy, transportation, and communications bottlenecks have reached critical levels in many area of the Delta. As China gives priority to infrastructure development, business opportunities appear especially promising in energy, telecommunications and transport sectors.

Around the world, we will see a major increase in private ownership of transportation infrastructure such as airports, seaports, railroads and satellite navigation systems.

Higher energy costs and greater traffic congestion will create more political pressure for public mass transit, particularly multimodal systems that offer greater transportation options to the public. This political pressure, coupled with greater construction costs, will lead to more efficient mass transit in densely populated high-traffic areas.

The United States will designate high-speed rail corridors in congested areas with the greatest economic potential. Light-rail systems will replace the expensive underground subways. Trains will rocket across Europe at up to 180 miles an hour and by 2020 will serve every major European city from the Baltic to the western Mediterranean.

TREND

IT'S A CLEAR WINNER—LIQUID CRYSTAL DISPLAYS (LCD)

The United States is lagging behind in one-third of the key cutting-edge technologies, according to the Council on Competitiveness.
The most horrifying example of our technological tardiness is in liquid crystal displays. This lag is sowing the seeds for future problems with our sophisticated competitor Japan.

Flat panel displays will be used in everything from autos to fighter planes and on every entrance ramp on the information highway. They are found on most notebook computers, and they will power the television sets of the future. The LCD industry is expected to expand from $5 billion today to $20 billion by the year 2000. Registering spectacular growth in particular are thin film transistor (TFT) mode LCDs. All the LCD makers have placed their sights on the growth rate of the TFT LCD market and will compete fiercely for a share of the expanding market.

IMPLICATIONS

Japan owns 95 percent of the global market. Sharp Corporation of Japan is the acknowledged LCD leader, and only a couple of small American companies are struggling to keep up. Companies like IBM are forced to go offshore to buy displays, dropping even more dollars offshore.

To get back into the game, the Pentagon will spend $1 billion on a national flat panel display initiative to provide incentives to get to full-scale manufacturing. To get around international trade agreements that bar such government intervention, the Pentagon will pay half the cost of a pilot plant—about $100 million plus an additional $100 million in matching industry research funds.

PREDICTION

The TFT LCD market appeared in 1986. After being developed for use as a display on 3-inch-sized televisions, the display was mainly used on 3-inch- to 5-inch-sized televisions. Large-sized panels of around 14 inches to 17 inches are now being manufactured on a limited scale for practical use. Parallel to their enlargement, the uses of LCDs will expand steadily. Along with the establishment of technology for producing large-sized panels, the competition among the manufacturers, who are mostly Japanese, will intensify. Foreign governments are sure to challenge the U.S. trade subsidies.

TREND

AIR TRANSPORTATION AND DISTRIBUTION TAKES OFF

The shifting focus of business to the Far East will make the air transport and distribution sectors high flyers in the next decade.

In the past decade, the volume of air cargo worldwide has doubled, and it's projected to grow two and a half times by 2005, with the strongest growth patterns expected in trade with the Orient. Air cargo currently accounts for $1.1 trillion or one-third of the dollar value of goods shipped globally. That figure will more than double to $2.5 trillion by the year 2000.

IMPLICATIONS

Today's companies are increasingly using air to carry high-value, time-sensitive products that were shipped by ocean 5 or 10 years ago such as chemicals, medical equipment, computer hardware and software and fashions. Logistics specialists stress that companies should figure precisely by how much air offsets its premium price as it lowers total costs—including such expenses as the cost of financing inventories, warehousing, manufacturing and purchasing.

Distribution space accounts for more than 3 billion square feet of the 7 billion square feet of industrial space in the largest metropolitan areas in the United States. As companies worldwide become more distribution efficient, the structure of those holding inventories will continue to change. Manufacturers will continue to hold less, and the number of independent wholesalers will increase. Independent whole-salers will continue to expand as producers downsize their facilities, providing niche development opportunities in those localities favored by the expanding wholesaler sector.

The thriving regional Asian economies have spawned a vast middle class that must travel for business and wants to travel for pleasure. New airlines are forming and old airlines are introducing new routes. Luxury hotels are opening in major cities, and middle level, budget hotels and resorts are appearing across the region.

After successfully breaking into other industries once dominated by the West—shipbuilding, cars, consumer electronics, textiles—Asians would like their fledgling aerospace industry to take off. Asian compa-nies already make components for western aircraft producers, but they want a bigger role.

Japan is planning its second attempt at building an airliner. South Korean firms are involved with many projects, including an Asian ver-sion of Europe's aircraft-making consortium, Airbus Industrie. China's aerospace industry already employs more than half a million people who spend most of their time keeping aging Russian jets from falling apart.

In America, where the average age of airlines is now 11, near bank-rupt airlines replace jets only when they wear out (or crash). In Asia, where airlines are profitable and new airports seem to open every year, the average age of aircraft is only 7.

By 2010, aircraft will be equipped to use global navigational satel-lite systems to ease the projected doubling of air traffic early in the twenty-first century.

PREDICTIONS

Asian airlines will buy some 3,000 airliners worth around $250 billion between now and 2010. Those sales will represent about one-third of the world's market for commercial jets. Japan alone is expected to buy more than 600 jets and China about 800. Every other Boeing 747-400 jumbo jet is now delivered to an Asian airline; many of the rest fly to or from Asia.

Asia's aerospace drive reflects the deeper eastward shift in many markets. In the airline market, the Asia-Pacific region already accounts for about a quarter of worldwide air travel. By 2010, the Asian region will have almost half of the world's air passenger traffic. The market for hotels in Asia will be increasingly domestic, and many long-haul travelers will be looking for less expensive accommodations.

Through 2010, African airlines will need $34 billion for replacement aircraft and growth—estimated at 7 percent annually. The airlines are being urged to buy rather than lease aircraft to build equity. The carriers must fund 15 percent of their investment in new aircraft to satisfy the export agencies' requirement for financing the rest.

Chapter 4

THE MOST IMPORTANT FINANCIAL AND LEGAL TRENDS AND THEIR IMPLICATIONS

·

A pinch of probability is worth a pound of perhaps.

JAMES THURBER

Be wary of the man who urges action in which he himself incurs no risk.

JOAQUIN SETANTI

There is no such thing as "zero risk."

WILLIAM DRIVER

Take calculated risks. That is quite different from being rash.

GENERAL GEORGE SMITH PATTON

·

Fundamental changes are at work in the international marketplace. Risks, both financial and legal, are increasing as operating complexities and

65

competition provide very real if not insurmountable concerns for managers. This chapter discusses the financial and legal trends that will have great impact on business: *Financial Markets in 2020; Financial Engineering and Particle Finance; Just Lawyers; Blurred vision—Negotiating with Third World Governments; Globalization of the Financial Information Infrastructure; The New Owners Are Big and Worldly;* and *Don't Bank on It.*

TREND

FINANCIAL MARKETS IN 2020

Contributor—Charles S. Sanford, Jr., chairman and CEO, Bankers Trust Company

Charles S. Sanford, Jr., chairman and CEO of Bankers Trust Company, clearly shares his fascinating prospective about the dramatic changes that will be affecting the financial markets. In the world of 2020, technologies will be on-line, and that will affect how basic financial functions will be performed. These functions are financing, risk management, trading and positioning, advising and transaction processing. Although financial functions will be the same, they will be looked at differently in the next century. Then, we will not refer to "loans," "borrowing" or "securities" but to "claims on wealth." A key to the system will be *wealth accounts* in which companies and individuals will hold their assets and liabilities.

IMPLICATIONS

Wealth accounts will contain today's relatively illiquid assets such as buildings and vehicles as well as what we know today as stocks and bonds. These accounts will also contain all forms of liabilities. Computers will continuously keep track of the items in wealth accounts and will constantly mark both assets and liabilities to market, making these items effectively liquid. Within an individual wealth account, the arithmetical sum of the items will be the net worth.

All seekers of financial "claims" will understand that to get full access to the financial markets, they will be legally responsible for keeping their wealth accounts current. These accounts will be electronically accessible to any authorized user, directly or through computerized analytic programs. Privacy will be maintained as with today's checking accounts. Wealth accounts will be the focal point for financial processing and reporting. The integrity of these accounts will be validated by institutions, much as checking accounts or mutual funds are today.

PREDICTIONS

Wealth accounts will be instantly tapped via "wealth cards." For example, you will be able to pay for your sports car by instantly drawing on part of the wealth inherent in your vacation house. Instant credit will be available to companies and individuals, secured by the current value of their wealth accounts.

Owners of wealth accounts will use automated analytic tools to help them determine their risk-reward appetites and suggest appropriate actions to achieve those targets. If the owner approves, the wealth account would automatically implement the program. Automated analytic systems will also provide customized investment management, making wealth accounts superior to today's mutual funds. In effect, individuals will have the option to manage their own mutual funds.

Global electronic bulletin boards will be the principal medium through which buyers and sellers will post their needs and execute transactions. Many financial claims (including loans and securities) will bypass middlemen (commercial and investment banks) and will be bought and sold via electronic action through global bulletin boards, with minimal transaction costs.

In effect, supplying financial assistance will be a free-for-all. It will not be limited to those calling themselves "financial institutions" because any organization or individual will be able to reply to needs posted on the bulletin boards. That means an organization that specializes in financial matters may at times find itself competing directly with its clients. In addition to the bulletin boards that will be open to anyone who pays a nominal fee, users and suppliers of financial claims will be networked to each other to exchange real-time data and documents (computer to computer) to automatically execute most day-to-day transactions and maybe to confer via virtual reality electronic meetings.

Other elements of the financial world of 2020 are harder to predict. What form will robbery and fraud take? Human nature will not change, and dishonesty will be around in 2020 as it is today. Voice recognition, DNA fingerprinting and secure data encryption will instantly verify transactions, preventing today's scams. But new forms of "information crime" will no doubt appear.

Today, we have only a few recognized rating agencies. In 2020, we will have hundreds—perhaps thousands—of specialized providers of news, data and analysis that will provide electronic bulletins, on demand, in real time and tailored to each subscriber's particular notion of risk.

Special retail financial branches will be unnecessary because individuals will have direct access to their financial suppliers through interactive TV and personal digital assistants. True interstate banking will be here at last! Or more accurately, true "global banking" will have arrived because every household will be a branch.

A key feature of 2020 is that nearly all services could be tailored to a clients needs or wishes at a reasonable price, including highly personalized ones from financial companies. Firms will be selling to market segments of one.

TREND

FINANCIAL ENGINEERING AND PARTICLE FINANCE

Contributor—Charles S. Sanford, Jr.

Revaluing knowledge resources for sophisticated competition are the themes in Charles Sanford's next interesting trend.
As finance becomes more like science and the arts, a convergence is taking place among scientists, business people, engineers, economists, mathematicians and lawyers. Financial theory is becoming increasingly important as theoretical advances have emerged in the last few years. These theories include portfolio theories, asset-pricing theories, option pricing and market efficiency theories.

A trend, particularly in Europe, toward "financial engineering" is occurring globally. Banks are hiring people with training in physics, engineering, and hard mathematics. These educational backgrounds are necessary because the financial models that develop derivatives are beginning to look more like engineering or physics problems and less like classical economics. These models will improve comprehension and risk management. The models deal with variables as straightforward as interest rates and as complex as the weather—all reason that have enormous impact on the markets.

The rapidly growing acceptance of derivative-based financial solutions to reduce risks for major financial organizations is an important example of the application of the physical sciences to the world of finance. Pioneers in the derivatives business are identifying, extracting and pricing some of the fundamental risks that drive asset values such as interest rates, currency values and commodity prices.

Now, however, the science of markets is at an extraordinarily early developmental stage. We are still in a "Newtonian" era of "classical finance" in which we look at financial instruments—stocks, bonds and loans—in static, highly aggregated terms.

Models based on classical finance analyze risk at the securities level (or options on these securities) and usually assume that the volatility is based on a highly aggregated bundle of many underlying risks that are unlikely to be stationary and that usually interact with one another. Classical finance also assumes that humans are rational economic decision makers—an assumption that often appears to be violated.

Most classical finance models concentrate on the "beta" of a stock—the stock's volatility relative to the market. These models have great difficulty in dealing with the multitude of critical underlying reasons that produce beta such as changes in financial market volatility, changes in global product, the volume of transactions, an earthquake in Japan, changes in consumer confidence in the United Kingdom or a change in corporate strategy. We describe these critical factors as "financial attributes." Beta ignores them or grossly summarizes them as homogeneous packets of white noise.

Theoreticians, however, have not ignored them. Researchers have begun to look for a theory—what we call "The Theory of Particle Finance"—that will help us understand an asset's financial attributes. Like quantum physics and modern biology, particle looks beneath the beta to identify an asset's financial attributes, including the attribute's individual and collective volatility. Efforts are being made to integrate these attributes into the desired financial claims.

IMPLICATIONS

This work is creating order from apparent disorder, providing building blocks that will allow the more effective packaging and management of risk in an economy whose structure is constantly changing. The research aims at reaching the most efficient balance of risk and return. Finding such a theory is not around the corner; but we are seeing interesting signs of progress, and by 2020 a much more powerful financial discipline will be in place.

Chaos theorists are attempting to find the underlying structure and pattern—if they indeed exist—of the apparent randomness of changes in asset values. Researchers are building neural networks that mimic certain properties of the human brain. It is hoped that when these neural networks are harnessed to massive computing power, they will find meaningful patterns in the "noise" of financial attributes and, by learning from experience, will strip away some of the apparent randomness of financial events.

"Fuzzy logic" is a mathematical way of drawing definite conclusions from approximate, vague or subjective input. Because it attempts to embody certain human perception and decision-making skills, fuzzy logic may help us understand complex systems that involve human interaction (like financial markets).

Combinations of these and new methods may produce the answer. For example, information gleaned from the neural networks might be used to define "fuzzy" relationships in the system and then to write fuzzy rules to control the process or predict the behavior of the system in new situations.

PREDICTIONS

Pioneers in the derivatives business are successfully identifying, extracting and pricing some of the fundamental risks that drive asset values such as interest rates, currency values and commodity prices. New derivative applications are on the runway; for example, credit derivatives and insurance derivatives.

Long before 2020, credit risks will be broken down into discrete attributes that will be readily traded, unbundled and rebundled. Intermediaries will manage a large book of diversified long and short positions in credit attributes. They will make markets in credit risk attributes and in bundles of attributes customized to suit the particular needs of their clients.

In 2020, as particle finance evolves, the primary job of financial institutions will be to help clients put theory to practical use. Implementation may be done through automated analytic tools that will provide much better allocation advice than is available today—allocating positions across many financial attributes rather than just picking the stock and bond mix.

TREND

JUST LAWYERS

Contributor—Some predictions by Connie Bagley, Stanford Graduate School of Business

Lawyers and their politician cousins are easy targets because both are sowing the seeds of future problems as they experience sophisticated competition in their fields. Constance Bagley, who teaches law and management at the Stanford Graduate School of Business, shared some of her insights about legal trends in 2005.

As the number of lawsuits in the United States has tripled in the last 30 years, we realize the desperate need for legal reform. The business community is scared to take the risks it needs to take for survival and feels abused by staggering legal costs, huge judgments, excessive lawyering and costly delays.

IMPLICATIONS

The United States has gone overboard in protecting individual liberties at the cost of endangering the future of the economy. Indeed, a poll of corporate executives revealed that 83 percent say their decisions are increasingly affected by the fear of lawsuits. Small wonder with law firms grossing well over $100 billion according to Department of Commerce estimates.

The legal system is rigged in favor of big business—lawsuits are a devastating competitive weapon for those who can afford them. Indeed, tort reform, including ending class-action suits and preventing people from suing a company if they misuse its product, would spark an explosion of productivity in America.

The legal profession is more specialized and more diversified than ever, not only in race or gender, but also in the range of cases. The disparity between the highest and lowest salary of new law graduates also continues to spread; some graduates make $80,000; others make $20,000. Moreover, an allied legal profession similar to that of the medical profession has developed that has created roles for paralegals, contract attorneys and permanent associates.

PREDICTIONS

To loosen legal strangleholds, expect companies to look for alternatives to litigation such as arbitration and mediation, including binding arbitration in all legal documents; efforts to severely limit the number of lawyers passing the bar exam; judges not juries setting damage awards and strict limits on the amounts of awards; and efforts to prevent the law from being used for determining priorities among broad social, economic and political interests. The discovery rules will be changed dramatically to cut back on the amount of paper, interrogatories and dispositions.

Globalization will open many markets to American lawyers if they're culturally flexible. The lawyer's principal service consists of keeping the form of a business transaction on the beaten track because the more regular a transaction is, the less danger of an upset in court. The chief merit of lawyers is an almost unconscious familiarity with the trade. However, the reverse is true in international dealings, where the prime requirements are a conscious appreciation of different ways of doing business, a flair for explaining one way in terms of another and an imaginative resourcefulness in devising new methods that are acceptable to businesspeople of different cultures.

Competition from foreign lawyers and law firms will grow. Globalization will also force transcontinental cost comparisons: If, for example, the Germans are able to produce a car with lower legal costs, they will put pressure on American manufacturers to lower their legal costs, adding pressure to reduce attorneys' fees.

Directors and Officers Liability Coverage (D&O) can expect increased international exposure over the next decade as economic borders give way to the global economy. We will see the demise of the old-boy network in choice of directors. These boards today are composed mostly of white men in their 50s and 60s. Shareholders are increasingly saying, "Look at all the women and minorities that buy your products and deserve representation on the board."

Also, the tendency to have the CEO choose the directors will be challenged, and directors will be chosen by an independent nominating committee that is not chaired by the CEO. In addition, we're going to see a global governance drive as the market for capital grows increasingly more global. Companies can no longer afford to be insular. For example, in the past in Switzerland, non-Swiss citizens were denied a vote on their shares. Now, big pension funds investing in Swiss companies register shares, giving shareholders a vote.

By 2005, we will see takeover and proxy contests in Japan. Pension funds simply will not invest in Japanese companies unless they have a corporate governance structure that is responsive to shareholders. And being responsive to employees or just to other members of the keiretsu will no longer be enough.

New U.S. laws such as the Americans with Disabilities Act and the Civil Rights Act of 1991 will continue to generate a growing number of employment-related claims. Discrimination and harassment claims are being filed in unprecedented numbers, resulting in unprecedented damages awards. A California jury recently took revenge on the legal profession by slapping a law firm with a $7-million-plus verdict after a partner put M & Ms in the blouse pocket of a secretary. Ouch!

U.S. insurance carriers can expect to see increased claims activity in the United Kingdom, Europe and Japan as those countries make their court systems more accessible. Court systems will continue to be overwhelmed and costly. Alternate dispute resolution (ADR) to solve problems through out-of-court mediation will continue to grow. In addition, there will be a global effort to protect intellectual property to promote increased global trade in services.

Franchising of basic legal research will grow. With the current system, an in-house counsel calls a local outside law firm when a research question arises and has that firm do a memorandum, usually researched by a junior associate who has never fielded the question before. Instead, what we're going to see is a tendency to "batch" research. Basically, you call into a number and say "I have issue XYZ," and the research company in their file will have information on that issue and will generate a tailor-made memo to rely on for a fraction of the cost to pay a junior associate who is first going down the learning curve. Clients will increasingly be unwilling to have their money used to train junior lawyers.

Furthermore, the future holds less hourly billing and more project- or subject-related billing; more work brought in-house; more advertising, price cutting and client stealing.

More business will be taken away by nonlawyers, do-it-yourself guides and computer programs. Higher levels of education in the general population will also reduce the information advantages of professionals. Although 60 percent of the members of the U.S. Senate are lawyers, many members of the House of Representatives are not. The trend for nonlawyers as U.S. law-makers will continue.

TREND

BLURRED VISION—NEGOTIATING WITH THIRD WORLD GOVERNMENTS

The culture gap between the rich and poor nations requires a shifting focus in management thinking.

Because of growing obligations of their companies in developing countries, large numbers of American, Japanese, and European executives will be entering into economic negotiations with government bureaucrats in Asia, Africa and Latin America. These negotiations will be increasingly demanding as deliberation about what is a "fair" division of proceeds continues to be a premier concern to both parties.

IMPLICATIONS

Third World government negotiators characteristically make two kinds of calculations. First, how much the country must give up to captivate the foreign investor and, second, what the terms were that investors in other developing countries obtained in similar circumstances. In the economic calculation, the government negotiator will frequently have a rate of return in mind just high enough to appease the foreign company and will strive for an agreement that will siphon as much of the return as possible above this minimum as shared revenue and taxes for the host country.

Government negotiators are always interested in more than financial flow. They, like labor leaders, also make political estimates. Indeed, the real restraint on many governments will be political as the appearance of terms beneficial to the investor will furnish the opposition a clear political target.

PREDICTIONS

On the surface, standard foreign investment contracts give some guarantee of stability for many years. But don't expect terms to stay unchanged; instead, expect renegotiation as a way of life no matter how solid the guaranteed terms look on paper.

Increasingly, being close to government officials will be the determinant of success in developing (and developed) countries. Expect government and military officials in former socialist countries to grasp the "everyone for himself" rules of capitalism. They will increasingly continue to divert country resources and opportunities to family and friends.

TREND

GLOBALIZATION OF THE FINANCIAL INFORMATION INFRASTRUCTURE

Contributor—Bernard Fleitman, vice president, Dow Jones Telerate

Writing a future trends book is akin to running to catch a moving bus—you try to publish trends before the future passes your stop. Bernie Fleitman shared his views about global change, valuing knowledge and derivatives before the media had begun to explore the subject. His insights about other trends thankfully are still several stops ahead of the bus.

As the cost and efficiency of computer power comes down and connectivity increases dramatically, information that affects financial markets is being received simultaneously throughout the globe. Dow Jones provides factual information such as the current price for GM stock while CNN sends information about a single story or event around the world.

IMPLICATIONS

Everyone's a player, so the game is over. Foreign exchange trading profits used to be made by staying ahead of the crowd and putting information into meaningful facts. But with the cost of computing power coming down and with increased connectivity worldwide, everybody sees information so fast that moneymaking on simple foreign exchange transactions is difficult.

We create more complexity to create opportunities. Computing power will, however, allow individuals and firms to perform highly complex transactions that offer opportunity for financial gain. The simple foreign exchange transaction of trading Deutsche marks for francs for profit could become a complex four-way arbitrage, where Deutsche marks might be traded for yen, then pounds sterling and dollars before converting into francs to make a satisfactory conversion or to turn a profit.

The finance community will take on a hidden but increasingly powerful role in some of the events that will happen, especially in emerging countries. New, evermore complex financial instruments and transactions could potentially have big effects on countries worldwide, perhaps less so on the U.S. government, but much more dramatically on a country like Portugal. Some large bank or financial institution could sell enough of your currency or create derivatives to include enough of it to change the economics of your country. Large financial institutions could decide, for example, to alter the exchange rate of your currency, which could drive prices up or down on imports, exports and domestic products. With the big five currencies that's hard to do—it's very hard to drive the dollar or the yen or even the French franc. But in emerging countries, it's not so hard considering how highly leveraged these transactions are.

These transactions by banks and large financial institutions are not a global conspiracy—quite the opposite, it's a form of free enterprise at work on a global scale. Some banks, particularly in Europe and Japan, are very secretive about what they're doing. They could drive the global markets without us knowing how or why the markets are being driven. How could we know? In some cases, the central banks of developed countries get involved in these games—albeit a dangerous one. At the far end of this spectrum, political upheaval is possible but not very likely. Generically, causing a war is not in the best interests of any financial institution. Putting aside questions of ethics, such institutions probably will not knowingly cause that kind of destabilization because they can't control the effects—but the potential still exists.

These complex deals will often not be public nor subject to much government regulation or review. Basically, if the institutions don't break any laws they're completely legal. My trading house and your trading house make a deal. We honor the deal and don't tell anyone. We could be very happy and satisfied with that deal and send out our year-end annual report showing that we made money without the details. We're all happy; however, that deal caused the price of oil to go up. This scenario is a possibility from some of these clandestine transactions, probably not from a single deal, but people do jump on the bandwagon.

Most of the large players are multinational. Merrill Lynch is considered to be a U.S. firm, but it has trading rooms in 40 countries around the globe. If Merrill Lynch wants to do an operation from Singapore, the firm will do it from the Singapore trading room instead of from New York. Depending on the tax treatments and local laws, structuring the transaction this way may be very clever. The legal constraints are not the same as the ones for a true U.S. corporation. The legal systems that exist in the United States or any other country are not structured to deal with such financial meganationals.

Economic fluctuations will be very hard for economists to understand. Economists often look for underlying primary reasons and these complex speculative transactions are not primary. Underlying these deals is enrichment or depletion of resources in finance because of things that are synthetic and not natural to supply and demand models. For example, why does the price of copper go down? too much supply? too little demand? This is how economists think but, of course, in more complex terms today.

The complex deals and transactions made possible by the increased computer power and globalization of financial information, however, are not visible to economists even on a micro level, and because there's so much going on, even on a macro level. For example, a good fraction of copper goes through the New York commodities exchange. What happens if a couple of investment houses decide to hedge copper against winter wheat or something else. I don't know if economists can understand that fluctuations in the price of copper were caused by that transaction. But, they definitely cannot understand the fluctuations in our economy as these deals happen all over the globe.

Since the financial markets are affected by world change or perception of world change, information whether correct or incorrect affects change. For example, an incorrect news story about damage to a Columbian oil pipeline drove the prices on the spot oil market.

PREDICTIONS

The public will face an increasingly complex unintelligible world, and government intrusion into that world will become less effective.

More companies will get involved in direct foreign exchange. If a large company is doing business around the globe, why should it pay the bank to trade dollars for yen? The bank is a business that charges for the transaction. Why not just do business directly—pick up the phone and call a counterparty Bank X and say, "I need dollars for yen. I have this amount of dollars. How much yen will you give me?" You will get the best rate because you're a primary part of the game.

Life insurance businesses will get very involved in financial market-places. They have always been involved as investors, but now they will become market makers by creating insurance derivatives to syndicate their risk. Japanese life insurance companies seem to be somewhat aggressive in this arena—they're building trading rooms around the world.

The small players will be squeezed out or become marginal. Opportunities for them will decrease because understanding these complex issues requires many people, and the money involved is a large amount—you don't trade small amounts. The greatest impact of the globalized financial information infrastructure and increased computing power will be on the large global investment houses: Merrill Lynch; Morgan Stanley; Lehmann Brothers and the other big investment houses.

TREND

THE NEW OWNERS ARE BIG AND WORLDLY

The movement from small to big and from fragmented to together in the control of corporations may be a move toward sophisticated competition or could be sowing the seeds for future problems.

Control of the world's corporations will continue to shift from individual investors to financial institutions—investment companies, foundations, mutual funds, trust and banks pension funds. In the year 2000, such institutions are expected to own 80 percent of all the equities on the New York Stock Exchange. Today institutional trades constitute almost 90 percent of the NYSE transactions (by both volume and value).

Global investing is the way these groups will go. Approximately one out of four equity trades conducted worldwide today involves either a foreign share or a foreign buyer or seller.

IMPLICATIONS

The trend from individual investors to financial institutions has far-reaching consequences because individual investors primarily look for long-term performance, while institutions pursue short-term profits.

Indeed, the fundamental focus of the stock market has been transformed from long-term investing to short-term speculation. Individual investors whose primary objective is long-term investment, turn over only half their stock holdings annually. Financial institutions, by contrast, turn over four times as much as the individual investor's annually.

Institutions own so many equities that they exert a powerful presence in the stock markets. And corporate executives are often at the mercy of their demands. Indeed, institutions own more than 75 percent of the stock of the nation's one hundred largest corporations. Only a few global organizations will have sufficient profits and assets to make the commitment to long-term global competitiveness without sacrificing shorter term earnings.

The flow of equity across borders (not counting direct investment) rose from $42 billion in 1986 to $159 billion in 1993; most of the investment was in developed nations. But the most impressive growth was registered in newly industrialized countries.

The United States is the largest net investor in emerging markets of the Pacific Rim and Latin America, providing about $20 billion in 1993, followed by Britain ($9.5 billion) and Japan ($6.8 billion). The investment power of the emerging nations is growing as well. They invested about $2 billion in other nations' stock markets in 1992 and over $20 billion in 1993.

PREDICTIONS

Corporate liquidations—where raiders join with pension funds to buy and liquidate firms whose stock is priced below salvage value—will increase, adding to the global unemployment woes. As more managers and investors borrow heavily to take companies "private" and to avoid stock market pressures for quick results, leveraged buyout activities will increase. Merger and takeover activity will increase as pension funds continue to provide much of the financing for this speculation.

Large block trading will continue to soar. There will be federal taxes on short-term gains on pension fund stock trades and regulations to change fund management compensation from transaction costs or management fees to some long-term fund performance measurement.

TREND

DON'T BANK ON IT

The banking industry with its conservative past will experience dramatic change.

International banking may once have consisted of frock-coated gentry, filing in and out of Swiss meeting rooms. It's come a long way from that now. The banking industry finds itself under enormous pressure throughout the world. Banking and money were once synonymous; now even the ordinary citizen is beginning to see money as an item that one buys and prices competitively. The bank is merely one of the variety of places where that can be done.

IMPLICATIONS

Corporations are lending money and charging lower interest rates than the banks. Americans are borrowing money from English banks and lending it to Third World customers more cheaply than the English banks can. Of course, making loans to the less-developed countries requires a willing suspension of disbelief.

The World Bank Revisited

Today the world's largest engine for economic development is the World Bank, lending $24 billion a year, mostly to poor nations. A bank review of 82 projects showed that almost half failed to meet their goals, with many leading to environmental havoc, displacing millions of poor and tribal people.

PREDICTIONS

Central Banks

The role of central banks will change as financial markets change. Two basic functions of central banks will be to protect us from systematic risk and to keep inflation in check.

The mechanisms by which central banks deal with inflation in the next decade are not clear. One method might be the use of margin requirements to control the amount of credit extended. Capital controls and fixed exchange rates will be relics of an earlier age.

Another mission will be to avoid systemic collapse. Central banks will have the tools to prevent systematic collapse in the world portfolio similar to the tools that financial institutions will use to manage the corporate risk in their portfolios. These tools will include real-time data and automated analytic tools.

Retail Banks

At one time, 24,000 banks existed. The bank holiday in 1933 cut that number substantially. When the consolidation began, about 15,000 banking companies existed. Due to some bank failures but mostly through consolidation, the number of U.S. banks has further declined to 8,500 today. That trend will continue and indeed accelerate. By 2005, there will only be about 3,500 banks.

While consolidation of banks takes place, branch networks will remain steady. In 1960, 23,000 banking offices existed; today, 65,000 exist. The banking assets in the United States will be concentrated, with as much as 90 percent of those assets in the top 25 banks.

Some banks but not many will be truly national in scope, operating in 40 states or more. Super regional banks will gain strength. Small banks will need to find a special niche to survive.

Banks will expand their product offerings. In 1993, banks accounted for over 20 percent of the mutual funds sold (remember, six years ago banks weren't even in the business!). Total mutual fund sales will grow by another $60 billion by 2010 as the population ages and people look for higher returns on pensions and other retirement-related assets. As long as this trend continues, depository institutions will try to do a better job of marketing their own mutual fund offerings. Currently, only 29 percent of customers go to their financial institutions for investment information. Householders aged 45–54 are leaders in contributions to insurance and pension plans. Baby boomers have been poor savers. Boomers who are forced to play catch-up will be attracted to risky, high-yield investments. Some will voluntarily reduce spending to increase savings, and a few may get bailed out with inheritances.

Expect a few large banks to become major players in the brokerage and investment banking fields. Banks will be significant providers of insurance products, selling casualty, life and annuity policies as well as being important underwriters. More emphasis will be placed on fee-based products and broadening of banks' service range. Traditional products will become less strategically important. At the same time, pricing strategy and tactics will receive greater attention than before. In the sluggish lending climate, institutions will target their advertising to specific market segments, particularly the consumer loan business— the most popular consumer credit products are home equity loans and lines of credit.

Banks will be driving on the information highway in businesses such as travel services and real estate brokerage. Banks will concentrate enormous amounts of data about businesses, individuals, municipalities and other facets of the economy.

The banking staff of 2005 will have a more efficient ratio of employees to assets and will be dominated by commissioned sales people. Geography will be less of a constraint. Many employees could be dispersed geographically such as those engaged in processing (for cost advantages), in sales and marketing (to be close to the customer) and in handling local problems that require local solutions. But the people responsible for creating products and overall strategy will be located in major cities. Banks will pursue higher levels of productivity with parallel reductions in cost and traditional management infrastructure. Branch systems and back-office operations will be particular targets. *A significant reduction in banking-related employment will result.*

Micromarketing segmentation, customer information data bases and market–price sensitivity analyses will take hold in bank marketing departments. Banks will evaluate specific customer segments based on revenue contributions and internal resources required to manage risks inherent in customer transactions. There will be a very few large credit card banks, fewer than 25. In this highly competitive business, look for some recent entrants to drop out as their profit margins drop.

The spread business, that is, taking deposits and making loans, will be gone. Smaller companies will have better access to the capital markets with the banks acting as a helper and not a lender. Other commercial loans may be accommodated through a mutual fund concept. Auto loans will be completely automated, and the paper sold to the highest bidder, not to a bank. The banks, however, will manage the process.

Within the next 10 years, a few banks will give up their banking charter and FDIC insurance and strike out as less-regulated financial service providers. This decision will either trigger a substantial rethinking and revamping of the banking laws and regulations in the United States or accelerate the departure.

Foreign banks have some advantages over the biggest U.S. banks: Operating from large domestic bases (since most financial and banking systems are not as fragmented as in the United States—five Canadian banks have 90 percent of the domestic business), the foreign banks could use their domestic profit base to support foreign expansion. Their shareholders require lower return on investments and their loan to equity ratios are not regulated like in the United States. Foreign banks will cause a threat to the banks in emerging countries. In Thailand, 22 foreign banks have arrived, determined to corner business with the country's biggest companies.

An exceptionally pessimistic view of the next decade emerges for European banking. Profitability will be seriously undermined by deregulation and competitive pressures, and a radical restructuring of the industry will be necessary. Average return on equity will fall to about 10 percent in 2005, a level considered to be unacceptable. Mergers and acquisitions will increase, resulting in fewer European banks in 2005. Large banks and specialist banks will be the winners in the new environment. The worst hit sector will be corporate banking.

TREND

WORLD MARKETS—WHERE THE ACTION IS

The focus of the investor is shifting from the United States to the world.
Like the hundreds of U.S. companies that have expanded to Asia, Europe and Latin America to generate growth, investors will increasingly look to global stocks to build wealth. Indeed, with the United States now accounting for less than 40 percent of the global equity market, investors risk cutting themselves off from some of the hottest prospects if they don't think and act globally.

IMPLICATIONS

Looking for double-digit gains for their investors, U.S. pension and mutual funds are sending billions of dollars of investors' money overseas. In fact, global U.S. mutual funds take in a billion dollars a week.

In the past, going global might have required immense amounts of legwork, but the reintroduction of American Depositary Receipts (ADRs), certificates that show ownership of equities issued overseas and pay dividends in dollars, saves investors the trouble of converting foreign currencies into dollars every quarter. Though ADRs trade in dollars, they represent shares that are actually denominated in marks, yen and other currencies, so a sharp move in the dollar against the currency of the ADR's home country can produce speculative gains or losses.

Wall Street will turn into the stock market for the world, where companies like Israel's Teva Pharmaceutical and China's Ek Chor motorcycles will trade and report their financial results on equal footing with IBM and General Motors. Accounting methods differ sharply from country to country, making comparisons of price to earnings ratios and book values difficult if not impossible.

Though U.S. funds invest have invested over $100 billion outside the United States, U.S. investors have a long way to go before they can be considered global players. For example, only 5 percent to 7 percent of the roughly $500 billion in Merrill Lynch customer accounts are invested overseas.

PREDICTIONS

Global stock picking is on the rise among individuals. Expect U.S. investors to have 20 percent of their asset portfolios in overseas investments by the year 2000.

More than 1,000 companies now list ADRs in the United States from massive companies like the German Daimler Benz (Mercedes) and Bridgestone Tires in Japan to Aladdin Knowledge, a small software maker in Israel. Expect this number to double by the next decade.

When it listed its ADRs on the American Stock Exchange, Daimler Benz had to dramatically change its financial disclosures to more closely approximate United States generally accepted accounting principles (GAAP). U.S. investors will increasingly demand financial statements and security rules according to U.S. standards, and since they're such major players, they will get what they want.

TREND

WHY START-UPS CAN'T GET STARTED

Two Yin and Yang themes, "rich-poor" and "big-small," characterize the problems of start-up companies.
Most small businesses are privately held and thus immune to the pressures of the stock market. Because they are unable to secure long-term debt financing, small businesses are also forced to operate with the same inflexible short-term orientation as public companies. Contrary to popular belief, the much publicized explosion of venture capital has done little to provide such funds. While assets of venture capital firms soared, only a small percentage was available to start-ups. Indeed, venture capital and government loans are the primary source of capital for only 1 percent of the nation's entrepreneurs.

IMPLICATIONS

At least 7 out of every 10 Americans starting a business rely chiefly on personal savings and loans from relatives and friends—as they always have. More than 75 percent of the companies in America are family owned or family controlled.

When small businesses do rely on banks and commercial lenders for monies, most of the loans are personally collateralized, and thus are little more than an extension of personal resources. Obviously, a small business finds long-term thinking difficult in the face of such immediate repayment pressure.

Insistence on short-term results continues even if a small business does receive venture money. Pension funds and institutions provide most venture capital. Because of these funds' needs for short-term profits, venture capital firms are being transformed from providers of long-term money and technical support to speculators demanding quick results.

PREDICTIONS

The government will acquire a portion of individual and small-business loans from local banks and package them into a larger security that would be sold and traded. Since local banks would hold about 30 percent of the loan and thus share any losses, local banks would be prudent. The bank that originated the loan would be paid to service it and would recoup part of the funds for reinvestment. This arrangement would allow for long-term loans to small start-up firms, reducing the short-term financial pressure as well as providing large institutional investors a safe, convenient vehicle to channel billions of dollars into long-term, safe loans for small businesses.

Chapter 5

GLOBAL TRENDS THAT WILL SHAPE THE NEXT CENTURY

•

In today's highly interdependent world, individuals and nations can no longer resolve many of their problems by themselves. We need one another. We must develop a sense of universal responsibility. . . . It is our collective and individual responsibility to protect and nurture the global family, to support its weaker members, and to preserve and tend to the environment in which we all live.

THE DALAI LAMA

Nothing quite like the globalization of business has ever happened—its impact is similar to going from a rural to an industrial economy.

WILLIS HARMAN

•

The global business community has always been optimistic. That doctrine is not challenged in this book. However, optimism needs to be tempered with reality. With a sense of just how difficult it may be to make money in the twenty-first century, you can't assume that doing business in the same old way at the same old stand will be sufficient.

In this chapter, we take a "satellite trip" to develop a real-world awareness of the new global village in which we will live and work during the next century. Contrast is what we see as our trip makes us distant witnesses to the global dramas playing out below us. We see the contrast of distinct nations becoming increasingly interconnected. Most world trends presented in this chapter reinforce the theme of togetherness. But as Tony Finizza reminds us in his wild card trend about the possible breakup of China, fragmentation is occurring and will continue in many parts of the world.

TREND

ENHANCED COMMUNICATION—THE KEY TO GLOBAL MARKETS

Contributor—Lou Platt, CEO, Hewlett Packard

Lou Platt shares how smaller-faster technologies will shrink the globe. In this TIP, we also see the themes of shifting focus and rich-poor coming into play on tomorrow's stage.

We're entering a period where communications are going to be immensely enhanced and will have a major effect on both our personal and business lives. It will be possible 10 years from now, and perhaps sooner, to communicate very easily, no matter where you are in the world. I'm not just talking about voice communication, but also about having the ability to carry with you the tools that you will use at work—tools such as highly portable personal assistants, computers and measurement instruments connected to a communications network either wired or wireless. Those tools will allow you to access easily data bases and information that today you would normally get only at your office.

IMPLICATIONS

Enhanced communication will also have a profound impact on the way work is done and how we stay in touch with one another. I don't know if it will render the office obsolete, but it will change the importance of the office as a place where you come to do certain types of work. You will be able to do many types of jobs at your vacation retreat, hotel room or on an airplane as easily as you can do them today in an office.

The speed in which business is conducted will continue to increase. The speed has already improved a lot in the last decade with advances like voice mail and E-mail. These trends will lead to more competition; obviously, the spoils will go to the quick. The leads currently enjoyed from being first to market will be shorter lived in the future—competitors will catch up more quickly. All these advances lead to a tremendous acceleration in the pace of business and to changes in how it's done.

PREDICTIONS

Plenty of work will exist, but you won't need as many people to do it. White-collar productivity, something that's been a bit elusive, has the potential to change. Because the kind of work done today is so different from the kind of work done 10 years ago, the traditional productivity measures hardly apply. Perhaps *effectiveness* of the white-collar workers is a better word than productivity because a lot of the delays will be removed from the system. You're not going to have to wait two days to get information to make a decision.

Growth will come from economies that will develop during the next decade. China, Vietnam and Indonesia—these are large countries with tremendous potential. And certainly, this decade will be one of development in Eastern Europe. Also, Latin America will experience dramatic growth as government stability increases and enhanced communication technologies and business practices flow into those economies. These are major new markets with opportunities for strong economic growth that will perhaps offset slower economic growth in some of the better developed countries.

For growth in the undeveloped world to happen, the people there must have disposable income. Therefore, companies like HP will find some role that the Third World can play in manufacturing the products that are going to be needed for the next decade. Whether it's Coca-Cola or computers, U.S. companies will be building products in underdeveloped countries as well as exporting to them. Business must be involved in providing real value added in the country, but there are lots of major opportunities to grow a business (particularly in places like China) at the same time you're helping to build the economic structure.

TREND

Going Global to Find Growth

Contributor—Jack Welch, CEO and chairman, General Electric Company

---

An old Russian proverb says that the wolf eats because it has legs. Jack Welch had the keen eyes and good senses to know that the future of General Electric required a "shifting focus" to a new hunting ground.

With blinding speed, economies everywhere are becoming market based in form and middle class in lifestyle. We are fast becoming a major part of a market system that embraces the entire world. As new capitalist countries race to catch up, their growth rates surpass those of older market economies.

Look at the Numbers

Corporate leaders become ecstatic over the highly optimistic forecasts of U.S. economic growth reaching 4 percent in the next few years, significantly higher than the average 2.5 percent during the 1980s. Though 4 percent growth is great news for the United States, it's anemic by East Asian standards. The growth rate in China averages above 10 percent, and other Asian countries are racking up growth rates of 6 percent to 10 percent. Even elephantlike India will outpace U.S. growth.

IMPLICATIONS

Corporations will have no other choice but to go for the growth—no matter where it is. Economies like India, China and Mexico, for example, may well determine the future of $60 billion giant General Electric as prospects for strong U.S. growth will continue to be marginal.

Companies will generate greater revenues and profits as the "center of gravity" of U.S. companies shifts from the industrialized world to Asia and Latin America. By 2000, these markets could provide GE alone $20 billion in revenues—double the current level.

Having ignored Third World countries like India, U.S. firms will have to play catch-up with the Europeans and Japanese. Indeed, in 1991, GE had just a sliver of India's $80 million market in medical equipment. Now, a joint venture with a local computer maker has the goal to boost sales tenfold to $200 million, by the year 2000. General Electric is coming on strong in ultrasound devices, including a 20-pound portable unit being developed especially for the Indian market. Service companies that provide technical consulting, training and capital to underdeveloped countries will provide growth opportunities.

PREDICTIONS

Continued loss of thousands of jobs in the United States will create growing pressure from unions to narrow the kind of work that goes overseas.

By 2000, 80 percent of the computer market will be outside the United States.

European nations will continue to tighten political ties with Asia for economic opportunity, particularly in the important aerospace industry, which is likely to remain flat in Europe and other parts of the world.

> •
> DO YOU OR YOUR ORGANIZATION POSSESS EXPERTISE THAT WOULD BE SALABLE IN THIRD WORLD COUNTRIES?
> •

TREND

VEGGIE POWER

Contributor—Roger Kilburn, former president, Protein Division, Archer Daniel Midland

I consulted for Roger Kilburn before his recent retirement from Archer Daniels Midland. Roger was constantly traveling the world, and I've always found his insights interesting and his predictions right on target. He's a good example of a CEO who understands you must get into the world to know what's going on. Roger, in his illuminating TIP summary about food, shares how by not preparing to feed the world will sow the seeds of future problems and that a shifting focus is required and is beginning to happen.

A major trend with continuing worldwide implications is the move toward more vegetarian foods. The three basic reasons are health, scarcity of natural resources and an improvement in convenience and taste of prepared foods.

On the health front, avoid animal fat because it contributes to heart disease, one of the major killers in the developed world. As the population continues to age in developing countries, the emphasis on health maintenance is going to put further pressure on reduction of animal fat. In a number of studies, fiber, found in large quantities in a vegetarian diet, has been shown to reduce cholesterol and colon cancer. Soy protein, often used as the primary source of protein in a vegetarian diet, has been shown to reduce breast cancer as well as cholesterol levels. These results are starting to be recognized. For example, the new food pyramid now used by the U.S. government moves away from the old four-square program and puts more emphasis on grains and vegetarian types.

Currently, about 12 million Americans are vegetarians. That's about 4.8 percent of the population, up from 3.4 percent in 1985. Beef consumption is down from about 81 pounds per capita in 1970 to about 68 pounds today. These statistics are indications of the growing trend toward vegetarianism.

Resources are finite. The world population will grow by about 1 billion people in the 1990s and has doubled since the 1950s. Crop land per capita has been about constant since 1988, but it's down 35 percent since 1965. Simply put, most of the arable land has all ready been put under the plow, and as the population grows, the amount of arable land per person is going to decrease.

Grain output has been dropping 1 percent per year since 1984, another indication of the almost full utilization of crop land. In Africa, for example, output has declined yearly for 20 years, leading to chronic malnutrition in that entire continent. Fertilizer is no longer a substitute for new crop land. Fertilizer use per capita is down 11.5 percent since 1985.

IMPLICATIONS

Normally as GNP increases, meat consumption grows. But how can the world supply the amount of protein that's going to be demanded? A protein shortage in seafood, meat and soybeans exists.

The total world fish catch has dropped since its high absolute tonnage in 1989. Right now it's about 17.8 kilograms per capita, down 8 percent since 1989. The world's oceans are being fished out, indicated by the current ban on fishing within a 200-mile limit of New England and Newfoundland reefs. The growth in fish protein is going to require fish farming, which requires feed protein of some sort. So seafood has declined in absolute terms and has certainly declined on a per capita basis.

Meat production uses about 37 percent of world grain output. Cattle, sheep and goats are rumens; they can convert grass to protein. But the worlds range land is already in full use; in fact, productivity is falling due to overgrazing. Beef production per capita is down 4 percent since 1990, mutton is down 2 percent. These declines also reduce the amount of milk and cheese available. Raising pigs and chickens is a growing trend, but because they are not rumens, they require a concentrated feed like grain or soybean meal.

Soybeans will be required to increase in fish, farming and meat production. Soybean production per capita grew three times from 1950 to 1979, but since then growth has been flat because of little available new land. In Brazil, rain forests have been cut, burned and slashed, so available new land for soybean production will be virtually nonexistent. Moreover, because soybeans are legumes (nitrogen suppliers) soy bean production doesn't benefit much from the use of fertilizers.

An increase in demand for meat with reduced grain and, at best, flat soybean production is an equation that does not compute. *Take China, for example: one kilogram increase in meat demand for the population would increase world usage of grain by 4 percent.* So something has got to change such as a phenomenal technological breakthrough. And even that would probably only impact grain because meats are an inherently inefficient way to produce protein.

In the past, taste, convenience, diet fatigue, reliance on beans as a basic source of protein, preparation time and ignorance were reasons for going off a vegetarian diet. But technology advances, consumer demand and health concerns have all lead to a decrease in meat demand and will increase demand for new soy products. Technical improvements in the taste of soy protein has and will continue to lead to wider use.

PREDICTIONS

The growing world population simply won't have enough grain available to feed itself and maintain a high degree of meat culture in the developed countries. The world can't support a meat protein food chain and a growing population.

As much as 25 percent of the population of developed countries will be vegetarian in the next 15 years due to increased cost—the method that will be used to allocate the meat—as well as health concerns demanded by individuals and governments.

Expect opening and expanding markets for consumer food companies. Companies like Con Agra, ADM and Campbell Soup will have major markets open for them not only in developed countries, but also in developing countries as an alternate to simple beans and grains as a food staple. Health concerns will reduce animal fat consumption, pushing more people toward vegetarian usage, and improvements in processed vegetarian foods will further expand consumption. Education and the school lunch program in the United States and in other developed nations will train young consumers to accept the concept of vegetarian meals. Improvements in technology will give foods a taste and structure that allows kids to accept them.

TREND

CHINA—WATCH OUT WHEN A GIANT SNEEZES

In China, all ten megathemes come into play, as well they should since that megacountry will be the stage upon which the world's future will be played out. Identify the following themes as China is discussed throughout the book: dramatic change; sowing the seeds of future problems; revaluing resource; shifting focus; sophisticated competition;

smaller-faster; forward-backward; together-fragmented; big-small; and rich-poor.

The international business community is paying serious attention to China's long-term prospects and current economic revolution as the most important trend in the world for the next century. China is the fastest growing economy in the world. The United States has possessed the world's largest economy for over a century, but at the present rate, China will displace it in the first half of the next century, and become the number one economy in the world.

IMPLICATIONS

There is much media hype about the changes taking place in China but very little specific analysis of the effects of its growth. China is becoming the fourth pole in world trade, market size and sheer economic power; the United States, Japan and the European community are the other poles. Indeed, China will be the biggest pole of all.

In 2020, "Greater China," including the People's Republic, Hong Kong and Taiwan, is expected to have net imports of $639 billion, compared with $521 billion for Japan, with a projected gross domestic product of $9.8 trillion compared with $9.7 trillion for the United States.

China's present economic boom started about 1978 and has resulted in real annual growth averaging about 9 percent per year. The economy grew at about 13 percent last year but will cool down as the economy becomes more efficient. But 7 percent to 8 percent growth rates for two decades is possible if political stability exists and the global trading system remains open to China's exports.

Though the Chinese live much better than the official statistics of $370 per capita GNP suggest, China is still a poor country. Businesspeople must be careful when extrapolating optimistic market projections based on the thinking, "if every Chinese just bought one of my widget."

China does, however, think big. The country announced over 200 large projects in two dozen different industries. Through the year 2000, China will be seeking foreign technology and equipment. The Chinese have a high regard for U.S. products and want to see more

U.S. companies in the Chinese market. Potential for U.S. exports to China has been enhanced greatly by recent United States–China agreements on the protection of intellectual property rights and market access.

PREDICTIONS

China will replace the United States and Japan as the largest user of steel and will cause a global scramble for certain types of steel; the country will continue its recent dominance over the United States as the leading buyer of gold and will use more energy than the United States, making it a net oil importer before the year 2000.

The bad news: By the year 2025, China will produce three times as much carbon dioxide as the United States. In fact, China is already the third largest contributor of greenhouse gases, even though it does not rank among the top 50 countries in per capita emissions. While the West is making efforts to curb greenhouse gases, China will not sacrifice economic growth for the sake of its own environment or the world's.

China's retail market, currently estimated at about $200 billion a year, will triple by the year 2000. Hong Kong will remain the commercial center for South China. But its dominance in China's economy will decrease because Shanghai will serve central China and Tianjian, and Dalian will serve the north.

The Chinese province of Guangdong has changed from a largely undeveloped area into China's wealthiest province. The transformation is a result of China's economic reform program, which led to the establishment of three special economic zones in the province, economic interdependence with Hong Kong and autonomy from Beijing to experiment with market-oriented measures. Western-style products such as black lingerie and greeting cards are beginning to brighten the dull existence. Guangdong's ambition is to catch up to Asia's Four Dragons—Hong Kong, Singapore, South Korea and Taiwan—by 2010. The province will give top priority to high-technology projects, investments that generate foreign exchange and the restructuring of large and midsized state enterprises.

After the death of its aging leader, China will elect a triumvirate of 60-year-olds, backed by the army. Within a year a leader will emerge from its ranks. The quality of life will remain poor because of inadequate housing, transportation, parks, museums and unavailable home energy.

TREND

CHINA CAN BREAK (WILD CARD)

Contributor—Dr. Anthony J. Finizza, chief economist, ARCO Corporation

I've been consulting many years for ARCO and have always been impressed by Tony Finizza's willingness and ability to think creatively and encourage others to do the same. Tony introduces one of the wild card trends that could dramatically affect what hand the future deals.

The countries that went cold turkey into market economies will be in a better position in the new world than those countries where change was managed. China will not be as dynamic as Russia will be. I think that view is a change from the common perception. Only going cold turkey allows all views to percolate. China will still fall back to the same device it has used for the last six dynasties or the last 5,000 years—that is, it will always fall back to authoritarian rule.

IMPLICATIONS

The whole sum and substance of Chinese democracy in the twentieth century is the one month before the Tiananmen Square massacre. I think China's managed economy will not be the way to enter the twenty-first century.

China, which had been a federation in many ways until the Emperors brought the various warlords together, could potentially dissolve into smaller countries. The Chinese do have a common written language and that may hold them together, but Finizza wouldn't rule out many Chinas.

The central government rules territories—such as Tibet and Xinjiang—inhabited by ethnic minorities who yearn for independence. Moreover, the government still has not dared to expose much of its huge state sector (accounting for half of industrial production) to the cruelty of market forces. When it does, the government could face strikes and revolts by disgruntled workers. Over the next decade, China may possibly face military coups, chaos and even civil war. For business to neglect these possibilities would be foolhardy and dangerous.

PREDICTIONS

As freer economic and social conditions continue, crime and corruption in the coastal provinces will increase. Beijing will conduct a blitz to restore public confidence. Episodic political shakeups will slow China's growth.

TREND

AN UNHEALTHY ENVIRONMENT

Besides the world-class corporate executives and consultants who contributed their insights, I'm fortunate to have the input from four renowned futurist colleagues. One of them, Willis Harman, a pioneer in futurology, adds some penetrating insights to my review of yet another trend that is sowing the seeds of future problems.

The human population of the world with its pace and scale of demands on the earth is reaching *carrying capacity*. This term refers to the largest number of any given species that a habitat can support indefinitely before the habitat declines along with the population.

IMPLICATIONS

As countries of the world become economically linked, they must also deal with another form of interdependence, environmental interdependence. Problems such as global warming, resource depletion and over-population cross borders without passports. If a German factory pollutes the Rhine, someone in the Netherlands may suffer the consequences.

Technology creates as many problems as it solves. Problems caused by technology are increasing while our skills to deal with these problems are decreasing. There is more questioning of the value of technology in our lives. For example, not-in-my-backyard (NIMBY) grassroots groups are effective at stopping unhealthy situations. Even situations we take for granted such as living near high-tension power lines are starting to be questioned. Living close to strong electromagnetic fields may or may not be good for us—but put the lines in someone else's backyard. On the other hand, environmental laws are also being attacked for forcing out entrepreneurial competition because only big business can afford costly "environmental impact" studies.

Willis Harman shared his concern that political leaders do not take pending environmental problems seriously enough. He noted that parts of the world are fast turning into desert partly because of the economy growing exponentially. Harman warns, "This predominance of economic logic over other forms of logic is tearing the earth apart."

Harman has observed how we squander resources to build products and then get rid of the "junk" so that we can create some more. "We've pushed other cultures aside as we develop a western 'economic monoculture' around the world because we were all taught that this would be a good thing." There is no strong diverse counterculture to balance the system. A consequence of this monoculture is that native cultures are being destroyed; people who lived on the land become impoverished and flock to the cities, where there is nothing for them. Environmental degradation correlates with poverty just as it does with consumption.

The good news is that most Americans believe that environmental pollution is a very serious threat to the country. Furthermore, over 95 percent think more should be done about environmental degradation by both public and private sectors. Almost 90 percent of Americans support recycling efforts. Products in packaging that helps consumers cut down on solid waste, pollution and degradation of nonrenewable resources are growing 30 times faster than all new packaged goods. More than half all Americans believe that if a tradeoff were necessary between economic growth and the environment, the environment should be given the nod.

PREDICTIONS

Environmental degradation will remain considerable throughout Asia, except in Japan. In their dash for industrialization, Asian countries will skimp on antipollution measures.

The jobs versus environment tension will continue to grow. Pressures will be brought on business and government to solve environmental problems and to cut down on economic growth that does not contribute to societal well-being such as the attitude that we've got to keep on consuming, for it's the only way to create jobs. In the long run, these pressures will bring about dramatic changes in how we look at the economy. In the short run, they will bring about a lot of conflict and chaos.

Green labeling such as West Germany's "Blue Angel" to assure environmentally correct products will become important globally. Companies will be more constrained when using old or new technologies, particularly where waste water and other environmental issues are concerned. In the European community, ministers have set a goal of recovering 50 percent to 65 percent of the boxes, tins and crates in which goods are transported and sold. A minimum of 25 percent and a maximum of 45 percent of all packaging must, by 2000, be recycled. Moving to a zero waste environment, the Germans are requiring manufacturers to be responsible for their products from cradle to grave.

The more educated, affluent, politically and socially active will continue to see the environment as a top priority for government spending. More young people will become involved in environmental cleanup projects as well as choosing environmentally related careers. Harman believes that pockets of indigenous people will teach us something about living with the land. Their voices are already being heard even in successful well-to-do circles in this country—the present generation of young Rockefellers, for example, are actively involved with this issue. Most minorities, however, will be more worried about economic issues than about the environment.

TREND

MULTINATIONAL CORPORATIONS (MNCS)—ONE COMPANY, ONE WORLD

The next trend highlights the themes of sophisticated competition, big-small, rich-poor and togetherness-fragmentation. The trend may also be an example of sowing the seeds of future problems.

About half the world's present industrial output is generated by MNCs with their widespread production facilities. Indeed, if all the conflicts about the power and purpose of MNCs are resolved, MNCs will be seen as the world's first uniquely global institution. The growth of the global corporation will continue in response to increasing trade, foreign investment and economic integration. The influence of global competition will make being an "American" or "Japanese" company less important than whether the company can meet the worldwide demand for corporate skills and insights.

IMPLICATIONS

Assuming that multinationalism is desirable or inevitable for all companies anywhere in the world would be a mistake. Frequently, companies enjoy a strong position in the domestic market and a record of failure overseas. Nevertheless, for more and more companies—whether American, Japanese or European or from emerging nations or former socialist countries—multinationalism is considered the route to survival, growth and profitability.

Organizing to operate internationally has been a major problem for business executives to confront—the difficulty is that no one answer can suffice for every kind of corporation. However, the preferred organizational design will continue to be centralized responsibility for strategic planning and control and decentralized responsibility for local planning and operation. One form of this design is the global product structure, which takes power out of the hands of international division managers at headquarters and foreign affiliates and gives it to central product managers. CEOs will view their own responsibilities as global in scope and organize their organizations in such a way that major decisions are considered and made in light of world conditions and opportunities.

PREDICTIONS

The debate over a multinational company's responsibility to its home market will intensify as U.S. companies seize the opportunities presented in the developing world.

American science, research and inventive flair will remain unsurpassed, and American multinationals will remain a major force in the economies of East and Southeast Asia. Their Asian operations—with research and product development capabilities—will become integral parts of their business. Except for Japan, no Asian economy has the technology or organizational ability to sustain such high-quality organizations around the world, and American multinationals have the edge over Japanese MNCs—they employ, promote and absorb foreigners into their midst better than the Japanese do.

TREND

THE BRIDGE OVER THE CULTURAL GAP

The yin and yang confusion and inherent problems of the theme together-fragmentation are exemplified in the following trend.

As more executives travel to other countries to do business, they will learn firsthand that they must deal effectively with the cultural differences that provide the backdrop against which all international business drama is played out. Executives will frequently be shocked to discover how much the many variables of foreign behavior and custom complicate their efforts.

IMPLICATIONS

Adapting to local cultural differences will continue to be a difficulty for noncountry managers. Foreign cultures have different views about business arrangements, friendships, material possessions, dress, time and space. For example, all over the world people use time to communicate with each other. There are different languages of time just as there are different spoken languages. In the United States, we use deadlines as a way of indicating the importance of a transaction. In parts of Africa, the time required for a decision is directly proportional to its importance, while in the Middle East, giving a deadline may be seen as being overly demanding and exerting unreasonable insistence. Moreover, in

Japan, a delay of years does not necessarily mean a loss of interest in a deal.

It takes years to develop a sound foundation for doing business in a given country. The common error will be in not allowing enough time for representatives to develop sufficient familiarity with the culture.

PREDICTIONS

More and more companies will require their offshore managers to be more strategically responsive rather than just operationally oriented. This requirement will include periodically reporting back to headquarters on changes in the social, political and economic situations that might change both offshore and domestic operations.

TREND

PARTNERING—FORMING ALLIANCES

Both sides of the global yin and yang megatheme together-fragmented are at work in the next trend.

Alliances and joint ventures (JVs) will become more common as competitors learn the many advantages of cooperation. However, there will also be a growing countertrend for company ventures to be as wholly owned as possible.

IMPLICATIONS

Collaborative ventures look as though that is the way businesses and government will interact within the global economy. Established Western countries will form alliances with ambitious Asian firms, whose market clout is already to important too be ignored. Some countries are so small that they cannot achieve high living standards on their own, but they can prosper by integrating themselves into global production systems.

Among the advantages to tying up with a local partner may be immediate access to marketing and sales channels as well as access to domestic suppliers. But with local operations and early stage entry into markets, companies can gain the benefits of alliances without the mess.

Joint ventures, strategic alliances and other such cooperative arrangements are, however, notoriously difficult to manage. The problems in managing joint ventures stem from one cause: there is more than one parent. The owners, unlike the shareholders of a large, publicly owned corporation, are visible and powerful. They can—and will—disagree on just about everything: How fast should the joint venture grow? Which product and markets should it encompass? How should it be organized? Because of such difficulties only about half of all JVs can be considered successful. Despite the hassles, there are a number of sound reasons for companies to form such alliances—cutting costs, reducing risk and gaining access to established markets are the reasons most often cited.

Do these problems point to less JVs? Not in Asia! For example, alliances to build airplanes are taking place throughout Asia. Indeed, Korea's Hyundai is planning a joint venture with Russia's Yakovlev; Samsung (Korea) leads a consortium with America's Lockheed; Daewoo (Korea) is trying to have a plane built by a possible consortium, including India's Hindustan Areonautics and Singapore Aerospace; and Taiwan Aerospace signed a $2 billion deal with America's McDonald-Douglas.

Even the Japanese who remain determined to build an aircraft have lined up four foreign firms to take part in the project. One of the firms, Boeing ATR, is itself a regional aircraft joint venture between France's Aerospatiale and Italy's Alena. Other members of the alliance are Saab-Scania of Sweden and China's AVIC.

It is not only in air transport that the Asian alliance megatrend continues: To help in the important microchip wars, Japan's NEC and South Korea's Samsung Electronics will jointly develop a new generation of advanced semiconductors. Ford Motor Company created Ford China operations to set up joint ventures in China. Japan's Kobe Steel and U.S.-based Alcoa Aluminum will help China National Non-Ferrous Metals modernize two smelters and will exploit China's aluminum market.

PREDICTIONS

Considerable attention will continue to be paid to the development of public and private partnerships throughout the world. A growing number of governments across Asia will make it easier for foreign investors to own local operations 100 percent, and an increasing number of companies will take advantage of the opportunity.

Chapter 6

DEMOGRAPHIC AND LIFESTYLE TRENDS IN THE YEAR 2000

•

The U.S. obsession with statistics is so deeply rooted that it takes an occasional error to remind users that some figures might as well be pulled out of a hat.

JOHN COBBS

All is flux, nothing stays still. Nothing endures but change.

HERACLITUS

•

Everything is in a state of flux. Nothing, as Heraclitus taught, ever stays the same. Americans are constantly changing, both demographically and psychographically. These changes will force business and government to constantly adapt to us. Companies that fail to respond to changes in the marketplace are in danger of losing market share or even going out of business. Choosing the appropriate response isn't easy because so many trends are occurring at the same time, often working against each other. Changing values, lifestyles and life phases have become as important a targeting tool for merchandisers as demographics.

Our search has uncovered the following lifestyle and demographic trends that will have an impact on the way we will do business in the next century: The global population demographics and implications (*Population Balloons and Pops*); increased immigration and the growth in the number of minorities (*The Sun Belt Bursts Open*); youth, alienation and crime (*Watch Your WAY [Wild Alienated Youth]*); the graying of the world (*The Fountain of Third World Youth Saturates the Old West*); the new family (*The Post Nuclear Family*); leisure (*Give Me a Break*); education (*When Will We Learn*); health (*A Healthy Outlook*); home (*Tech Sweet Home*); and cities (*A Bushel of "Big Apples"*).

TREND

POPULATION BALLOONS AND POPS

A growing population is sowing the seeds of future problems. Of all demographic trends, population growth and shifts are the most crucial in determining our future on this planet. These shifts offer startling insights into the social, political and economic problems and potentials that will shape life and work in the next century. A global struggle exists between production and reproduction. While production has long been predominant in industrialized countries, three-quarters of the world's people live and reproduce in developing nations, and reproduction is winning over production.

Indeed, world population is likely to exceed 7.8 billion by 2020. Nearly 95 percent of this growth will occur in less-developed nations. To understand the enormous implications of this "so what" statistic, let's give it some perspective. This staggering increase of nearly 2 billion people is twice the population of China and eight times that of the United States.

This extraordinary population rise is not precipitated by higher birthrates, as occurred during America's post–World War II baby boom era, but rather by a drastic decline in Third World death rates due to foreign aid programs providing public health programs and assistance. Another reason is the large numbers of young women having children.

IMPLICATIONS

Every 24 hours enough people are added to the earth to fill a city the size of Newark or Akron and most are Chinese women. Indeed, one out of eight people in the world is a Chinese woman.

We will continually be bombarded with press reports of famine and deprivation in Africa, Latin America and Asia as the Malthusian predications of a permanent excess of population over available resources is actualized and forever dooms millions to subsistence living. Population growth will overwhelm the capacities of underdeveloped nations and newly developed nations. Starvation and war will continue to threaten hundreds of millions of lives in Africa and parts of Asia.

On the other hand, U.S. population growth will slow down to 5 percent in the first decade of the next century—all-time lows, except for during the Great Depression. As the birthrate declines, the potential for conflicts are huge. Since rich nations represent a relatively small share of the earth's population, future population growth—which is occurring mostly in poor countries—will intensify tensions.

It will not be business as usual. Though experts have cried wolf before, what these figures actually mean is that the earth's resources cannot feed, clothe, house and educate a population that in the next 25 years will be almost 30 percent larger then the earth's present 5.6 billion people. *Perbaps the most important but least heralded and understood challenge to the global business community is to discover and develop new sources of food, raw materials and energy in time to address the problems of an overpopulated planet.*

PREDICTIONS

It took 4 million years for humanity to reach the 2 billion mark. That figure was reached in 1927. It will take just 70 years—the span of one lifetime—for that number to triple!

By 2020, the population of Africa will grow to 1.4 billion; Latin America's population will nearly double to 750 million; and the population of Asia will increase from 3 billion to 4.3 billion. In the next two decades, the Philippines will increase from 59 million to 92 million; Nigeria, from 105 million to 216 million; Mexico, from 83 million to 125 million; Brazil, from 144 million to 207 million; and global troublemaker Iran, from 53 million to 95 million.

The largest developing nation, China, appears to be gaining effective control over its population. Despite the remarkable success of China's harsh one-child-per-family campaign, the Chinese population will expand from 1.1 billion people today to nearly 1.3 billion people by 2020—a significantly lower rate, but an absolute increase, approaching the projected population growth of all Latin America.

The extraordinarily high Third World birthrates will come down as Third World nations continue family planning efforts, despite the Vatican pushing its self-serving, anti-abortion agenda. Today, nearly half the Third World's population lives in nations where women have five or more children during their lifetimes. However, fertility is falling in most places. In Indonesia, fertility rates dropped from 5.6 children per woman in the late 1960s to 3.3 children today; in India the drop has been from 5.7 children to 4.3 children.

Despite the prediction of a decline in birthrates, the population explosion will continue unabated because 40 percent to 50 percent of the developing world's people are under 15. The number of births will remain high as these people pass through their childbearing years.

TREND

THE FOUNTAIN OF THIRD WORLD YOUTH SATURATES THE OLD WEST

Young-old is clearly the megatheme for our next trend.

As a nation, America has never been as old as it is now. In the United States, people are living longer and retiring earlier. Indeed, over the next half century, the populations of many developed countries will become predominantly aged. By 2010, Japan's over-65 population is expected to jump from 12 percent to 20 percent of its total, and West Germany's will rise from 15 percent to 21 percent, while the United Kingdom will remain the oldest population within the European community.

At the same time, Third World populations will not only be growing larger, but also will continue to consist overwhelmingly of young adults and children.

IMPLICATIONS

The Third World incorporates many impatient societies. The huge age differences are bound to cause more immigration as the poor and young move to rich and old countries. We see this happening already in Europe and the United States. (The effects of this movement into areas of the United States are discussed in the next trend.)

Employers especially will feel the economic effects of the young/old split as health care premiums continue to rise along with the expense of funding their pension systems. Elder care is already a problem for many Americans. One-quarter of America's workforce now provides care for an elderly person; almost all employees think elder care is difficult to do while working. Over one-half the workers who are caring for elders report feeling extra stress; other complaints include having to be on the phone more and being less productive.

Retirees will compete with younger age groups for government spending and jobs. People over 65 receive 29 percent of federal spending, while children under 18 get 7 percent. The main reason for the high senior spending is the indexing of social security benefits to the cost of living. Proposals to raise taxes or cut benefits on social security are politically incorrect to seniors, who more consistently exercise their right to vote. By 2000, half the voters will be 48 or older.

The traditionally pyramid-shaped workforce will be replaced by a more even age distribution, and compensation structures where earnings increase with age may change. It is estimated that over one million Americans over 50 want to return to work, and this trend will increase as the population ages. Pension benefits and marital status strongly affect decisions to keep working, particularly for older women. Divorced older women and those without pensions are three times as likely to be in the labor force than married people or those with pensions. Two out of three men over 65 attempt to return to some kind of money-producing vocation; and over one-third of those 60 and older would like to open a home-based business.

Marketing to Gray Markets

People over 65 hold 50 percent of U.S. discretionary income and over three-quarters of all financial assets. But the older markets are complex and highly segmented, and there is jeopardy for marketers who are attracted by demographics alone. Senior consumer behavior is more accurately defined within categories of lifestyle behavior than within categories of age.

There will be more and wealthier older adults and fewer and poorer young adults. However, the graying of America will not lead to the great boom in the consumer economy that is anticipated. Older people spend less money on durable goods. They buy fewer homes, appliances, household furnishings, clothes and cars. Moreover, older people tend to be good savers; a good percentage of their income goes into passive investments, not into the marketplace. Other dollars go for necessities such as rent, health care and taxes, leaving seniors with less discretionary income.

Those just entering "seniordom" are the most affluent of all age groups, but in the 65 plus group, household income and expenditures drop significantly.

The 1980s were dominated by discussions of aging baby boomers. Now that the first baby boomer is approaching 50, however, the key concept is shifting from aging to preservation. In the middle of middle age, boomers want to preserve their health, the environment and financial assets. For many people, the focus has shifted from moving forward to not moving backward.

An aging population will value time, save more, move less, look to prolong life and place a high priority on personal comfort. Older adults are more resistant to peer group values than younger adults are. Inner self, not external events or material things, is the source of life's satisfaction. Psychological growth continues as physical attributes deteriorate. Mature consumers are motivated more by the capacity of a product to serve as a gateway to experiences rather than by the generic nature of a product or service.

Older adults want to be self-sufficient. Marketers should avoid talking down to them as if they're helpless—verbal or graphic images that emphasize their limitations and vulnerabilities will repel most health-minded seniors. Instead, older people should be presented as being endowed with creativity, intellectual involvement, experience, vitality, productivity, compassion for others, concern for the world about them and the wisdom they desire to share.

Mature consumers are very astute when it comes to ascertaining value and quality and take warranties seriously. Older adults have a strong aversion to embellished claims as well as marketing messages that emphasize selfish interests—rather reach out to them through cause-related marketing or programs that seek out older volunteers.

PREDICTIONS

An aging world will impose substantial economic costs, many of which will be borne by employers. Business will be increasingly hard-pressed as health care premiums continue to rise along with the expense of their pension systems. An early retirement trend will con-

> •
> WHAT HOME-BASED PRODUCT OR SERVICE COULD YOU MARKET TO SENIORS?
> •

tinue with concerns about pension benefits strongly influencing decisions about whether to keep working.

The age wave will crunch social security in the early decades of the twenty-first century. In 2012, the eldest baby boomers reach the traditional retirement age of 65. The number of workers per retiree will plummet from over 5 in 1990 to approximately 2.6 by 2030. Changing demographics also means that countries with state-provided social security systems are likely to have less money to pay out when the aging workforce retires. Therefore, more and more countries are encouraging employees to establish private pension programs. Government will have to restructure social security to compensate for the projected imbalance between retired people and workers. The social security safety net will be under additional strain as the mortality rates for the elderly continue to fall.

Both the 55–74 and the 75–84 age groups will include larger and wealthier segments of the U.S. population by about 2030. Twenty-one percent of the U.S. population will be over 65, and there will be more people 65 years and older than there will be under 18. The median age will be over 36 in 1999. In the first decade of the new century, the United States will pass 40 and continue to climb. The over 65 age group will explode in 2012, when baby boomers reach retirement age, and America's population of 85 plus is expected to multiply sixfold by 2050.

By 2020, a third of the people 65 or older in Japan will be over 79. Japan's current publicly administered pension system will create an intolerable burden on its workforce by 2025, when almost a quarter of the population will be above 65. Expect Japans bureaucrats to raise the retirement age from 60 to 65 and to fundamentally alter pension calculations.

In 2010, however, just 4 percent of the population of the Middle East will be over 65, and the share will be only 3 percent for Latin America.

Industries where sales, profits and employment will benefit from the maturity market in the next decade include health and fitness clubs; travel and hospitality; financial services; senior housing (the demand for retirement and nursing home space will double in the next few years); media and entertainment; health care; home computers and information; advertising and marketing services.

TREND

THE SUN BELT BURSTS OPEN

Despite spurious arguments about the needs and benefits of future U.S. immigration, we are sowing the seeds of future problems.

As the nation approaches the third millennium, the United States' demographic center will gravitate increasingly toward the South and West. The Sun Belt will be crammed by increased population in the first decade of the next century. Growth will be due to changes in births, slowing death rates, migration and the fertility of a fast-rising immigrant population that continues to move into the Sun Belt. The United States is the only nation that accepts hundreds of thousands of immigrants each year. In the past five years, we've absorbed more immigrants than all other industrialized nations combined. California will be the first state to have a "minority majority" early in the next decade. Los Angles already has a minority majority.

Despite recent restrictions, liberal U.S. immigration policies will become a time bomb that will change American society dramatically. There will be problems galore. Sun Belt states like California, Florida and Texas will become Third World states with huge immigrant and black inner-city populations divided from white America by poverty, violence, education and racial tension. Finding the right level of welfare support that will provide a safety net without undermining immigrants' incentives to succeed will be particularly difficult. Education and job creation will also pose major problems for government at all levels. Americans are assimilating into one society, but the rate will continue to be painstakingly slow.

IMPLICATIONS

We will not have the predicted labor shortages that have justified our lax U.S. immigration policies. Severe underemployment in newly developing nations will fuel the migration of millions of workers to industrialized nations, particularly to the U.S. Sun Belt. In the United States, zero-population growth will be reached in the second decade of the new century with only immigration accounting for population increases. Immigration will account for half all U.S. population growth by 2015. Without volatile birth, death and immigration rates, the U.S. population will peak at about 300 million about 2038 and begin to decline for the first time ever. However, unless increased immigration from Asia, Latin America and Eastern Europe is checked, a decline is highly unlikely.

U.S. immigration is approaching the record levels of the early 1900s. While Asian Americans grow at a rate eight times that of whites, Hispanic immigration and birth will increase at a rate four times that of whites and will double that rate in the next decade. African Americans, currently the largest minority group, are also growing at a rate faster than that of whites but not as fast as Asians and Hispanics.

As minorities become a majority in many congressional districts, the Congress with Hispanic and Asian surnames will exert political pressure on business to supply money and jobs to solve the problems of their unmanageable states. This demographic trend will continue to exert what Robert Dahl called "minority rule," in which public policy is arrived at by neither a majority nor a minority but rather through compromises of various organized and vocal minorities. The old squeaky wheel syndrome is the oil that will move our politicians through an ever-widening sphere of vocal minority influence.

Business, having major problems of its own, won't be able to provide the resources necessary to solve the problems of states like California and will locate in areas geographically away from Sun Belt cities, further eroding tax rolls.

Markets

Growth in immigration will have a profound effect on household markets. Immigration from Asia and Latin America now accounts for one-third of U.S. population growth. Immigrants are likely to be young adults, so they have high rates of household formation. As a result, in the next decade, a large share of new householders especially in cities will be Hispanic or Asian.

There is a growing market in minority communities. The number of Hispanics in the United States will increase by 50 percent to 30 million people by the next decade. Hispanics will continue to comprise an ever larger proportion of the youth market in the United States and will provide a growing share of both skilled and unskilled job entrants.

Marketers must cater to the growing influence of Hispanic and Asian food, fashion and customs. Business must be aware that the food we eat, the music we hear and the clothes we wear will have a Latin flavor. For example, tacos surpassed pizza for the first time to become the most popular ethnic food in the 1990s. Business will begin exploring opportunities in the exploding Hispanic and Asian markets, using community leaders and consultants who specialize and have pull in these markets as guides.

Rather then assimilating into the economic melting pot, we will see a cultural mosaic, where there are highly concentrated Asian- and Hispanic-speaking markets, requiring marketers to deal in Spanish, Chinese and other languages. This language diversity will lessen the need to do business in English. Computer software that converts U.S. software source code into foreign languages will also reduce the need to learn English to conduct business.

Advertisers trying to reach African Americans will continue to use TV as their media source because this group's television viewing is above average. An increase in advertising targeted to African American TV viewers will lead to a significant increase in the number of television shows featuring African Americans. Wealth has risen steadily in this group with more than one-third of African American households living at middle-class income levels or above and little percentage change at the poverty levels. However, poverty levels have been increasing for whites and Hispanics. Expect a widening philosophical and cultural gap, between middle class and disadvantaged blacks.

Public education systems will be radically upgraded to help inner-city Americans break out of the ghettos. The increase in immigrants will provide career opportunities for people who can teach English as a second language. There will be disruptive and misguided pressure to require school districts to provide teachers who speak the numerous immigrant languages. Business may have to offer English courses to recently arrived employees and some job training for immigrants will be funded by government.

PREDICTIONS

The wide cultural diversity reaching our shore will generate a distinct culture of its own that will be neither traditional American or identical to the country of origin.

In 2040, whites will have a median age of 45, while Hispanics will have a median age of 28, reinforcing the tendency for diverse groups to stay apart from each other. The growth of separate ethnic groups and gangs will provide the social backdrop in our schools and universities. The loss of the traditional American way of life, coupled with political impotence to reverse the trend, will spawn a conservative backlash over the next decade.

By 2088, U.S. minority populations will become the majority. California will have twice as many people in 2040 as it does now. No racial group will be able to claim majority status, but Hispanics will account for almost 50 percent of California's population. Asians will triple their share of U.S. population in just two generations.

Hispanics will surpass African Americans as the largest U.S. minority group by 2015. Though Hispanics will continue to have an ever-increasing share of poverty, they will also show strong increases in the number of upper- and middle-class families.

Asian Americans will become continually more visible in business and education on the West Coast and will have higher rates of success as entrepreneurs than any other minority groups.

Almost nine million people will immigrate to the United States in the 1990s. It is estimated that immigrants will form 262,000 new households in 1995 and 360,000 a year by the end of the decade. By 2000, they will account for more than one in four households, and their life expectancy will increase from 76 to 82 years.

TREND

WATCH YOUR WAY (WILD ALIENATED YOUTH)

While society has been fixated on the old side of the young-old megatheme, the ranks of teenagers, fueled by the children of baby boomers and immigrants, have started to grow again. One growing segment of this new crop of young adults is sowing the seeds for future problems.

Teens are the leading edge of a demographic wave that will wash over the United States during the next two decades. In the United States, the population 13–19 inched up by 70,000 to over 24 million, ending a 15-year decline. Now the pace is picking up and will grow at twice the rate of the overall population during the next decade. By the time the bulge peaks in 2010, it will top the baby-boomed teen explosion of the 1960s and 1970s.

For several generations to come, expanding numbers of young people will become alienated as they try to enter the labor force in nations in which combined unemployment and underemployment rates will often run as high as 30 percent to 50 percent. These wild alienated youths (WAYs) have an anomic, nihilistic and defeatist view of life and the future.

In broad areas of the globe, a widening societal chasm will grow. Those with wealth and access to all manner of advanced technology will be juxtaposed against a growing alienated, illiterate, sociopathological underclass. As society becomes increasingly polarized, this phenomenon is already occurring all over the world, especially in urban areas. Tracking the WAY across the urban landscape, we see increasing racial brawls, growing gang membership, abandoned and orphaned children (in the past 30 years, the birthrate among unmarried women 15–19 has almost tripled), drug dealing, AIDS babies, malnutrition, homelessness and crime (the number of juveniles arrested for violent crimes is up over 55 percent from 1982).

The perception of a growing number of people who nightly watch stories of gang violence and occasional riots is that Anthony Burgess's science fiction novel, *A Clockwork Orange*, in which young barbarians rip apart society, may become a chapter in our future.

IMPLICATIONS

By 2020, at least a billion jobs will have to be created to absorb the youth coming of age in the developing countries outside China. Most of the youth of the world will be trying to move out of Third World countries into richer countries.

The WAY resent the baby boomers whom they see as the "Happy Days" generation having partied though the 1960s and 1970s, leaving today's youth to pick up the check. The WAY are part of the neglected latchkey generation that saw their parents divorce in droves. (One in four U.S. households with kids is headed by a single parent, up from one in eight in 1970.) Among minorities, one in three is a teen compared with one in four in the general population.

The WAY will not participate in bringing about peaceful changes in government. Left unmoved by most political events, their rhetoric is anti-establishment without alternatives. They lack education though some attend universities. They are followers and look for direction from radical and revolutionary agitators and cultural heritage teachers who make up historical "facts," and encourage blaming others for their problems. They feel society owes them for historical injustices and admire those who are publicly hostile toward the establishment and those outside their group.

In China over 70 percent of those in jails are youth. Many in the recession-racked countries in Europe feel shut out, angry, neglected and pessimistic about their future prospects. They don't expect to own a home or hold a good job. Except for their collective anger, foreboding, alienation and attitude that blames others for their problems, the WAY have little in common with each other. Indeed, they include radical elements of both political poles, including right-wing skinheads and their rival left-wing counterparts.

But Most Teens Are Great!

Teenagers now are responsible for more decisions than previous generations, including what to buy and what's for dinner. More are graduating from high school and a greater percentage of young women than men are attending college. Those in China, India and Southeast Asia are optimistic about the future as they foresee having better lives than their parents have.

Despite their many hardships, young people in their teens contribute to an annual spending power of some $90 billion and influence more than twice as much in purchases in the United States alone. They are essential to the success of many major categories—music, beer, soft drinks, fast food, cosmetics, athletic shoes and electronics such as compact disc players, portable phones, VCRs and video games. Moreover, young adults are the best market for appliances such as microwave ovens and should represent 23 percent of the refrigerator market by the year 2000.

PREDICTIONS

Marketers will use more black cultural idioms such as hip-hop dance, rap-oriented music and black music and sports superstars to reach teens in the United States.

The new "street wise" like to think they live on the edge, though most still live at home. Expect ads aimed at this group to include images of wild, death-defying stunts. Despite the rise in global media, differences in tastes among teens remains, complicating the marketers' jobs—European teens prefer a closer relationship with their parents and a more irreverent ad style.

With marginal educations, the WAY will have to settle for what author Douglas Coupland calls "McJobs," mundane and marginally challenging work that provides a paycheck and little else. Expect increasing violence toward immigrants as even these marginal jobs become more competitive and scarce in a bad economy.

Assume an increased focus on security with more involvement by local business as their facilities and other assets are endangered by youths rioting and looting. There will be increased opportunities for private security services and equipment. As more younger offenders are brought to justice, expect increased amounts of tax dollars to be used for more police and teen violence prevention programs.

TREND
THE POST-NUCLEAR FAMILY

Fragmented-together is the megatrend seen in our new family portrait.

In the past, blood lineage defined family, and the bigger the family the better it could protect its own. But as the United States economy and family size continues to shrink, a proliferation of nontraditional household types will be the norm.

IMPLICATIONS

The number of U.S. households is expected to increase 11 percent from 1995 to 2000. Growth of household formation will slow to less than 2 percent, slightly over the overall population growth rate of less than 1 percent per year between 2000 and 2005. Since new households purchase disproportionately more of many durable goods, consumption of durable products in the United States will be negatively affected. However, fragmentation into nontraditional households will alleviate the negative economic impact somewhat.

Controversy over the deterioration of family values and the changing structure of families will continue. True, the turbulence in family structure has been great in the past decades, but it will subside, giving way to a new norm rather than a return to old standards.

Emotional, financial and physical needs will be met by a variety of caregivers, advisors and supporters who will become more important as the traditional family structure continues to fragment. The friends and associates you can count on in troubled times will evolve into the extended family of the future. There will be continued pressure for redefining the family to provide benefits for the nontraditional family.

PREDICTIONS

Comprising 56 percent of all households in 1990 and accounting for 70 percent of all consumer spending, married couples are the largest and most powerful consumer segment.

Although the size of this segment has been shrinking and will continue to do so in 2010, married couples will still make up half the households and account for two-thirds of consumer spending. Families in the next decade will experience a wider age gap between parents and children. In 2010, the volume market will remain among younger parents, with married parents younger than 45 accounting for 7 in 10 married households with children.

Record numbers of Americans will stay single longer, lessening the family influence on society. The percentage of people who will never marry will triple in the next decade. By 2005, single people will account for more than half the U.S. population. Of those who are single today, 25 percent are separated or divorced and 56 percent have never married. We will see rapid growth in the number of roommates and singles as members of the baby boomlet generation begin their adult lives. Getting voter support for education and family service initiatives will be more difficult as the number of single people increases.

Important characteristics of single parents include a busy lifestyle, lower-than-average incomes, lower-than-average spending on most things and a greater likelihood of dwelling renters. Households of related people not headed by married couples, referred to by the Census Bureau as "other families," are divided into two major groups. The households with children under 18 are known as single parents and the remaining households are a conglomeration of siblings, grandparents and other relatives living together. The total number of households classified as other families could reach almost 19 million by 2010. Single parents represent 56 percent of other families, and single mothers comprise 85 percent of single parents. Single mothers are expected to grow 18 percent between 1990 and 2010 and will remain the majority of all single parents in 2010 at nearly 8 million households.

Nonfamilies include 23 million people who live alone and 4.3 million households of unrelated people who live together. This segment of households is expected to grow, thereby providing an important target market for businesses. In 2010, one-person households will be 27 percent of all households, while other nonfamilies will remain constant at 5 percent of households. Although the proportion of single-householder men under 45 will plunge over 1990–2010 from 54 percent to 35 percent, the proportion 45–64 will increase dramatically.

Households with adult children are important to businesses because they spend more than any other household type: Couples whose eldest child is 18 or older spend 9 percent more than those whose eldest child is 6–17. Spending by these families is high for food, entertainment, personal care products and services, education, vehicles, fuel and maintenance. People will have children later in life and form smaller families. Thus, married parents 45–54 should present a growth market, and there will also be a record number of single-parent families, families with stepchildren and childless couples.

High divorce rates, delayed childbirth, high teenage pregnancy and liberal welfare benefits and social acceptance of alternative lifestyles will reduce the imperative of being married to raise children. The number of children born to unmarried mothers will increase. This year, some

40 percent of all U.S. babies are expected to be born out of wedlock. Only 14 percent of never-married mothers received any child support in 1989. Since the mother's own resources are slim, the government has to step in, adding to welfare and indirect costs such as health and law enforcement. More than 60 percent of black babies are born to unmarried mothers. The percentage of whites born out of wedlock is lower but rising at a higher rate. But family values are different even in countries with similar living standards. For example, in Japan 1 percent of children are born out of wedlock while in Sweden nearly half the childeren are.

TREND

GIVE ME A BREAK

It's time to stretch and shift our focus.
People will continue to trade time for money. The majority of Americans under 50 believe they have insufficient leisure time but more leisure time than their parents had and a right to as much free time as needed. As the baby boomers age in the Western industrialized nations, a voluntary "simplicity" counterculture will sprout as people say "I have enough to scrape by and am willing to trade time for money." In contrast in the developing world, you will have masses overworking as they try to get out of poverty.

IMPLICATIONS

More women than men complain about scarce leisure time, as do over 60 percent of two-income families. Parents spend two-thirds more time cleaning, cooking and doing laundry than those without kids. Competent child care will be a primary concern in the twenty-first century. Leisure and chores lose out as time with kids remains a priority.

As desire for material things wanes in middle age, the desire for new experiences grows. Mature adults often use their free time and disposable income to travel. Indeed, this market segment buys more travel products than any other segment. Travel, concerts, culture, theme parks and other such activities are expected to grow as the global population ages. But seniors are not the full-time leisure junkies that advertisers overdepict. For seniors as well as for the rest of us, the purpose of leisure time is to refresh life, not to validate it.

For almost two-thirds of all Americans, leisure is best spent if it is focused on achieving some kind of goal. Over three-quarters of executives play sports with business associates or clients. Almost 40 percent use sports to generate business. Golf ranks number one in popularity and is played by over 80 percent of executives. Walking has the highest participation rates of any fitness activity as fitness becomes an ever more popular goal.

PREDICTIONS

Home is the focus of leisure activities for most Americans, who are reading more but also watching more TV—providing high-definition television (HDTV) with good growth potential toward the end of the decade. Conversely, the audience for cinema admissions is declining among the under 30 set, but the average moviegoer is watching more films.

Participation and attendance in formal religion as an activity will decline, but the majority of people will believe in a universal spirit. Religions will segment just as markets do. An intellectual and social orientation will appeal to the growing ranks of the highly educated singles. While the popularity of Eastern religions such as Buddhism and Taoism increase in the West, Christian sects will make active gains in the Far East and Russia. In the United States, by the year 2000, Hispanics will account for about half of all Catholics.

TREND

WHEN WILL WE LEARN?

The decline of learning in the United States and its ripple effect on the economy and society leads many of us to believe that education can no longer be entrusted to the educational or governmental bureaucracies but instead requires a major shift in focus.

The answer to when will we learn? is when "edutainment," the combining of education and entertainment through interactive multimedia, saturates the classroom and corporate training rooms. Interactive education will be a huge business as global competition, new technology and other forces continue to provide occupational growth in areas requiring more training and education.

IMPLICATIONS

When manufacturing was an increasing source of employment, job opportunities were available that offered access to higher paying jobs without a high school education. As restructuring in manufacturing takes place, more jobs are likely to require postsecondary education than in the past. Indeed, more than half the jobs in the United States will soon require education beyond high school, and the skills of the workers have not kept pace with occupational change.

Immigrant populations will exacerbate the skills gap. Many immigrants do not possess the job skills that will be demanded by the next economy. Education will be the hot issue for Hispanics because low educational attainment along with limited English language proficiency will continue to be barriers to the higher incomes enjoyed by Asian Americans (who achieve higher levels of education than do native-born Americans).

Though the United States keeps spending more on students, performance keeps declining.

An identifiable rise in illiteracy among the young is also producing a growing segment of the population with limited skills in mathematics, English, history, geography and general culture. A recent study of mathematics proficiency of the country's 12th graders showed that only a very small percent of 12th graders are operating at the highest level, and less than half are able to handle the math traditionally taught in the first few years of high school. Yet many occupations projected to grow most rapidly by 2005 will require at least this level of proficiency in mathematics. These include not only science and engineering, but also many of the occupations in health care and the highly skilled blue-collar trades such as tool-and-die maker.

PREDICTIONS

Business will move to higher and higher levels of education reform involvement. This will include adopting schools, supporting policies that promote a national curriculum, tougher testing, more vocational and apprenticeship training for students, public preschool and better paid but fewer teachers in reengineered interactive classrooms.

By the year 2000, parents will be spending over $1 billion on home-learning software. Education will be the driving force behind a predicted increase in CD ROM–equipped multimedia personal computer sales. Expect explosive growth in educational software as multimedia textbooks become de rigueur and inner-city test scores begin to improve.

There will be great opportunity for providing training programs, particularly in Asia. Many of the growing organizations in developing countries will send employees overseas for international training at offshore branches, and universities will offer university extension courses beamed by satellite.

TREND

A HEALTHY OUTLOOK

Another revalued resource will be our health.
Consumers the world over are learning more about health and fitness and are responding by taking better care of themselves.

IMPLICATIONS

Life-threatening habits such as smoking and drinking are on a long-term slide. Baby boomers entering their peak family-forming years will start a new brand of traditionalism. Expect more conservative attitudes about sex. Less smoking and drinking in the United States will force distillers and tobacco companies to continue to exploit foreign markets, particularly in Asia. The likelihood of college or high school students using illicit drugs is only half what it was a decade ago. Moreover, the occupancy rate of hospitals has been dropping, causing an increase in health care advertising and hospitals to pay doctors for patient referrals.

Here's the bad news: Industrial relations executives in the United States say drug abuse is now the number one problem in the workplace, and almost three-quarters of all employees support an employer's "right" to test employees for drugs. There are twice as many work-related disability claims among blacks than whites and Hispanics. There is also a steady rise in the number of people who feel they are under stress. The top five causes of stress all come from the office, and stress-related illness and burnout are responsible for 75 percent of lost workdays in North America. Business travel that last five days causes stress when it interferes with the traveler's personal life. Women feel travel-related problems more than men. However, the more years one travels the less stress is reported.

Food marketers will have to upgrade products as consumers become more aware of ingredients, calories, fat content and such. Older and more affluent people in the United States (incomes over $40,000) spend about 40 percent of their food expenditures eating out and tend to eat healthful foods. Affluent Americans are healthier than average-income Americans: they eat smarter and exercise more. However, Americans in general are fatter than ever: almost two-thirds are overweight and two-thirds of children 6–17 can't pass a basic fitness test.

PREDICTIONS

For the first time, by 1998, increases in health care spending will consume more than half America's economic growth. Moreover, if health care reform legislation is not enacted, health care could equal 18 percent of the GNP by 2000. Most Americans are dissatisfied with the health care system. In the next decade, health care providers that can lower cost of services to employers and consumers will be rewarded.

Baby boomers are more health conscious and more likely to use preventive care. Expect more use of alternative medicine approaches, surgery and birthing centers to meet the cost and convenience needs of this group. Women make the health care decisions for more than two-thirds of U.S. households. Baby boomers are demanding more information about health care services and relying less on a physician's advice as the sole source of health care information.

By the year 2000, India will have more people with AIDS than in all the world to date since AIDS first appeared. Moreover, worries over pesticides and other chemical contamination will be a major concern of consumers worldwide.

By 1999, scientists will succeed in identifying hundreds of gene abnormalities and their relationships to environmental influences. By 2005, some 26 states will have passed laws that restrict insurer use of genetic test information in risk selection and classification for life, disability and health insurance. As they become more aware of the genetic basis for disease and disorders, people will become more sympathetic to those with such diseases.

TREND

TECH SWEET HOME

Homes will be smaller and built more quickly, and selling them will require "out teching" your sophisticated competition.

If the current trends persist, the number of U.S. households with personal computers will increase from 16 million in 1992 to 26 million in 2000. There will be personal computers in more households, allowing computer-assisted home buying—potential home buyers can key in criteria such as location, price range and architectural style.

IMPLICATIONS

We will find viewing-center kiosks in malls and retail stores across the United States where virtual reality will enable a person to "sample" a new home—without leaving home. Individuals will turn their heads and see different aspects of a particular room—or feel the texture of wallpaper from afar by using an electronic glove.

The outlook for multifamily housing will remain positive into the next decade because of high demand and low supply. Information about household formations and historical home ownership rates makes it possible to project renter households.

PREDICTIONS

Of the 93 million households in the United States, approximately two-thirds, or 60 million, own homes, while the other one-third, 33 million, rent. The number of renter household formations in the 1990s should average approximately 275,000 annually through the year 2000. The 2000s will see rapid growth in the number of roommates as the baby bust generation begin their adult lives.

Projected shifts in size, age and distribution of the U.S. population suggests that net domestic housing investment will decline 22 percent from 1995 to 2005 before increasing again and that factory-built housing will outpace traditionally built housing for the next decade and beyond.

As the U.S. population ages, community associations in which homeowners voluntarily accede to noise control, landscaping and other aesthetic rules will gain popularity. Nearly one-quarter of the population is expected to live in a community governed by such a neighborhood association by 2000.

TREND

A BUSHEL OF "BIG APPLES"

Big is the megatheme when you think about tomorrow's cities.
Urban centers suffering the consequences of the unadulterated pursuit of wealth—traffic congestion, air pollution, inadequate sanitation and infrastructure—are being stretched to the breaking point by rapid urban growth. Moreover, there is an obvious spreading and melting of the rural, suburban and urban landscape over vast areas, and the growth of "rurubania" will continue.

IMPLICATIONS

The World Bank recently reported that many of Asia's cities are degrading faster than the region's robust economies are growing. Problems in the cities will slow economic development throughout the world. Indeed, in Bangkok, nearly a third of its potential gross product is lost because of delays caused by traffic congestion. Moreover, pollution in metropolitan Bangkok is estimated by the World Bank to cost the Thai economy as much as $3 billion a year.

As Asians are pursuing the Western view of the good life; they want running water, flush toilets and air conditioners, despite all the changes that go with that. That same Westernized view from Asia's growing middle class is responsible for the groundswell support for "green issues" relating to the quality of air, water, light and the environment in general.

PREDICTIONS

The flood of people pouring into Asian cities is not about to stop. By 2020, a staggering 1.5 billion people will be added to the urban centers of Asia. Unemployment will persist in the underclass areas of most cities in the world. As a result, Asia will become a region of megacities each with populations of over eight million people (the world's largest city is still Mexico City with a population of 19.4 million). These huge populations will have a major influence not just on Asia's long-term economic health, but on the world as a whole.

Mixed use satellite cities will ring major cities such as Tokyo. Surface transportation will be limited to walking, monorails and electric cars. Ultra high-rise buildings will be linked by skyway, escalators and "urban ropeways," dramatically cutting the space and energy that would otherwise be wasted on elevators and surface transportation. Distinct residential, commercial and cultural zones will be linked by wide promenades and pedestrian skyways. These new towns within cities will also place heavy emphasis on teleconferencing in the hope of reducing strain on transport systems and on the people who use them. Planners know that a city's transport problems are inextricably linked with how it uses space.

Some future city planning will turn the high-rise concept on its head and move everything that need not be on the surface very deep underground. Most of the surrounding land would be covered with trees and gardens that bury below ground any impact on the environment.

Urban sprawl will increase primarily located along major vehicle transportation corridors and public mass transit routes. A denationalized Europe will grow up along the rocket train (Eurostar) rail line. More municipal authorities will follow the examples of Singapore, which charges drivers for coming into the city center during rush hour, and of Jakarta, where no car may enter the city without at least three passengers.

More and more governments will use a "trade-off" system, requiring developers to build public facilities in return for the right to lease or develop state land. Another approach will be to draw up and enforce policies for managing and limiting growth such as a "floor area ratio" system for each new district, limiting land use density on new construction.

Cities will witness greater "infill" development in already urbanized areas. Land areas that were once marginal will be bought and upgraded for new development. Older land uses such as outdated commercial and industrial facilities will be upgraded to make them more marketable. By the year 2020, the total U.S. bill for earthquake damage in the United States will be approximately $245 billion, and hurricane expenses will reach $281 billion. As a result, expect Congress to enact legislation that encourages damage prevention through such techniques as better building code enforcement and incentives to build away from coastlines, floodplains and fault lines.

Continuing high land values will lead to increased gentrification, further exacerbating the need for low- and moderate-income housing. More state and federal laws and court decisions will usurp the home-rule powers of elected officials and serve to limit discretion in many areas. Public officials will stress economic development as a vehicle to raise revenues without increasing taxes. Highly urbanized cities will have to resort to redevelopment for their financial survival. Jobs, however, will not be found in the downtowns but will be expanding in "edge cities"—typically, areas where 24,000 or more jobs are concentrated outside traditional downtowns. Edge cities are fun, having lots of restaurants, drinking establishments and nightclubs.

Limited government revenues will be earmarked for those cities with large low-income populations and related social and housing problems. New ethnic neighborhoods (ghettos) will evolve in metropolitan areas as residents will stress maintaining the cultural traditions, values and customs of their homelands. A greater number of smaller households will require more high-density residential developments such as condominiums, townhouses and apartments, placing greater demands on existing public services. More public meetings will be aired on public access cable TV stations. These stations will be used to educate citizens on available services and major issues facing their communities.

Chapter 7

HOT TECHNOLOGICAL TRENDS

•

We know what we are, but we know not what we may become.

SHAKESPEARE

All that's different about me is that I still ask the questions most people stopped asking at age five.

ALBERT EINSTEIN

•

Tremendous changes have occurred in the twentieth century. More mind-boggling discoveries in science and technology have altered our lives in the past 100 years than at any other time in the history of the world. As we barge into the next century, the pace of change will continue. Thus, science and technology are often the wild cards of the future.

The world can be divided in many ways, but the technologically aware and the technologically ignorant will be the dichotomy that will have the greatest impact on our quality of life. Like understanding your native language, you must become fluent in technology to be successful in the twenty-first century as it becomes an ever more important commodity to trade and ever more difficult to protect.

The answers to the following science and technology questions examined in this chapter will provide exciting business opportunities: How do we think? Where will miniaturization of computers and microprocessors lead us? Are expert systems real? How will satellites change our lives? How will speech switch on the next century? What are the trends in optical transmission technologies? Will biotech fulfill its promise? What's a ceramic turbo? How will ceramic-cogeneration technologies power our future? What are the new laser applications?

TREND

UNDERSTANDING HOW WE THINK—SMART DRUGS

Contributor—Steven William Fowkes, managing director, Cognitive Enhancement Research Institute (CERI)

In 1992, *Time* magazine published a feature article about vitamins. The cover boldly proclaimed, "New evidence shows they may help fight cancer, heart disease, and the ravages of aging." Ten years ago, such a statement would not have been made by a mainstream publication. Yet today, Americans spend over $3 billion a year on vitamins and nutrients, and that figure is growing. Steven Fowkes of CERI shared his view that "smart drugs" are now where vitamins were 10 years ago and that dramatic change is ahead as these drugs become part of our reality.

Science is changing our understanding of the human brain and intelligence. There is a whole new concept of what intelligence is and why certain people are more intelligent than others. Scientists no longer believe that our intelligence is fixed or determined strictly by genetics. It's now known that you can develop and increase your mental performance with so-called smart drugs and nutrients.

More businesspeople and scholars will be looking for the kind of edge that athletes get from science. The competition in business is every bit as real and intense as the competition on the playing fields. Many career paths require that people continue to educate themselves. Some professions require regular testing to establish that their members are staying abreast of new developments, and some corporations are structured so that employees must compete intellectually for promotions and raises.

Faced with information explosion and sensory overload in a world of constantly increasing complexity and competition, memory sharpness and increased thinking ability become imperative.

IMPLICATIONS

Smart drugs will become big business in the coming decades. Over 140 types of smart pills are being developed by the American pharmaceutical industry, more than 160 worldwide, making them the 10th largest class of researched drugs. (The top category of drug development, anti-cancer agents, comprises only about 260 drugs worldwide.) The total smart-drug market will top $2 billion per year before 2000. A single brand of one of these drugs Nootropil (Piracetam) reported 1990 worldwide sales of $1 billion.

Currently, no legal basis for approving performance-enhancing drugs exists in the United States. The U.S. Federal Drug Administration (FDA), drug companies and the medical establishment do their work by targeting a particular disease and then developing, testing and administrating a drug to deal with that disease. This disease-oriented approach can stifle innovation. Performance-enhancing drugs can be approved, but only if they can be demonstrated effective for the treatment of some disease. Therefore, to broaden their market, drug companies have defined a new disease called "age-associated memory impairment" (AAMI).

It doesn't take a smart pill to realize that there is a large market for people who want to have their memories improved. Memory impairment often interferes with our job performance and social lives; certainly, there is a large market with Alzheimer's disease alone. We can all think of an 80-year-old with crystal clear memories. On the other hand, some people in their early 50s have difficulty remembering telephone numbers or putting names to faces. It is estimated that at least 4 million people in the United Kingdom suffer from AAMI, and the possibility of 10 to 50 million healthy Americans using drugs to enhance memory function presents a large investment opportunity.

In studies done in England and California, giving vitamin supplements to school children produced nonverbal IQ increases on the average of 6 points. The IQ difference between an American with an average IQ and a doctor, lawyer or professor is only about 11 points. The gain observed in one out of three (study participants) is the same as might be required for an American with an average IQ to aspire to be a doctor, lawyer or professor.

Publicity about the study triggered such buying enthusiasm in England that many of the stores' shelves were stripped bare of vitamin supplements in days. Indeed, up to 300 million U.S. dollars was spent in one week, and this by a population only twice that of the state of California.

The most popular smart drug for normal healthy people is Piracetam, a broadly effective enhancer of many aspects of human performance. Another smart drug, milacedmide, can be absorbed into the brain (like a molecular Trojan horse) and subsequently broken down to release glycine, which acts on the receptors that are critical for long-term memory. In numerous studies, milacemide has been shown to improve human selective attention, word retrieval, numeric memory and vigilance.

Unfortunately, since milacemide appears useful only for memory enhancement in normal healthy people and not those with cognitive disorders, it may languish on laboratory shelves because of the FDA's catch-22 policies of only approving drugs for treatment of diseases.

Also, milacemide does show negative synergy when used with deprenyl, producing dramatic negative learning and avoidance behavior in tests.

Pregnenolone is a steroid-hormone precursor that has unusual memory-enhancing activity that has been found to be 100 times more effective than other steroids at improving memory and learning activities in mice. However, there is currently a lack of data documenting this drug's memory-enhancing effect in humans.

PREDICTIONS

After decades of safe use and millions of prescription and over-the-counter sales in many countries, the United States will join the rest of the world and approve Piracetam for its citizens. The attribute of Piracetam of reducing metabolic stress under low-oxygen conditions will make it popular with high-altitude sports people (skiers, rock climbers, mountain bikers and hikers) interested in better and safer performance.

As the U.S. federal government tries to control health care costs, it will move toward the German model that allows nontraditional homeopathy and other preventive care treatments to fit under its health care umbrella.

TREND

BRAIN ON A CHIP—
VERY SMALL WILL BE VERY BIG BUSINESS

Sophisticated world competitors understand the importance of the megatheme smaller-faster.
Advances yet to happen in computing are going to change the world. The new age of computers and semiconductors is dependent on the pace of device miniaturization. Trends in microelectronics will drive trends in the evolution of computer hardware, displays, printers and other accessories needed to manage multisensory information, including pictures, sound and text (and some day, smell and touch).

Driving down the size of microelectronics puts humans in a strange new world of size and space dimensions beyond our comprehension and senses. The human brain contains about 100 billion neurons; currently, ventures are underway where parallel computers would have as many transistors as the brain has neurons.

IMPLICATIONS

The drive toward miniaturization will have profound effects on many industries, particularly computers and telecommunications. Microprocessors will do what they do now only better: faster searching through stored information; more efficient control of manufacturing; bigger, faster, easier to use networks of computers; better computer models of complicated phenomena such as aerodynamics of advanced aircraft, the earth's climate, the economy, the genetic code and the structure of the universe.

Microprocessors will do what is envisioned now but cannot be done yet: Smarter and more friendly user interface with spoken natural language will recognize and "interpret" word language; visual systems using artificial intelligence will discriminate among distinct objects in a visual field; while full digital television and chips with the power of PCs will run faster, flashier computer games.

Computing will depend on the concept of microcomputer clusters—very large clusters that today already realize a processing power of 10,000 MIPS (millions of instructions per second). Just 20 years ago, by contrast, mainframe computer designers were struggling to attain just one MIPS! The price of executing computer instructions will continue to fall and will vary greatly from mainframe to minicomputers (middle-range multiuser systems) to microcomputers (general purpose work stations, the "PC"). Minicomputer MIPS cost half as much as mainframe MIPS. The principal difference is that mainframe users want to concentrate large amounts of computing capability in one place. To get maximum processing capability, the silicon chips employed in these computers use complex bipolar transistors.

On the other hand, to make them more compact, economical and energy efficient, chip makers use a logic circuitry made of field-effect transistors (FETs). The least power hungry of them are known as CMOS (complementary metal oxide semiconductors). FET circuitry is also used for all the memories for both large and small computers.

One step in constructing transistors is to etch lines in silicon wafers to form outlines of circuits. This etching is accomplished by sending electromagnetic radiation—such as visible and ultraviolet light—through a mask (a type of circuit blueprint processing the patterns of the desired circuits). The narrower the lines forming transistors, the greater number of devices that can fit on a single die, and the faster these circuits can accomplish their task.

For the last two decades, microelectronics have attained smaller, cheaper, faster and more functional devices, allowing companies to put a lot of devices on a silicon chip. Companies have moved from large-scale integration (LSI) to very large-scale integration (VSLI). We will soon have ULSI ultralarge-scale integration, where the minimum dimensions will move from today's devices of about $3/4$ of a micrometer to dimensions of $1/4$ and $1/10$ of a micrometer—invisible to an optical microscope.

Driving down the size of these microelectronic devices allows electrical current to be driven through the chip at higher frequencies or *clock speeds*. Frequency is a rough measure of the speed information can be processed at a given time. Today, advanced microprocessors run at clock speeds of 25—100 megahertz (MHz), and bipolar transistors switch in about $1/2$ to $1/3$ of a nanosecond. There are as many nanoseconds in a second as there are seconds in 32 years.

PREDICTIONS

Bipolar transistors will operate at speeds of about 50 picoseconds. We're talking small and fast—there are as many picoseconds in a second as there are seconds in 32,000 years (light travels only 1.5 centimeters in 50 picoseconds). We will have conventional transistors measuring 400 atoms by 400 atoms each.

Today, molecular beams (laser, layer-ion, and electron) are used to perform microsurgery to construct microelectronic devices. The minimum dimensions of devices on today's chips are just under one micrometer. With the wavelength of light just a little smaller than one micrometer, optical lithography is reaching its ability to pattern devices.

Two prime candidates for lithographic processing of subhalf-micrometer dimensions are electron-beam (E-beam) and x-ray lithography. The next frontier may be based on single electronic devices whose behavior is described by the laws of quantum physics as applied to single particles. By 2010, such new devices will begin displacing some conventional devices.

The *word length* refers to the size of a unit of data in bits that a central processing unit (CPU)—where the computer computes—can process at a time. Now, 32-bit computers are commonplace. In the future, we can expect chips to be designed with 128 or even 256 word lengths. By the year 2000, line width should reach 0.25 of a micrometer. To put this in perspective, the length of the average bacteria is one micrometer. The area occupied by a single transistor will be a thousand times less than what it was in 1971.

Today, the densest memory chips used in most products have a million bits (1 Mbit). Around 2000, expect billion-bit chips. By 2010, the trend will have matured with chips containing a few billion components each for highly packed circuits such as memory. By 2000, a single processor should be able to run at 700 MIPS, and microprocessors will have a clock speed of 250 MHz or more.

Possessing the power of a PC on a chip will mean having a computer with the power of a multiprocessing mainframe in a box the size of a handheld calculator. We literally will have a world of information at our fingertips—such a chip could reasonably store the equivalent of 500 books and could find any piece of information in those volumes in half a second. If you wanted to have more information available, say what is stored in the 8,000-volume public library, a slightly larger but still portable 16-chip system would do. If the average book is an inch thick, that's the equivalent of 650 linear feet of books.

The actual components per chip produced may be constrained by economics rather than physical limits. Fabrication lines to make such complex chips will cost up to $10 billion each. For that reason, there may be only 5 to 10 such lines in the world. Today, the design of microchips requires an array of design automation tools that has greatly reduced the need for human labor. Because defective dies in a batch of silicon wafers are getting sparser (currently about 200 defects per million), the semiconductor industry has been able to quadruple the density of memory chips roughly every three years. Expect a wafer defect rate of nearly zero on these lines by the year 2000.

TREND

SOLAR-POWERED SATELLITES (SPS) PROVIDE CLEAN, ABUNDANT ENERGY (WILD CARD)

What's that in the sky? It's a bird, it's a plane, no it's SPS!
Global energy represents a trillion-dollar-a-year market. Japanese strategic thinkers know that energy technology can keep Japan an economic superpower well into the twenty-first century. By using their experience in the commercial appliance market, the Japanese have acquired the industrial ability to construct solar cells and microwave systems that they will assimilate into an SPS program.

IMPLICATIONS

Solar-powered satellites introduce an opportunity to privatize parts of immense government space programs, and the potential for being profitable will secure their survival. The United States, Japan, China, Europe and Russia will join a new space race to be first to deliver electric power for a profit. Electricity will be inexpensive in the long run. While SPS costs plenty to build, fuel cost is minimal—the sun sends no bills.

Structures up to 15 miles long, the size of Manhattan, would be required to supply the 10 billion watts of electricity needed to power New York City. A 1-billion-watt system will be required for commercial viability. The United States may buy Russian heavyweight rocket boosters to lift the huge parts of the satellite into space, providing hard currency and a growth industry for the Russians.

PREDICTIONS

The controversy about health dangers from relatively small amounts of microwave energy will be intensified as huge amounts of solar energy are transmitted via microwave. The microwave beam would be so dispersed, however, so that birds could fly through it without harm.

The Japanese will take the lead on SPS, starting this year with a one-kilowatt test from a spacecraft to a satellite.

By the year 2000, the Japanese will succeed in testing a 10-megawatt system in orbit.

Oil-rich countries will invest heavily in these projects and will use their vast arid lands as receiving stations for microwave transmission from space. Antenna farms will be placed in remote areas of the United States and on floating platforms off major coastal cities.

TREND

ROBOTICS—REAL EXPERT SYSTEMS

When I worked at SRI in the 1970s, my kids couldn't wait to visit me and see "Shakey" the robot, who would roam the laboratory of Charlie Rosen, a pioneer in robotics. Will robotics revalue or de-value human resources?

The loom developed by Jacquard in 1804 could be programmed to make different designs according to punch cards fed into it. Later computer numerically controlled machines have wittily been referred to as the "fruit of the loom." When computer control went beyond simulating human control of a tool and began feebly mimicking a human, industrial robotics emerged.

IMPLICATIONS

To be competitive in a global environment, companies must automate and integrate or disintegrate. In fact, the service sector, which employs more than two-thirds of the American workforce and includes such industries as hospitals, retailing, banking, insurance and finance, has already automated most business functions.

The technologies needed to automate most of the world's manufacturing work exist but have not been integrated into comprehensive applications in most industries. Computer-aided design (CAD) and computer-aided manufacturing (CAM), for example, are used by most manufacturing firms as well as computer-controlled machine tools, robots, automated inspection, quality control, procurement, inventory control, production-line scheduling, material handling and warehouse systems that are now found in many upgraded facilities. The problem is these automated processes have typically been introduced piecemeal because the software and process engineering needed to link them have not been available.

In 1980, the United States possessed 15 percent of the world's robots, but today, Japan has three times as many. Regardless, in the years ahead, there will be more advanced automated manufacturing technologies, and America will excel in software and will process engineering systems to integrate technologies. Machines that can see, touch, speak and hear are now being used by such companies as General Electric, Ford and Texas Instruments.

Issues such as standards, operational performance and system integration capabilities have hindered the development and implementation of expert system applications.

Artificial intelligence (AI) researchers are addressing most of the technological limitations of early expert systems, yet companies are still waiting for software standards and development methodologies. These tools are essential for successful applications.

PREDICTIONS

The direction in manufacturing is toward the unmanned factory. However, robots will not displace men and women (robots often do assembly work traditionally done by women). Robotics has been introduced in some areas of the manufacturing environment, but despite the publicity and hype, its use thus far has been limited. Robotics is already in use to string tennis rackets, wire lights and fit rubber padding around car doors. Mainly, robotics is used for work that is unpleasant, physically demanding and dangerous—spraying, welding and so forth.

The demands of the future will be for flexibility and easy-to-program robots that can quickly move from task to task. Flexible manufacturing systems that use the same machinery to produce a wide variety of components that can be assembled into customized products at a profit—will profit. By 2000, for example, multitask robotic harvesters may replace human crop pickers.

The new generation of information systems will most likely use AI and other advanced technologies. Computer-automated design (CAD) is the most important step in a product's life since half the life cycle cost of a product is fixed by the original design. Fuzzy logic, case-based reasoning and common sense modeling are among the new research areas that hold the most promise for a second wave of smart systems for business use.

TREND

SPEECH TECHNOLOGY—SWITCH ON THE NEXT CENTURY

Now, the only time I talk to my computer is to express some expletives when it decides to impress me with its complexity and my human frailties. By doing something horrendous to my text, "old blue" makes me commit more time to our relationship than I care to. A dramatic change is needed in how man and machine communicate, and perhaps it's coming.

Speech recognition and speech synthesis are guaranteed interest technologies because they support direct communications between humans and computers through a communications method humans commonly use among themselves. Both manipulate speech in terms of information content: computer recognition changes human speech into text to be used literally (e.g., for dictation) or to be interpreted as commands to control applications; synthesis allows the generation of spoken utterances from text.

IMPLICATIONS

The scale of integration for silicon speech-processing chips is increasing by about 33 percent a year. At the same time, the speed of individual components is growing by some 20 percent a year. The trends make it possible to use fewer and fewer components to implement the processing associated with a specific speech-recognition or speech-synthesis algorithm. One outcome: We can now construct a 100-word recognizer into a single chip.

Automated speech recognition (ASR) is gaining a significant measure of commercial success by assisting human operators or by replacing the human element altogether. Significant areas of ASR are dictation, personal computer interfaces, automated telephone services and special purpose industrial applications. Speech synthesis is a stable technology that is cheap and usable; however, generated speech still sounds unnatural and is less intelligible than human speech.

PREDICTIONS

The greatest potential application of speech technology lies in the development of systems that combine recognition and synthesis to support conversational interaction between humans and computers in complex task domains. Expect voice interface for both conventional desktop computers and for the coming generation of small portable devices PDAs (personal digital assistants) It is doubtful, however, that speech could completely replace the keyboard or the pointer.

Large vocabulary dictation will be used for business letters, newspaper articles, medical reports, insurance claims and so forth. Current vocabulary capacities store up to 40,000 words. Usability of dictation systems will increase because their ability to adapt to an individual's voice, vocabulary and tasks will be improved.

A 1,000-word recognizer will be on a single chip in the next decade, making speaker independent automatic speech recognition commonplace. These thrusts will explode into a variety of services based on the ability of intelligent machines to talk and listen much as people do.

By 2010, we will have the ability to transfer unique personal speech characteristics across languages to make customized speech translators. Speech in one language would be automatically translated into a second language, which will be synthesized with the voice characteristics of the original speaker, and this translation will be done in real time. Due to the difficulty of converting thousands of unique Kanji symbols into data, Japan will aggressively pursue development of audio input devices that convert spoken inputs into digital format.

The telephone companies will be the first to advance recognition-based services. Telephone-based recognition-operator services, including small vocabularies, interactive dialogue and prompting, offer enormous potential. Because of the pervasiveness of voice communication and lack of control over use, these services will prove to be technically demanding. Additional opportunities that will be promoted include credit card validation, catalog shopping and automated answering machines. These extensions, however, require progressively larger vocabularies and interface intelligence.

TREND

OPTICAL TECHNOLOGIES—SEE US THROUGH

The potential of fiber optics eluded my antenna in the early 1970s. I envisioned too many technical problems to overcome as well as limited applications for this new technology. Remember, computers then were still using punch cards and retrieving large paper printouts. Global communication using fiber-optic technologies evolved much faster than this guru ever imagined.

Optical fiber cables are now viewed as one of the great inventions of the twentieth century as well as a transmission medium to support the information-oriented society of the twenty-first century.

Optical fiber cables carry extremely high volumes of information with little attenuation. They are free of electromagnetic interference, thin, light and energy efficient. Most of the current systems employing optical fibers use a method of sending light pulses as a signal. The information-carrying capacity is determined by the duration of the intervals between the light pulses.

IMPLICATIONS

Market Pull

Our passion for entertainment will be the powerful marketplace incentive for the evolution of an all-fiber network, including fiber to the end user. The entertainment industry is gearing up for high-definition television (HDTV) as the best solution for marketing its products selectively through a switched fiber system that could feature pay-per-view programs. For HDTV to come into the home it will need optical fiber to allow the 40–150 megabits per second data rates required.

The local telephone companies and the cable television (CATV) companies are rapidly upgrading to fiber-optical trunking systems; companies who own satellite systems plan to lease their transponders for direct broadcasting of HDTV to small rooftop antennas. The outcome of the HDTV sweepstakes will change the shape of communications. If the vehicle is fiber to the home, then perhaps all other communications services can also ride that fiber, hitchhiking along with HDTV.

Technology Push

By 2010, electronics will mature, and instead of using electrons as the medium for information processing, optoelectronics (photonics), using photons instead of electrons, will take over many electronic functions. Trends in photonics are just evolving beyond that of generation and transmission, where the technology has had a major impact. By 2010, a trend toward the control of light by light, which is essential to photonic logic functions, will be well under way.

Even though the photonics function for light-wave transmission is well developed, trend data suggests we have another 20 years of progress. We measure the capability of light-wave transmission by the product of system data (bit) rate and the distance that signals can travel before needing regeneration or amplification. That capability has been doubling every year for well over a decade and will continue to double every year for the next two decades before known physical limits are reached.

In fact, today's most advanced research systems are only 1 percent of the known physical limits for light-wave technology. Today's practical in-service systems already transmit information at 3.4 billion bits per second—equivalent to nearly 50,000 simultaneous phone calls on one pair of fibers. This amount is more than twice the data transmission that takes place over the optic nerves that connect our eyes to our brain.

Moreover, photonic transmission technology is becoming largely independent of specific bit rates. This technology is a result of the emerging use of optical amplifiers, which use light to control light, and therefore eliminate the need for high-speed electronics to regenerate signals in electronic repeaters. These optical amplifiers will first be used in transoceanic cable systems, enabling signals, by the year 2000, to traverse the oceans without regeneration. The number of undersea fiber-optic communications links has increased dramatically. In 1993, for example, 46 new regional and transoceanic sub-marine systems were placed in service worldwide and will be added to the 136 existing sub-marine links.

LASERS

Industrial firms in Japan and Europe are more interested in developing high-energy lasers for industrial applications than are U.S. firms. However, the United States is developing niche industrial applications such as cutting methods for materials, laser enrichment of nuclear fuels and stereo-lithography. The United States has a slight lead in laser-based medical technology over Japan and Europe. Because of its potential for use in communications, ther-apeutics, chemical analysis and consumer electronics, the use of lasers as a transmission source to replace micro-wave frequencies will continue to be explored.

Other research in electro-optics is focused on the development of non-linear optics, self-scanning, detector arrays and optical fibers.

PREDICTIONS

The use of light-wave technology has increased the quality of international communication transmission significantly. The proliferation of undersea light-wave links will make international communications traffic less likely to be transported via satellite, which suffers from inherent delays.

Optical fiber to the end user—home or business—will be the last step in achieving an all-fiber communications network. Once it gains momentum, growth of residential fiber networks will be rapid. Within 15 years, the fiber network will grow to 100 million access lines.

Optical fibers will be extended to every household in Japan by 2015. In 1992, some 2.46 million kilometers of optical fiber were produced in Japan. The Japanese are developing resins for fiber coating that show practically no deterioration under extremely severe experimental conditions.

Laser beams combined with liquid crystal displays will dramatically improve pattern recognition, help robots pick out imperfectly shaped products, match fingerprints faster and eventually lead to an optical computer.

TREND

CONNECTIVISTS—MAPMAKERS LOCATING A HEALTHY FUTURE

I've watched biotechnology evolve over the past two decades, both as a consultant to biotech companies and as a contributor to the book *The Status of Biotechnology. Biotechnology* is a catchall term used to describe dramatic change in a wide range of industries. It includes genetic engineering to produce large quantities of valuable natural proteins for the production of monoclonal antibodies—the human body's defense against viruses and bacteria—as well as the cell fusion procedures used in plant agriculture. All of biotech will benefit from the next trend.

Within the spiraling strands of human DNA is a treasure trove of information such as who is likely to get certain types of cancer or heart disease and how can those diseases be prevented? The Human Genome Project is a $3 billion, 15-year effort to decipher the entire genetic human bluprint. In the United States, this coordinated effort is funded by the National Institutes of Health (NIH) and the Department of

Energy. The mapping project is billed as one of the great scientific efforts and a way to keep U.S. biotech ahead of such rivals as Japan, France, Britain, Canada and Italy, who are also involved in mapping efforts.

IMPLICATIONS

The two specific objectives of the genome project involve mapping 50,000–100,000 genes and determining their sequencing. Mapping gene sites along 23 pairs of threadlike chromosomes and sequencing involves the task of "reading" the order of the chemical subunits of DNA in any cataloged gene.

By the end of the last decade, fewer than 10 percent of our genes had been located. Most gene-mapping research has not focused on the Human Genome Project but rather on independent efforts to pinpoint genetic defects that cause the approximately 4,000 inheritable diseases. Scientific sleuths have already identified those genes for sickle cell anemia, cystic fibrosis, muscular dystrophy and a type of Alzheimer's disease. Finding the answers is a tedious, expensive job: The cost of identifying the gene that causes cystic fibrosis was $150 million. Such projects would move faster and cost less if we had a map to locate the genes within the chromosomes.

PREDICTIONS

New advances in machines that map and sequence automatically will dramatically speed the process and will provide a new infrastructure for biology. Once genes are found, expect quick commercial payoff in diagnostic tests for medical concerns such as predisposition to heart disease. New drugs targeted at specific genes will arrive further into the next decade.

The NIH touched off a storm when it applied for patents on over 300 pieces of human brain genes found by one of its biochemists. Expect the NIH to be required one way or another to share the Human Genome Project discoveries with U.S. biotech companies.

TREND

CERAMIC AND COGENERATION TECHNOLOGY POWER
OUR FUTURE

Contributor—Richard Carlson, futurist

Richard Carlson, futurist, author, consultant, public speaker and former colleague at Stanford Research Institute (SRI International) has been doing work on the economics of energy. He presents a trend that could drastically change utilities in the future.

New small, high efficiency, ceramic gas turbine power generation systems will become an economic reality in the next 7 to 15 years, dramatically impacting the future of electric utilities. Electric power generation will become much more decentralized as localized production of electricity occurs on a large scale.

IMPLICATIONS

What's about to happen to the electric power utilities will be the economic and technological equivalent of events that raised havoc with the telephone utilities, particularly AT&T. The core technology of AT&T through the 1950s was mechanical telephone switching. Mechanical switching systems were probably the most reliable mechanical devices ever built by humans.

In the 1950s and 1960s, a symbiotic relationship existed between AT&T and the public utility regulators who allowed AT&T a 3 percent to 5 percent depreciation rate that was moderately faster than the expected mechanical lifetime. This rate helped AT&T to book very large profits on paper. A problem surfaced, however, in the 1960s and overwhelmed the telephone company and their regulators by the 1970s. Simply put, the stuff that was built to last 50 years had quickly become technological junk due to high-speed electronic switching.

High-efficiency ceramic-based turbines is a technology that will have a similar revolutionary impact on electric utilities and our electric rates. We're already seeing ceramic coating on turbine blades, and in a 7- to 15-year time frame, the whole system will be built from ceramics, at least the hot part of the turbines that generate electric power. Ceramics will allow electric generating turbines to run at much higher temperatures, which by the basic laws of thermodynamics means higher efficiencies.

Let's put some perspective on the future ceramic revolution. Right now, the most efficient turbines have a 40 percent fuel efficiency, while experimental ceramic systems are in the 60 percent to 70 percent range. That fuel efficiency is so good that it will have the same impact electronic switching had on mechanical switching. *All the power plants considered excellent today will suddenly be technological junk.*

Deregulation and technology changes will drive down the cost of energy bills over time. A tidal wave of deregulation is about to hit U.S. electrical utilities. Starting in January 1996, California's largest industrial customers will be allowed to shop around for electricity rather than being required to buy it from the local utility. By 2002, even residential customers will be free to buy power from competing suppliers.

The growing trend of companies to bypass power utilities is apparent with cogeneration. On-site cogenerating uses a natural gas-fed turbine and provides both heat and electricity. The system generates light, which in turn produces heat, which instead of being exhausted, heats the building or can be used in the cooling system. Cogenerators using existing technology can provide energy more cheaply to commercial industrial users than can most electric utilities. They are killing the high-cost utilities by cherry picking just as MCI cherry-picked AT&T. They take away the high-volume, high-profit users, leaving the utility with the low profit if not the loss customers.

The cost-benefit decision for decentralization will be the economic equivalent of shooting fish in a barrel. The high-cost utilities, the ones that will be stuck up in the $0.12-per-KW range (some are already close to that for residential use) will be competing with these new technologies that will generate power for half that cost. If a utility has a high book value for existing generating plants, being depreciated at 2 percent or 3 percent a year, that means they're going to be stuck with a lot of investment cost by 2000. According to the books, there will be a lot of life, and the utility will be performing well by today's standards but not by future standards.

PREDICTIONS

The first really reliable turbines made primarily of ceramics will be small because of mechanical stress problems. Ceramic materials don't bend like metal. Instead, they break and explode when something goes wrong. Therefore, it's much easier to contain a small explosion than a big one. The small, early turbines will easily meet all the energy needs of an office building or small factory. With privately owned, on-site ceramic generating systems, the rates will be much better than those of the electric power utilities.

Some big-name utilities are not going to make it. Be wary of utilities with the highest fixed costs. *A key sign to watch is if a utility's commercial and industrial loads turn downward.* A downturn started to happen in the late 1980s and early 1990s. Some utilities were doing fine and others poorly, averaging out in the aggregate. But a downturn is significant when it's looked at on a utility-by-utility basis.

Cogeneration and ceramic technology will be forced by the larger industrial and commercial customers. Some unusual alliances will be formed to try to stop this technology. The public utility commissions and the utilities that they have been fighting will suddenly become allies. They may use the air-quality rules to stop or slow down decentralized generation. Because emissions are low, however, that strategy will fail.

The regulators will also team up with existing residential customers to try to slow technology because most utilities lose money on residential customers and make up the money from nonresidential customers.

Who will pay for already-built power plants that competition makes economically untenable or unnecessary? Big industrial users argue that utility shareholders should be stuck with the bill, but most likely, customers who shop around for power will pay some transition charge to compensate the utility for uneconomical capacity.

TREND

TECHNOLOGY AND PEOPLE

In Japan, foreign guests with a sense of urgency trying to understand the operating directions in Japanese on the electronic keypad of the

"Smart" toilet (i.e., a paperless toilet that sprays warm water like a bidet, then blows warm air to dry and even dispenses a scent) would agree that it may be time to revalue and perhaps shift our focus away from technology.

The future will not be determined by technology alone. In recent years, scientists have had dreams of new services such as information and education in the home, the videophone, appliance control and so forth. They have all been technologically and economically feasible but have been rejected by society. For years, people have been talking about displacing travel and working at home through telecommunications, but the actual displacements have been small thus far. Human beings are complicated and finicky. We will be hard to satisfy even with future technology.

IMPLICATIONS

Ken Colmen, head of SRI International Technology Management Group, asks: Do we need major discontinuity all the time? Without a major breakthrough like computers, there may be problems in the short term for individual firms. But in the overall quality of life, how much difference does it make? Isn't it possible to have a happy, heathy, educated world without the constant turmoil because of technological change? Indeed, Colmen envisions a world where there are fewer and less important major technological breakthroughs but there is a slow steady improvement in the conditions of the masses.

More High-Tech Answers to Low-Tech Jobs

Everyone heard how Teflon migrated from the space program to the kitchen, but conversions of military and aerospace products to the private sector have been rare. Now, an array of new composite materials—tougher graphite, carbon fibers and boron filaments—are getting a share of the consumer markets from autos to fishing rods. Falling prices due to depressed military demand and overcapacity have cut costs to where composite fibers will replace steel as the material used most in U.S.-built cars. In 1990, plastics worldwide accounted for 11 percent to 13 percent of the weight of a car, approximately 230 pounds, a figure growing by about 8 percent per year, which could possibly reach 20 percent by 2000.

South Korea's Goldstar Company claims to have invented the world's first consumer product to exploit the chaos theory, which holds that there are identifiable tendencies of movement amid the randomness of, for example, weather patterns. Goldstar has analyzed the movements of water in a standard washing machine, identified those that produce cleaner, less-tangled clothes and then built a washing machine that produced these motions.

PREDICTIONS

Human factors—how people interact with machines and products—will be of increased concern because of the inability of many people in the workforce to cope with new technologies.

Most countries of the developing world see modern technology as the answer to almost all their problems. In the future in many nations, the pendulum will swing the other way. Governments of developing countries will see advanced technology as the cause of one of their most perplexing problems, massive unemployment. Expect foreign business to clearly be a candidate for blame. Companies will adjust their automated equipment downward to create intermediate technologies that are better suited to the real needs of the developing country.

TREND

WILL SOFTWARE GET SOFT?

The next trend illustrates how productivity will improve in an area of ever more sophisticated global competition.

Despite growing global competition, software is one of the fastest growing and most profitable American business segments. America exports the dominant operating systems for desktop machines, including Microsoft's DOS and Unix (AT&T and others). The principal micro-computer software packages for word processing, data base management and thousands of other uses are supplied usually in English to a growing worldwide computer market.

IMPLICATIONS

Though IBM relinquished the operating-system and application-software business to Microsoft and others, it still offers four mainframe products that account for $1 billion in annual sales.

Today's major software problem is to increase programmer productivity to meet exploding demands. For some types of software, expect productivity to increase dramatically from a range of 5,000 noncommentary source lines of code to over 50,000 lines per programmer year. The increase will come mainly from the growing reuse of previously developed and tested software modules. In the next two decades, standards for software should be pervasive and widely deployed.

Software design will also change dramatically. For example, conventional programmers will have graduated to other important jobs. The generation of software will, for the most part, be automated like today's computer-aided design of integrated circuits. Software jobs will be heavily concentrated in work-in-process, bringing discipline to the creation of new software platforms and eventually to new technologies like photonic-based software.

Emerging information technology trends are influencing how companies will use software to plan, organize, analyze, manage knowledge and reengineer business processes. These trends include widespread use of PC-based local area networks to link computers and management users that will provide flexibility and easier multidimensional modeling and analysis; graphic user interfaces such as those provided by Windows, which will greatly expand managerial computer usage and will improve "user friendliness" with easily usable commands that give the same look and feel to all applications no matter what the underlying software; and the realization that software is more application-dependent than was previously understood.

PREDICTIONS

The sales pace of North American microcomputer application software will slow. An erosion in software prices will mean thinner profit margins for software vendors. In 1994, there was $5 billion in software acquistions. Expect the pace to continue for the next few years.

Mainframe computers that require specialist environments and support staff will decline as organizations transfer to small decentralized powerful networked PCs and minicomputers. Due to the decline of the mainframe, chief information officers (CIOs) will suffer increased turnover and stagnant or decreased budgets. The average information service budget is 1.7 percent of company revenue. The majority of applications, nearly 70 percent, still use a mainframe platform. This percentage will diminish to less than 50 percent before 2000.

TREND

THE CERAMIC CAR (WILD CARD)

Contributor—Richard Carlson

Richard Carlson shifts our focus about the electric car in this wild card trend.

I'm (Carlson) not a believer in electric vehicles (EVs). I think that technology stinks. Battery technology hasn't progressed as fast as the backers with a quarter of a billion dollars of federal monies had hoped. The battery isn't a magic wand. Hundreds of companies are trying to come up with a good battery, and they're all failing. Short driving range and problems that develop in severe cold weather will continue to weaken consumer acceptance. Incentives will be required to offset the higher price tag consumers would have to pay on electric cars. Furthermore, with electric cars, air quality gains may be minimal since coal- and oil-fired generating plants will have to ramp up to power the new cars, emitting nearly as much of some pollutants. Natural gas vehicles and incentives to retire old, high-polluting cars make more sense.

The auto companies are also experimenting with ceramics for internal combustion engines as well as turbines. There are experimental internal combustion engines running around with great fuel efficiencies.

IMPLICATIONS

Interest in advanced ceramics is growing. Three factors are driving current activity: (1) competition among ceramic companies; (2) improved consistency of ceramic materials; (3) the belief that structural ceramics may be the only way to achieve certain design improvements such as greater fuel economy, longer life and reduced emissions from engines. Among the advantages of ceramic part manufacturing are high strength at high temperature, chemical resistance, wear resistance and ultrasmooth surfaces.

Design engineers will continue to exploit the properties of ceramics in power transmission equipment. Electromechanical clutches and brakes with ceramic friction surfaces last longer and are easier to control than conventional fiber resin surfaces. In Japan, advanced ceramics with heat resistance, corrosion resistance and wear resistance are attracting attention as the new materials for structural applications to high-performance machinery such as engines.

PREDICTIONS

Watch for the development of a very small, high-efficiency electric car using a ceramic turbine combined with some modest energy storage device. We would then have a small turbine that would cruise the car fine but would need a battery to kick in the acceleration. This "hybrid" engine could force a review of the air-quality laws because the engine will have a nitrous oxide problem but minimal ozone emissions due to running at a high temperature.

The electric utilities are hoping to be saved by the inefficient battery-operated electric car. Their profits would rise as you drive home in a car that would need to be plugged into an electric socket overnight in the garage to recharge the battery. *With the hybrid car you also need to plug in the car; however, the car will supply energy to the home, not vice versa.*

TREND

BIOTECH BREAKS (UP) THROUGH

Biotech manipulates the very processes of life, and therefore dramatic change is possible and probable.

After a decade of high flying, biotech will first face a major shakeout. Billions of investment dollars have created an industry choked with copycats—capital hungry companies lacking the critical mass of technology to survive. But by 2005, biotech will emerge as the driving force in medical technology.

IMPLICATIONS

In 1987, of the approximately 300 companies in the biotech field, few if any were profitable, However, through venture capitalists, public offerings and the like, start-up biotech companies had raised about $4 billion. In the 1990s, less than 25 percent of the over 1,000 biotech companies are profitable. Indeed, only about half the companies have enough money to last until next year.

PREDICTIONS

Contrary to the predictions, 2020 will not be the "bioeconomy." Instead, expect more than half the existing biotech companies to consolidate, merge or go out of business. Most companies will survive as parts of large drug companies rather than as an independent industry.

Expect an industrywide sales increase of over 25 percent by 2005. Almost all companies will have a product on the market before the end of the decade, but most product breakthroughs will be in areas that have relatively small markets. Some of the more promising areas where breakthroughs might happen include anti-clotting drugs, cardiovascular drugs, septic shock, rheumatoid arthritis and diabetes. The cancer treatment of choice may be monoclonal antibodies, specialized versions of the body's own intruder-fighting substances that could provide the vehicle that will hone in on tumors and deliver potent anti-cancer drugs without harming healthy tissue.

Other breakthroughs include a tiny plastic disc that will release an enzyme that destroys collagen, a basic component of the hard coat of the eye. This enzyme disc glued to the eye in the doctor's office will replace surgery in the treatment of glaucoma. "Designer drugs" will home in and disable "rhinovirus 3C protease," the enzyme that all cold viruses need to replicate. By 2005, a method will be developed for converting Type A blood and Type B blood to Type O blood, resulting in Universal Blood.

Chapter 8

HOW WE WILL MANAGE ORGANI-ZATIONS IN THE YEAR 2000

●

If we could first know where we are and whither we are tending we could then better judge what to do and how to do it.

ABRAHAM LINCOLN

The never ending flight of future days.

JOHN MILTON

●

Everything that has been said and will be said in this book leads one to believe that this era may well be called a *hinge of history*—a term coined by late SRI colleague Mike Levin—one of those times when the world holds its breath not knowing exactly how the critical third act will play out.

There have been other periods like this. For example, in the 1530s, when Carlos V made a series of political decisions that kept Spain out of the modern world for four centuries; at the same time, Francis I of France tricked the Moslems into a treaty that kept them from expanding past Hungary; King Henry VIII of England commanded and got the first Bible printed in English; the Portuguese reached Japan; Erasmus was publishing; Joan of Arc was executed; Machiavelli had just been buried; the Hundred Years War was just winding down; the Moslem empire under Babur had just taken control of Delhi in India; the Shi'ites and Sunnis were battling in Persia; the Jesuits were founded by Loyola; in Germany, 150 years of religious wars started with a peasant uprising that Luther helped suppress; the Polish Copernicus was proving the earth was not IT; Michelangelo was in the thick of things artistically; the Incan Empire was at its height just as Pizarro's "visit" occurred; Brazil was first settled; and DeSoto landed in Florida.

Now, that really is not what you could have called your normal decade. One could almost say that the decade of the 1530s set the tone for much of what was to follow for almost the next 400 years, taking us to that funeral of King Edward VII in 1912 and the beginning of the modern era.

The 1530s was a swing decade, one of the hinges of history, and the chapters of this book attest to the fact that the first decade of the new century may be another.

The ego of each generation demands that its period be nonpareil. And yet, there is indeed something very particular about the coming decades that's going to make them a time of travail. In the next decade, business must be more vigilant than ever before of the many tangled tradeoffs that will lure the unwary into a maze of tiger pits. Indeed, corporations that were the success stories of the 1990s may find their management methods are not working as they cope with the intricacies of the coming decade of the "Terrible Two Thousands." Being vigilant requires an understanding of the trends discussed in this chapter that will effect the management of businesses.

TREND

TOOLS FOR KNOWLEDGE WORKERS

In the 1970s at Stanford Research Institute, I worked for a time with Doug Englebart, who many consider one of the major contributors to the broad field of information technology. Englebart spent years developing what he called "power tools for knowledge workers." Frankly, at that time few people were able to understand what Doug was trying to achieve, but tomorrow's worker owes him an enormous debt.

Tomorrow's workers will be computer literate and have a vast array of automated tools at their disposal. The toolbox of the future will be crammed with information technology—"info-tech" for short. Info-tech consists primarily of computing, combined with telecommunications and networking, and also includes expert systems, imaging, automation, robotics, sensing technologies and mechatronics (microprocessors embedded in products, systems and devices).

The info-net backbone consists of digital signals carried through a fiber-optic network, supplemented by satellite and wireless technologies—the so-called information superhighway.

IMPLICATIONS

Ride the Information Highway

The fast lane on the superhighway is company and media hype about being able to sit with zapper in hand and net surf through hundreds of television shows, data banks and electronic shopping malls. But the reality is that the electronic market and interactive playground for consumers is years away. Still, the truck lane

> •
> WHAT INFO-TECH SKILLS DO YOU NEED TO DEVELOP OR UNDERSTAND HOW TO USE?
> •

that will help companies conduct business electronically is taking shape. Businesses are recognizing that a high-speed information infrastructure can play a big part in speeding the pace of operations and in cutting costs.

In 2000, workers will do more of their jobs through "assistants," expert systems and computers. Jobs will be redesigned to take advantage of these powerful tools. Groupware—software that enables workers in different locations to share information on their computer screens—and videoconferencing will be important tools for managers and scientists.

PREDICTIONS

The growing army of consultants will use software assistants called "knowbots" to search through an ever-increasing network of data bases for information desired for projects or for an individual task.

On-line catalogs will advertise and describe parts and services using text, drawings, sound and video clips. They can be updated daily to keep abreast of changing markets.

Hypertext software will make it possible to sort through product data or bid specifications and combine information from many computers on a network. Shopping agents will automatically search for the best price and availability on a specified item. They'll "know" the owners' preferences and budgets.

Collaboration Software–Groupware and videoconferencing and video-phone service will allow engineers and scientists located around the globe to work on similar problems, exponentially increasing the number of engineering and scientific breakthroughs. Information about what's happening throughout the world of science will be readily and almost simultaneously available throughout the globe. Scientists will use computer-aided molecular design (CAMD) to design drugs that will act as keys that fit into the body's receptor locks to release natural healing substances. Engineers will use CAD to build products like Ford's new world car.

Data graphics will be particularly important for converting huge amounts of data into attractive, easy-to-grasp pictures. The power of the computer will dramatically improve the colorfulness of presentations and the crispness of the images. Easy customization of software to suit a variety of applications and languages will be a very important feature.

Salespeople will convert their cars and vans into mobile offices. Many routine meetings will be videoconferences, freeing salespeople for more face-to-face calls. E-mail and voice mail will handle less urgent communications. These trends will further erode the market for commercial office space.

Computer simulations will help customers take remote "test drives" of components that are waiting to go on the production line. After simulating your products and applications during a sales presentation, contracting systems using advanced cryptographic technologies will make it possible to sign business deals that have legal standing and move money securely through cyberspace, then transmit orders directly from the customer's site to the factory.

Farmers will work primarily indoors, managing information that will come from smart sensors. Sensors will analyze soil conditions, plant health, fertilizer mix and proper animal feed as well as determine by the condition of produce, commodity prices and trends the best time to bring product to market.

Police work will be transformed by info-detectives using networks and massive data bases to hunt for clues. DNA sampling will supplement fingerprints. Electronically monitored house arrest may be more prevalent, using satellite-based global positioning systems to locate the nearest officer. The squad car will become a mobile crime lab, enabling an officer to make quicker and more accurate decisions.

Utilities will exchange human meter readers for super computers that can exchange data with traditional meters or build energy systems. In plants, virtual reality images will oversee automated operations: A worker will manipulate an image of a part needing repair, while tele-operated robots carry out the worker's commands.

Expert-systems assistants will supplement and enhance physicians' skills, filling knowledge gaps and helping physician assistants confirm routine diagnoses. Patients may dial up expert on-line systems that feed in the medical history and provide a diagnosis and home remedy, alerting the doctor if a serious problem is suspected. Videoconferences will enable live assistance from one or more physicians located anywhere in the world for more difficult procedures.

TREND

THE DIVERSE WORKFORCE

Contributor—Lou Platt, CEO, Hewlett Packard

Lou Platt shares how dramatic change in the workplace will affect management in the next decade.

By the year 2005, we're going to see quite a different workforce than we see today, a much more diverse workforce in the United States. Many more women and many more so-called minorities will be part of the workforce than are today. At Hewlett Packard, we're looking typically at people with a high level of technical education. Historically, these graduates were white males. But by 2010, the average person getting a technology degree will be a female or a minority male or minority female. Companies are going to have to learn how to thrive with a much more diverse workforce then we have today.

As more women and two-parent working families enter into the workforce, we have to come up with more flexibility to accommodate both the work and personal demands those people have for raising a family as well as for holding down a career. Today, we still think about a normal workday and a five-day workweek with flexible work hours and job-sharing, benefitting only a small fraction of the jobs that accommodate people with significant demands outside the workplace.

There will be great changes in the way we accommodate these personal demands. Historically, the worker has been asked to sacrifice almost everything to be at work during a certain period, and I think if we're going to do well with this new diverse workforce, that's going to have to change.

IMPLICATIONS

By 2005, we're going to have to have a different view of how people accomplish work. The communications revolution and new technologies will make it easier to accomplish work off-site and on a schedule that's more accommodating to the rest of the worker's life responsibilities. It will be easier to do productive work and stay connected to colleagues when away from the office or working outside a normal eight to five time frame.

> •
> WHAT ARE THE IMPLICATIONS OF A DIVERSE WORKFORCE TO YOU AND YOUR ORGANIZATION?
> •

PREDICTIONS

By 2000, holiday calendars may change to include holidays beyond the white, Christian holidays primarily recognized in business today.

Minorities will comprise almost 30 percent of all new U.S. job entrants.

Half of all jobs will require a college degree, and half of all employees will be at least 40.

Expect to see more flexible work schedules in the next decade, with job sharing, flex time, and home-based work becoming increasingly widespread.

Expect to see greater ethnic integration of American federal agencies.

The United States will evolve as a world leader in managing a highly diverse workforce. By comparison, competitors, led by the Japanese, will struggle to deal even with small amounts of diversity.

TREND

MANAGE CHANGE OR CHANGE MANAGEMENT

Our ability to deal with the megatheme dramatic change is the subject of the next trend.

Perhaps the single most important indicator for corporate success in the coming decade is the attitude of the company culture about change. The willingness of a structure to set itself up for change, to regard itself as a testing ground with daily battles, not just those that occur every planning period, is one of the best litmus paper indicators of eventual success or failure.

Today's information explosion is just beginning. The growing list of mergers, alliances and joint ventures and the rapid deployment of technology are producing change at a velocity that even the seasoned players in businesses can't surmise. The challenge for businesses will not be in how we manufacture or market change but how we manage it.

IMPLICATIONS

Business in the 2000s will involve converting change, whether social, economic, political or technological, into profit. There will be an urgent need for focus, flexibility and follow-through. In time of transition, a lean, purposeful operation will always find it does better because it is carrying less flab. Companies and individuals will identify the activities at which they're most able. Stripped to their strengths, they will not carry sidelines that can't pass a risk-benefit tradeoff analysis. The weak division will be dumped when compared with areas of useful future focus and flexibility.

The rule will be "dump any deadwood," deadwood being defined not just as operations that may not be making money, but operations that over the period of the next decade show growth potential of less than the minimum industry growth rate (MIGR). Companies will make more use of "zero-based planning" (i.e., at the start of each planning cycle, companies will look at a product line and determine whether they would invest in that line as if the company were starting over. If not, the question will be how to change the line so that they would. If they can't change the line, the issue will be how to dispose of it).

The 1990s assumption that large is efficient is being replaced by the view that "small is beautiful." This view is reflected in the dismantling of large, centralized administrative functions (hopefully, the U.S. federal government will follow this trend). The "downward" delegation of authority, responsibility and accountability within many organizations and the associated flattening of management hierarchies are all attempts to get closer to the customer.

PREDICTIONS

The days of the large-scale, vertically integrated corporation are numbered. The trend is toward smaller enterprises with increasing specialization of products or services: A leader in this trend is Richard Branson of the United Kingdom, founder of Virgin Records, Virgin Airlines, and Virgin Entertainment. Branson's approach is 50 people are the maximum for a company; if the staff gets above 50 people, he cuts the company in two. There is no place to hide in a firm of 50 people. These small companies know what's happening in their marketplace and with their competitors—they're not isolated from the marketplace.

TREND

SHORT SIGHTS TAKE AIM AT LONG-TERM CORPORATE RESEARCH AND DEVELOPMENT (R&D)

The next trend, one that illustrates the megatheme "sowing the seeds of future problems," is a reason for the "glass is half empty" crowd to justify their pessimistic future vision.

Globally, companies are responding to increasing shareholder emphasis on short-term profitability by abandoning longer-term R&D goals. Concurrently, companies are looking to buy or license R&D or to acquire smaller companies that have the research or technology required. The result is that companies are eliminating long-term planning projects and research activities, producing a broad decline in investment for future R&D across most business categories.

IMPLICATIONS

Long-term damage to the global economy has already started, and a "sameness" of products and a lack of new product development has already begun. For example, U.S. automakers have formed a consortium to develop an electric car, which will result in both a lack of innovation driven by market forces and a uniformity in the resulting limited number of product options available. The shift in R&D is away from long-term efforts that can produce major breakthroughs to short-term "safe" projects. The National Science Foundation reports a growing number of businesses are directing their research toward minor refinements of existing technologies rather than major technological breakthroughs. Rather than adding "bells and whistles" to existing products, we need research breakthroughs such as fiber optics that will create tomorrow's new industries.

> •
>
> WHAT INNOVATION OR BUSINESS OPPORTUNITIES CAN YOU PRESENT TO YOUR CLIENTS? WHAT PRODUCT INNOVATION IN YOUR INDUSTRY OR OTHER INDUSTRIES CAN BE AP-PLIED TO YOUR BUSINESS?
>
> •

Shareholders are increasingly demanding short-term results. These results will be created at the expense of longer-term investments in R&D and market development for the products that result from basic research. Shareholders no longer care for—if they ever did—balanced companies that produce consistent returns over long periods. Even institutional investors are on the short, "hot track" now.

As the allocation of resources (such as capital spending and new hires) devoted to basic research declines, there will be a *dramatic decrease* in corporate and governmental grants to educational institutions for basic research. Researchers will be pressured out of their ivory tower environments to work more closely with operating units, with outside customers and with partner companies that they will share new technologies with. Indeed, scientists working in the United Kingdom fear that by the year 2000, the United Kingdom will be relegated to third-division status in the world science league. Their remedy is more government money and more company support for pure and applied science.

PREDICTIONS

R&D will change into a technical support service for existing products and technologies rather than providing basic research into new areas of knowledge.

The emphasis on short-term performance will result in less product diversity, more emphasis on quality within existing products and a decline in real choices available to consumers.

Technically astute suppliers will develop new products, technologies and innovations in materials and processes to add value to the commodities they supply.

The Japanese will expand their product horizons and focus on proven existing technologies and shorter marketing cycles. They will, however, continue to search for longer term research despite the recession and bad investments financed by and now owed to Japanese banks.

The role of the chief technical officer (CTO) will continue to decline in the corporate hierarchy while that of the chief financial officer (CFO) and other cost cutters will grow dominant.

A growing chunk of R&D resources will be consumed by the continuing increase in governmental rules and regulations relating to products and services. Complying with these regulations reduces the resources available to develop new technologies and product innovations.

TREND

POWER-SHARING MANAGING AND MOTIVATING WORKERS

Contributor—Dr. Willis Harman, futurist and CEO, Noetic Institute

Willis Harmon's future vision of bringing a diverse fragmented workforce together to meet corporate as well as global needs is described below.

The enthusiasm for management buyouts (MBOs) as a source of corporate rejuvenation and power sharing has been replaced by worker cynicism about the financial gains made by the key players. As managers and banks realized the potential profits in buyouts, they attempted increasingly ambitious deals. However, in the United Kingdom and elsewhere, studies have found that the financial performance of MBOs between four and seven years after the buyout was worse than the industry average, despite the fact that performance was better than average in the first three years. In the longer term, nonpersonnel cost-cutting measures have had increasingly marginal effect on the figures, and to sustain profit growth, even businesses where employees own the company or share ownership will be forced to cut personnel.

IMPLICATIONS

There will be a new compact between management and employees—willingness to share a sense of ownership, psychological ownership sometimes accompanied by financial ownership. They will share a sense of stewardship not only for the company, but also for the full range of company responsibilities such as the environment, the self-sustaining growth of the world's economy, world population, technological change, income inequality and so forth.

PREDICTIONS

Restructuring of power will effect the stockholders' ability to pressure CEOs to put financial considerations first. Furthermore, as employees share in the ownership and responsibly, they will reject attempts to treat them like chattel—sold when the ownership changes to a new master, whose values may be entirely different. Ownership and power go together, the prerogatives of the owners in a financial sense will have to be diminished, but it's not clear how this will happen.

The trend toward more shared responsibility between workers and management will continue, and there will be shifts even in the legal prerogatives of owners. However, forget power sharing in China; the head of most Chinese companies will continue to make all key decisions. Unions will continue to lose clout as employees share power and ownership, and many jobs are likely to shift to nonunion subsidiaries. More employee responsibility means more versatility, and hard work will be required of employee owners. Expect high levels of dissatisfaction and stress when younger Americans are required to work longer hours as they share power with management.

TREND

WILL PARALYSIS BY ANALYSIS BE REPLACED BY EXTINCTION BY INSTINCT?

Contributor—Dr. Hewitt Crane, Bio-Engineering Program Director, SRI International

---

As one who has always valued and trusted instinct, I am intrigued by the shifting focus away from analysis toward instinct that will affect management in the year 2000.

To be able to sift through the confusion, contradiction, mixed and weak signals of the next decade, senior managers are going to have to be able to make better "gut level" decisions. I know that flies in the face of "let's get more numbers before we make a decision." I generate a whole lot of numbers, so I'm not at all antinumbers. But there are going to be other ways to get executives where they need to be more quickly.

IMPLICATIONS

When a company is in trouble, often it can profit from the services of an outside business analyst. The problem may not be immediately apparent to the analyst. He may listen carefully to each of the "inner voices" of the company, to which he has access only through the cooperation of high-level management. Suppose the analyst is granted access only to the chief executive officer. With more freedom, he might find out directly that one department is sabotaging output because of a series of unresolved conflicts, but now these conflicts have to be deciphered by deduction. The CEO will have to dredge up episode after episode from memory, and the analyst will have to sort and shift until he finds a pattern. This takes time and assumes the CEO is highly cooperative and fully aware of the past history.

At the individual level, formal analysis can be complemented and balanced by developing better access to our subconscious levels so that the necessary information propels upward, so to speak, more on its own. What we call gut level is really the accumulation of our personal experiences and thousands of years of the collective experience stored in our cells—no supercomputer could begin to duplicate the inputs that give us intuitive insights.

A good designer, scientists or engineers operating in one of the complex fields of the next decade must have a good awareness of their less analytic, subconscious processes. An experienced designer understands that although categories are an important aid to teaching, learning and implementation, it's creativity, intuition and subconscious processes that provide the successful unified whole—the gestalt. A physical design might pass such familiar criteria of success as economy, quietness, safety and salability, yet not please the designer.

PREDICTIONS

The limitations of analysis at the intellectual level and the difficulty of exploring what goes on at the lower levels is why in the next decade even more conventional managers will turn to meditative practices and the development of enhanced conscious and subconscious interaction. If through meditation, awareness is restricted to one unchanging source of stimulation such as breathing, a "turning off" of the external world follows, and one can then reach and explore different levels of the mind.

Schools will de-emphasize the simple world of subjects, to emphasize the relatedness of all things. Perhaps subjects are not over-emphasized, but are presently missing the "other half"—training and developing the intuitive, subconscious processes will be added or greatly expanded.

Experience rather than reliance on numbers and reports will become the key inputs for decision making. By 2010, virtual reality, building on widespread interactive telecommunications and entertainment, will enable people to indirectly and remotely experience a place or an event in all dimensions. For example, if in 20 minutes I could give you a good accurate feel for the earthquake in Los Angeles, you would have a much better idea of how you might shift your operations or make other decisions. You are less dependent on the views of others when you can feel like you're in the action.

Moreover, it will allow you to attend meetings without travel. Although such a telepresence will not displace all travel, individuals will be able to sit at their desks and attend perhaps a dozen simultaneous meetings in remote locations, choosing which meetings to join by flipping channels—much as people do now with remote-controlled TVs.

TREND

THE COMPANY GENERAL IS A GENERALIST

As evidenced by the large number of hyphenated terms throughout this book, I believe that the next century will bring together many fragmented disciplines, specialties and people. Diverse businesses will require generalists who can see how the puzzle pieces fit together.

The champion for single combat, the prime element on which future success stands or falls, is the CEO. Moving into the future takes leadership, and only the CEO can take on that burden. If that individual shirks it, disregards it or fails to handle it properly, the company is condemned to stumble its way through the next decade, no matter how well upholstered its present profit line.

Given the flux of business changes, the CEOs operating in the 2000s will have to be very astute, capable generalists. Time was a CEO was expected to be very good at just one of the disciplines (e.g., money, marketing, manufacturing) and then could rely on his staff to bolster lack of familiarity with the other elements of the business. This mode of management will no longer be adequate.

International business is not going to be a tea party in coming years. For that matter, it will not be easy to find any cozy domestic arena in which to hide. Any domestic market large enough to be attractive is going to be subject to the normal activities of the large international companies looking for additional markets. The companies who emerge least bloody from the upcoming decade-long scrap will be those who have CEOs who understand the stakes, can orchestrate firmly conceived poker tactics and be skilled enough to know how to take risks in a cool and calculating fashion.

IMPLICATIONS

Many CEOs see their job to be reactive, to listen to suggestions from the juniors and to assume a judicial mien to render a decision on what should be done. This strategy may be adequate in a mature industry but is not sufficient leadership for a company that needs to grow. Mediation is not leadership; companies without leadership in the 2000s are going to find it difficult to hold their place, let alone carve out new territory.

Another major problem for business in the tough times ahead is the omnipresent concern with process as opposed to planning. Most business leaders have risen from the process ranks as engineers, financial experts or new business getters. They view business as the act of making the process work better, being more efficient or finding ways to get there "firstest with the mostest." This approach is dynamic for the present but can be disastrous for the future.

Thus, the first essential in dealing with the future is for the CEO to recognize his responsibilities and leadership requirements. Without that, all else is dross.

Yet the average president spends about 75 percent of the time overseeing the day-to-day operation of business. That leaves just 25 percent of the time for the following:

- Dealing with the future;
- Establishing and maintaining a public activities posture;
- Dealing with the complexities of all the stakeholder requirements;
- Motivating the proper utilization of all company resources;
- Coping with the need to enhance company image.

Insofar as a CEO is principally concerned with the present, he cheats the future. There are many managers properly charged for performance in the present, but only a handful charged with the future. If the CEOs don't get the maximum from the managers and from themselves, the future will resemble the return of bread cast upon the waters: soggy.

The Japanese top management, on the other hand, do not share the American concern for involvement with operating problems or process at the top layers of the company.

They instead manage relationships. These include the interplay with business, labor, ownership and government as well as the face the business will present to the outer world in policy, trade and investment. All of this is done with considerable regard and concern for the macro world and the future.

PREDICTIONS

More companies will create or expand the Office of the Chief Executive Officer (OCEO).

In some cases, it serves a very useful role that brings together under the aegis of one person a host of talents that the CEO can depend on for assistance in deciding the company's future direction.

If CEOs in the 2000s are to be a truly efficient and empathetic leaders, they will, among other things, be fluent in the following business "languages":

Strategic management: The vision of the future cannot come up from operating managers alone. When the CEO tries to delegate strategic management, it ends up as much talk and very little performance. The CEO must set the guidelines for managers, not vice versa.

Information sciences: The second language essential for the 2000s onward is information sciences. That doesn't mean the CEO has to be a programmer or a systems expert. It does mean being comfortable using information as a tool instead of a camouflage. In too many companies, top management accepts computer output because it has not had the necessary learning to query, probe and properly analyze the output.

Money: Money is still the prime present descriptor of business conditions, and the CEO must be able to understand and communicate the implications on the business of inflation, trade blocks, foreign exchange, capital formation and universal and local banking.

Many CEOs will have to be trained for some period before and after they take over the job to be able to operate rather differently from how they do today. Also, the selection of executives from outside the industry will require providing them in-depth understanding of the relevant markets, technologies, process, resources available and needed as well as a competitive analysis.

Expect more activity between outside directors and CEOs. The directors will use tracking systems to monitor management, production, sales, market share, liquidity and productivity. Directors will insist rapid remedial measures be initiated by their CEO when these systems alert them to a deviation from the corporate plan.

TREND

How Top Executives Will Get Paid

The sophisticated, competitive business environment will require a shifting focus about executive compensation.

Creating shareholder value continues to be the single overriding objective of CEOs in America.

The preoccupation of corporate executives with short-term results is heightened by the way they are compensated. Most companies reinforce the unrelenting pressures for short-term performance by basing pay and promotion decisions on immediate financial goals such as quarterly earnings. Partially because of activist shareholders and Securities & Exchange Commission disclosure rules, a mounting controversy over the growing paychecks of top executives will force reforms in how executives are compensated.

IMPLICATIONS

Shareholders are demanding that compensation be linked to performance. Boards of directors will be devoting more time to the issue of compensation, including a review of the CEOs goals at the beginning of the year and measuring progress at the end.

In addition, more companies will hire outside consultants to provide an objective assessment of executive earnings rather than rely on people who may have been hired by the executive whose compensation is being reviewed.

In the past, the best way to link pay to performance was the stock option. With the wild bull markets of today, CEOs are being rewarded for rising along with the stock market tide rather than the results of their own efforts. In the future, stock options will carry an exercise price above the price the stock is currently trading. This strategy will ensure that the shareholders will realize stock gains before the CEO does. Compensation will, however, continue to shift away from salary and short-term bonus into stock options.

CEOs and other top management are reacting to this new set of circumstances. More and more executives are taking their bonuses in short-term stock option programs, driving business developments that maximize profits in the short time frame.

PREDICTIONS

Corporate governance will change with investor-driven short-term goals and huge salaries for CEOs giving way to longer term competitive strategies. Moreover, the ratio between the compensation of the CEO and the ordinary rank-and-file worker will close. In the United States in 1993, the average CEO made 157 times what a factory employee made; but in Japan, the CEO makes less than 32 times as much as rank-and-file employees.

As the saying goes, "You can't be a prophet (or make a profit) in your own land." It will pay hugely to be an outsider CEO. The size of outsider pay packages will substantially exceed the pay of insiders. The compensation packages will include low-interest loans and relocation allowances as well as sign-on bonuses that would be the envy of any free agent athlete.

TREND

SHARP EYES AND FAST FEET

The next trend deals with whether a company has the culture to move forward against the tide of sophisticated competition.

Businesses, like societies, decline as they lose their capacity to adapt. Many business have become *arthritic freaking elephants* (AFEs), a term used by a CEO to describe his billion dollar plus consumer electronics company. Accelerating change and declining flexibility will have far-reaching implications for much of the developed world.

To meet increasing competition at all levels and within all parts of the economy, staff must be flexible and responsive. The reductionist approach of breaking work and tasks into meaningless and repetitive individual tasks is being increasingly replaced by emphasis on teamwork. The team is responsible for the complete task, often including creating its own organizational structure, solving problems, improving quality and constantly reviewing and refining its activities.

IMPLICATIONS

The structure of a company for the 2000s must be such that it can with some degree of ease move resources (raw material, human, financial and technological) from one business arena to another. The vertical rigidity that has characterized many industries in the past will make doing business very tough in the next decade. Companies are going to have to become more efficient and more flexible in maneuvering with the opportunities (being strategically and structurally responsive). This equation was unworkable with past management and manufacturing systems but will be possible with the flexible, modular and interchangeable systems ahead.

As an additional demand for flexibility, the company has to maintain a strategic reserve, an ability to move effectiveness to where it can create breakthroughs. A military analogy is perhaps odious, but nevertheless true. An opponent with all its resources committed is wide open to being beaten, given the right use of strategic force. The French Army had more tanks and was armed with more superior guns than the Germans in 1940. They simply had them all committed in such a fashion that there was no strategic reserve available to deal with a concentrated attack at one point. The simile applies to business for the 2000s.

Considering the shortness of time frames, remember, this year's success is next year's dog. Any business must constantly be looking for new opportunities, new products, new markets, new modes of keeping old business. Success should not be thought of in terms of an individual product or line of business, but rather in a continuing way, an approach to doing business.

Growth that comes merely from revenue increase of one kind or another may be useful temporarily, but over time in the next decade, it will be a diversion of resources and assets, which will sooner or later affect the business. An increase in volume is not necessarily growth. Volume increases can come from inflation, from price adjustments and from productivity. The first source isn't growth at all. The second may not be growth, depending on what happens to margins. Indeed, the only kind of growth that is solid and substantial is growth built on productivity gains.

Contrary to the popular dictum that market share is all, it may or may not be. There are an infinite number of businesses with very comfortable and very profitable market niches that have nothing to do with market leadership. On the other hand, being a marginal member of a market is often a sure portent for eventual loss. As a marginal member of a group of companies, an operation is often at risk in terms of its ability to withstand the competitive stress and economic distortion that will define the global business climate in the next century. Marginal companies will have a difficult time mustering the capital for reinvestment. If they slide down the curve, the operation simply won't ever be able to put together the financial package necessary to survive long term.

Once the proper focus has been established and the flexibility to maintain proper advantage has been created, the successful company in the 2000s will need a way to mount the proper follow-through to make its choice effective. Too often, capital goes for initial investment, and too little is left for the operating follow-through.

PREDICTIONS

Networking, particularly among small firms, will increase as the economies of sharing particularly within an industry cluster presents a wide range of possibilities—expect the development of new methods of customer-supplier cooperation, not the vertical Japanese "Keiretsu" relationship, but greater cooperation and openness than in the past. Size is no longer synonymous with success—corporate customers who used to give their business to one monolithic supplier will begin to shop around, allowing a growing raft of specialty suppliers to provide increasingly potent competition.

TREND

Remaking Manufacturing

Manufacturing will move forward from the backward management and production systems of the past to survive sophisticated global competition.

The United States is gradually learning how to survive without traditional smokestack industries and has instead become the world's salesperson, shipper and financier. A manufacturing component will exist in our economy for decades to come, but it will evolve into a new form of technologically oriented manufacturing, run by scientists and engineers rather than by shop foremen.

Manufacturing will be knowledge intensive rather than labor intensive. Rather than blast furnaces and punch presses and extruding machines, the tools of the future will be lasers, microwaves, fiber optics, nuclear power, artificial intelligence, semiconductors, gene-splicing equipment and other technologies now on the cutting edge of science and industry.

IMPLICATIONS

When manufacturing was an increasing source of employment, job opportunities were available that offered the possibilities of access to higher paying jobs for those with less than a high school education. But manufacturing employment, which peaked at 21 million in 1979 (I was the first to predict that it would peak in 1977), had fallen to 19 million by 1990, and it is projected to decline another 600,000 by 2005. Global competition, new technology and other forces have restructured employment in manufacturing so that manufacturing jobs are more likely than they once were to require postsecondary education.

The role of information in the business process dictates that the new plants and distribution centers on the drawing boards will be very high tech. Automated, computerized and operated with almost no people at all, manufacturing and distribution will be driven by a continuous flow of data coming from the field and fed into sophisticated information systems. There is a new technology on the distribution side as well that will control inventory costs through "just-in-time" techniques, whereby suppliers provide components just as they're needed. For example, at a 7-Eleven chain in Japan, the moment a 7-Eleven customer buys a soft drink or a can of beer, the information goes directly to the bottler or brewer.

In manufacturing, computing power is being used to assist in the design and modeling of new products, allowing flexible manufacturing processes that can respond quickly to market demands. Creative use of product development teams will get products to the market faster with fewer errors, more refinements and better manufacturability. These teams, pioneered by the Japanese, have been copied and improved on by companies such as Boeing, Xerox and Chrysler. Focus on the value stream within manufacturing facilities will increase, dramatically reducing work-in-process, space, tool costs and human effort, while improving flexibility and quality.

PREDICTIONS

A new breed of production manager will replace a whole generation of manufacturing managers who failed to display the strategic and structural responsiveness the new world order requires. More women will be hired for traditional male manufacturing management positions. Anticipate also the greater use of robotics rather than humans.

Operator interfaces will play an ever-greater role at all levels of plant management. Companies will be looking at higher functions such as enhanced alarm response, graphic displays, on-line process data and simultaneous communications for better real-time information as well as diagnostic and maintenance functions such as records of historic maintenance to help minimize downtime.

Advances in computer hardware and software will result in ever more sophisticated CAD models. Improved computer capabilities are among the forces that will driving rapid-prototyping (RP) factory systems that produce metal parts directly using a laser to create prototype objects.

TREND

WELCOME BACK MANUFACTURING

Contributors—Vic Para, consultant and retired Tandem Computer executive, and Dr. Charles Turk, president of OAI, a high-tech company

Vic Para and Charlie Turk are two bright executives with steel trap minds and excellent bottom-line thinking. I've collaborated with them on many projects over the years and was very interested in a trend that may signal a shifting focus in the economics of high-tech manufacturing.

As high technology and products become more complex and specialized, they require more innovative manufacturing techniques. While Third World countries were able to mass produce parts and products in the recent decades, the new highly automated technological innovations are often beyond their current capabilities but fit perfectly with U.S. strengths in automation, product design and technology innovation.

IMPLICATIONS

Manufacturing that had been contracted for offshore will increasingly come back to the United States, particularly to the San Francisco Bay area. U.S. high-tech companies are reevaluating if they should manufacture in-house, as 3-Com has decided to do, or use an onshore contract manufacturer. The decision is usually based on whether manufacturing is a "core competency," in other words, a major component of the business. If it's not a core competency, a joint team composed of executives, technicians and engineers from both the company and the contract manufacturer work together to devise innovative, cost effective ways to produce the product or component.

Dr. Turk believes that the assembly of printed circuit boards may continue to come back onshore due to "just-in-time" manufacturing, the making of smaller boards and new automated techniques. Indeed, companies like Solectron have shown tremendous growth in U.S. contract production of printed circuit boards. There is also a cottage industry developing in the Vietnamese and other immigrant communities on the West Coast performing high-tech assembly work at favorable prices for local high-tech firms.

PREDICTIONS

Manufacturing is a core competency of some IBM divisions. "Big Blue" has excess manufacturing capacity and unique specialized technologies such as ball grid arrays that eliminate the pins that secure components to circuit boards. Expect IBM to pressure its divisions to exploit contract manufacturing opportunities or face plant closures. Opportunities will grow for brokers to assist companies in identifying outside manufacturing opportunities that fit their core competencies.

Dr. Turk believes that a "yin-yang trend" is at work—though the assembly of printed circuit boards may return to the United States, more circuit board components will be produced overseas. Also, U.S. companies will sell their offshore manufacturing facilities and then contract back to these same facilities, allowing for greater financial and manufacturing leverage while reducing long-term overseas obligations.

Chapter 9

RETHINKING ROLES AND RESOURCES

•

The trouble with our time is that the future is not what it used to be.

PAUL VALÉRY

A generous and elevated mind is distinguished by nothing more certainly than an eminent degree of curiosity.

SAMUEL JOHNSON

•

Change is in the air above the optimism, confusion and despair.

As we accelerate toward the twenty-first century, responsive, resourceful change is the one currency that will be accepted, indeed, required in every business. Those who embrace it, prosper; those who resist it, stagnate or sink. Without a doubt, these times are confusing and turmoil and uncertainty reign in every city and corner of the globe. Stock markets hum along at a record pace, and most of the world's economies are rebounding. Yet government bureaucracies, also known as "Tyrannosaurus Wrecks," let massive layoffs, deficits, social problems and crime rage out of control.

Calling what's going on today "business as usual" is as shortsighted as were the buggy whip manufacturers in 1910 who saw the car as just a rich man's toy. The turn of the next century will be disastrous for unprepared businesses while offering great opportunities for those who understand the transitions taking place. This chapter explores changing business roles and resources.

TREND

WOMEN'S WORK

Large numbers of women in the workplace will dramatically change the way we do business. Whether these changes will lead to togetherness or fragmentation is a concern.

By the next decade, women will truly become major players in the workplace and will make dramatic strides in gaining economic and political power. In fact, by 2005, half the labor force will be women.

IMPLICATIONS

Men still dominate in business. In 1990, only 3 percent of senior executives in Fortune 500 companies were women. But mobility patterns for men will change, with only a third of men moving up in the business ranks in the next decade as compared with half moving ahead in the 1960s.

Women are the new changing force of influence in business—they have more degrees and are more likely to go to college than are men—business is their first choice as a major. Moreover, young women are rapidly narrowing the pay gap with men.

Women occupy only 26 of the 314 auto designer jobs at the Big Three U.S. automakers, yet female customers account for 46 percent of new car sales in the United States. The top two auto design programs, however, anticipate graduating the most women ever in 1994. Women's design concerns may often be more pragmatic than those of men, and women will be listened to since they will buy more than half the cars in the United States by 2000.

Split-shift parenting is on the rise due to the rapid increase in the number of married women with young children in the labor force. The service sector has the highest proportion of shift workers. Men will do more housework as families become more dependent on the wives' income. Time with kids remains a priority over leisure and chores. However, more than 50 percent of working parents spend fewer than two hours a week looking after kids, and 42 percent spend no time reading to them.

PREDICTIONS

Sixty-one percent of all working age women will have jobs by 2000. Expect about 75 percent of minimum wage earners to be women, up about 15 percent from 1990, and through the next decade, the percentage of working mothers will grow. One major reason is an increase in divorced women with children. Today over 65 percent of women with children under 18 are in the workforce. Expect that percentage to increase to 75 percent by 2000. As women feel they can earn their own living, the financial necessity for marrying will diminish.

Demand for child care will be a major social problem in the next decade. Only 1 in 10 workers receives child care benefits. Record level representation of women in politics will continue with a steady incremental increase in representation through the next decade. The Family Leave Act will give an edge to big business, which can afford to shell out millions in paychecks for people who aren't working—small businesses can't afford such benefits.

TREND

WHICH "WHO" TO KNOW—THOSE WITH *GUANXI*

Who you know and what you know will be important "resources to be revalued."
Trying to cut a deal in China? Get involved with a "red capitalist" and his *international trust and investment corporations* (ITIC).

The clout in many emerging countries is wielded by this new class of politicians, tycoons and deal makers all in one—a red capitalist. There is a trend across China and in most of the emerging countries toward local financial powerhouses. The decentralization of the economy leaves local governments the challenge of creating companies to finance infrastructure projects and compete for overseas money. In these circumstances, local financiers offer a crucial degree of stability as these countries complete their economic metamorphoses.

IMPLICATIONS

By developing new businesses and attracting foreign capital, these quasi-governmental ITICs are helping to create the millions of jobs required by the mass migration of rural people in search of work in the industrial sector. These ITICs do not suffer from hardening of the categories and are bounding into new fields and industries where they can cut themselves a piece of the lucrative financing of corporate and government deals.

Since many government banks are strapped for cash due to bailouts of unprofitable state enterprises that keep millions of workers employed, ITICs will raise money through investment funds that will buy shares in power plants, bridges and freeways. These ITICs have unequaled connections, or *guanxi,* and know how to work the system to get licenses and approvals quickly, avoiding typical bureaucratic delays.

PREDICTIONS

Ethnic Chinese with guanxi, scattered across Asia, will drive and dominate most of the dynamic Asian economies. They now number 55 million and in most countries are a tiny minority. In Thailand, for example, they make up only 8 percent of the population but own 80 percent of the commercial assets and half the banks.

TREND

MANAGEMENT EDUCATION IN A CHANGING WORLD

Contributor—Dr. David Palmer, OMT Group

Dr. David Palmer, a very bright and experienced management consultant, professional speaker and graduate business school professor, shares his insights about the need to shift focus and revalue what managers need to know.

Not long ago, you could assume that a set of skills or professional knowledge would equip you for your working life. However, because of the magnitude of changes taking place in the future, knowledge and skills will need upgrading several times during a person's working life. Moreover, the economics of telecommuting with E-mail and videoconferencing will reduce the number of face-to-face meetings but not end them. Having a limited amount of "in-person" time to work with colleagues or customers requires a higher level of interpersonal and sales skills because you have fewer opportunities for presenting your agenda.

IMPLICATIONS

As we move to a high-tech economy, interpersonal skills are becoming more important. Educators are finally realizing that many of the skills that are required for success revolve around interpersonal, communication, negotiating and listening skills. In the next decade, knowing how to interact with people, to work on a team and to form a team will be more important than ever before. Because today's educators don't consider these skills proper academic subjects, they aren't taught in schools. This mistake is allowing the multibillion dollar commercial training industry to teach skills that could be taught in a traditional academic setting.

As the value of an MBA continues to be questioned, the survival of business schools will require a complete reevaluation of their programs. Wharton has begun this process, and Harvard is going through a multiyear reevaluation program.

PREDICTIONS

MBA attendance will continue to drop in all but the top business schools. Schools that include interpersonal skills will move ahead in the race to recruit students.

The growing international orientation of business will induce schools to include a second language requirement for admission.

Academic research-oriented instructors with little real-world experience will fall out of favor and be replaced with adjunct part-timers with strong business experience.

How to start and run a small business will a very important and growing part of school curriculum as the immigrant community continues to swell. Already in Los Angeles, most people who work in manufacturing work in firms that employ 50 people or less.

As business school enrollments decline further, engineering and computer science will supply a greater percentage of MBA students. With pure research on the wane, engineering schools will be pushing students into business courses. MBAs with engineering and computer skills (techno-managers) will be in great demand.

TREND

I'D RATHER DO IT MYSELF

Having become fragmented from the organizational togetherness of the past, many former employees have shifted focus.

Jobs and career advancement were uppermost in people's minds in the 1980s. However, the recent wave of corporate layoffs has changed the focus from finding a good job with a growing company to personal enterprise. Moreover, as the cost of doing business continues to mount because of government-mandated programs, legal concerns, health and other benefits, corporations will continue to move toward out-sourcing. This trend will create an explosion of independent contractors, many working in family businesses or at home. Complementing this trend will be the growth of small businesses owned by immigrants that will market not only to the immigrant population, but also to established corporations.

IMPLICATIONS

One-quarter of all U.S. households have at least one person who works at home either regularly or occasionally. Over 26 million Americans now work at home. Nearly three-quarters are in households with dual incomes. In fact, there are some 36 million dual-career couples in America. Moreover, the world likes "all in the family"—in the United States, some 96 percent of companies producing over half the country's goods and services are family owned, while in Western Europe, family business accounts for up to two-thirds of GDP and employment.

PREDICTIONS

Businesses and government agencies are buying more goods and services from outside sources rather than producing them internally, and that trend will increase as about half of the purchase decision makers expect to out-source more by 2000. Out-sourcing will improve service quality as entrepreneurs obsess about winning and serving the customer.

> •
> WHAT PRODUCTS OR SERVICES DO YOU NOW HAVE OR CAN YOU CREATE TO SERVE THIS GROWING MARKET?
> •

The "floating office"—a management system that allows employees to set up their mobile offices wherever convenient, at home, in corporate headquarters or in a branch office, provides both cost savings and employee freedom. Four primary technologies—cellular telephones, personal pagers, laptop notebook computers and E-mail—are working together to make the floating office an increasingly popular trend.

Continued downsizing will increase the pool of middle-class unemployed available to work as temporary employees, which is another form of out-sourcing. Not having to pay benefits will also change corporate decisions to use temporary workers in the next decade. Several economic factors suggest a higher proportion of workers will be moonlighting. Currently, 6.2 percent of all employed people are working two jobs, most to meet routine living expenses and pay off debt. Wages will continue to stagnate as they have since the early 1970s. Working a second job will be required by a growing percentage of the population, over 10 percent by 2005. As corporations allow their employees more flexible work hours and the permission to work at home, expect a dramatic increase in moonlighting ventures funded by corporate paychecks.

The trend toward smaller enterprises will increase specialization of products and services. The growth in the number of home workers will provide a growing global market for word processors, copy machines, faxes, telephones, computer software, personal computers and office furniture. Enhanced communication capability will also dramatically increase the growth of cottage industries as well as provide creative marketing approaches to reach this fast growing market segment.

TREND

LEVERAGING KNOWLEDGE

Contributor—Tom Peters

I first met Tom Peters in Singapore in the early 1980s, when we worked together on a program for the government of Singapore. I've watched with envy his success as a consultant, speaker, and best-selling author to a worldwide audience. Tom shares an article he wrote that exemplifies the megatheme "revaluing resources," in this case, knowledge.

"We can no longer compete on the cost of labor with countries like China," says Olivetti chief Carl De Benedetti. "What we have to leverage is our know-how."

Right on! Unfortunately, we don't know how to do it.

IMPLICATIONS

The 17,000 Price Waterhouse consultants and accountants are using Notes, Lotus Development's new work-group technology system, *Chief Information Officer* (CIO) magazine reports. But most applications of the software have been mundane. Why? "Fostering the shared work-group vision that lies behind Notes has proved elusive," reporter Thomas Kiely concludes.

Devising the right sticks and carrots is the issue, says Sheldon Laube, the $3.8 billion firm's national director of information and technology. The following question must be answered affirmatively by a cast of thousands: "Was it worth their time to enter information—for someone else's benefit—on the gamble that somewhere down the road information would appear in Notes that is useful to them?"

Laube has sidetracked this issue so far and settled for practical uses of the system. Case in point, per CIO: "A banking consultant in Washington picks up regulatory gossip, and sensing an opportunity, broadcasts a message to the 200 or more Price Waterhouse banking consultants throughout the nation, who immediately broach the subject with their clients." That boils down to an E-mail use of Notes, according to MIT Professor Wanda Orlikowski, who studied Price Waterhouse. "It isn't the same thing as collaboratively working together on a joint project," she adds.

Brook Manville, co-director of information and technology at Consultants McKinsey & Co, understands the distinction Orlikowski makes. He's also overseeing a major implementation of Notes—but McKinsey's avowed emphasis is fundamental transformation of the company's professional practice.

McKinsey has typically thrown very bright, energetic folks at a client project. Manville calls it "we're smarter than everyone else and that's enough to maintain our advantage" strategy. But competitors are catching up. McKinsey's next step, according to Manville, is to leverage its collective experience by systematically developing and sharing institutional knowledge.

Knowledge development at McKinsey orbits around 30-odd "practice centers"—voluntary, virtual communities of consultant-specialists who offer their expertise to colleagues.

Getting these centers to view knowledge development in marketing terms is the first step. "They should think about growing their 'mind share' with consultants throughout the firm," says McKinsey exec Bill Matassoni.

McKinsey summarizes what it's learned from some 1,500 projects completed each year in computer databases. But these records aren't viewed as dusty electronic archives. Manville, a statistics nut, urges practice center leaders to measure usage of the data bases—and even publish "best-seller lists" of the most valued documents.

However, such tactics still fall well short of the mark. The Organization Performance Practice, the firm's largest, has gone much further. The centerpiece of its activities is the Rapid Response Network (RRN), manned by four people better characterized as consulting psychologists rather than technical support staff.

The RRN team instantly responds to internal customers' questions with referrals to McKinsey experts and customized material culled from numerous internal and external data bases. The human touch counts: Send too many documents and the already besieged consultant is overwhelmed; send too few and the consultant is disappointed. (Ducking such nuts-and-bolts issues is the Achilles' heel of most knowledge-management schemes.)

All 60 consultant-specialists in the Organization Performance Practice have also agreed to act as "on-call consultants" a couple of weeks a year. They guarantee a response, within 24 hours, to queries from consultants in any of 58 offices in 28 countries.

Finally, the RRN staffers perform extensive follow-up interviews and religiously track "customer satisfaction." They even publish an annual report on their activities!

The bottom line is trying to get harried consultants to routinely "use" the firm's knowledge in their client work and to take the time to "replenish" that reservoir. Beyond the practice-center activities, McKinsey is slowly developing the "cultural" value that measurable contributions to the firm's knowledge base are a must for satisfactory performance evaluation.

Manville has barely gotten started, as he readily admits. But he's asking all the right questions. Fitting together the pieces of the knowledge-development puzzle may be the foremost challenge for corporate America in the coming decade.

PREDICTIONS

An unfortunate fallout of the current economic disruption is that companies are dumping years of undocumented accrued experience as they lose armies of middle managers. Middle managers possess the knowledge base that becomes difficult to replace. Capturing knowledge assets before terminations and plant shutdowns will become standard operating procedure for the industrialized world because of increasing awareness of the value of information and intelligence. Indeed, the accountants of the world will begin to quantify the value of intellectual property.

> •
> WHAT IS BEING DONE TO PROTECT, DOCUMENT AND DISPENSE KNOWLEDGE ASSETS WITHIN YOUR ORGANIZATION? WHAT UNIQUE INSIGHTS HAVE YOU SHARED?
> •

TREND

THE SUPERSTAR EFFECT

In all professions, a small percentage of people rise to the top ranks. Sophisticated competition in the next decade will make the knowledge and business contacts of these "superstars" even more important.

The trend to pay extremely high salaries to a select group of top performers will become more important as globalization raises the stakes for businesses. A successful corporation now has access to markets all over the world. At the same time, the increasing number of foreign competitors leaves less room for mistakes. This combination, along with improvements in communication, will make it easier for a small group of top people to serve a wide market.

IMPLICATIONS

It is not just top business skills that will produce big income gains. Professions where a small number of top performers pull down the bulk of the compensation include Wall Street investment bankers and traders, television, movies, sports stars and journalists.

In law firms, partners garner 10 percent of all income going to lawyers, though they represent less than 2 percent of the entire profession.

PREDICTIONS

Superstars will proliferate and promote them themselves through specialized marketing organizations. With the MTV generation, marketers are finding that rock stars and athletes that personify the changing values on the street—the brash, "in-your-face" style will sell products. Eventually, however, there will be so many "superstars" that their value will decline. They will also put so much strain on their organizations because of their increasingly unrealistic salary demands that a perfomance-based compensation system rather than giant salaries will become the norm for both superstar executives and athletes.

In addition, there will be legal pressure to control the client contacts and knowledge base developed by superstar business executives to lessen the negative effects to the organization if they leave. With the emphasis on "teamwork" and minimizing individual differences within a corporate culture, the superstar will become a superheadache within many organizations.

TREND

THE NEW ENTREPRENEUR

Small entrepreneurs are becoming the big way to do business, while big business becomes smaller and more entrepreneurial in style.

The squeeze on middle managers and an aging, more educated workforce will increase the number of U.S. entrepreneurs in the 2000s. Another reason for growth in the entrepreneurial ranks is the movement away from the large business environment. Indeed, 38 percent of college students state that owning a business is the best route to a successful career, while only 24 percent state that they would prefer working for a large corporation.

IMPLICATIONS

The profile of the entrepreneur is changing. One out of five small-business owners are under 35, and women are forming businesses at twice the rate of men. Already 1 in 10 American workers is employed by a woman-owned company—most women entrepreneurs are drawn to the retail and services trades, in part, because of the low start-up costs.

> •
> WHAT BUSINESS WILL DO WELL IN THE NEXT DECADE? WHAT BUSINESS WOULD YOU LIKE TO DEVELOP?
> •

Expect even more pressure to rescind taxes. Between payroll, social security and corporate taxes, entrepreneurs are hemorrhaging one of their most valuable resources—investment capital. Workers' benefits—workman's compensation, unemployment insurance and health care—are also costs few entrepreneurial businesses can afford—they drive prices up and wages and profits down.

PREDICTIONS

A larger proportion of business schools will give courses in small-business entrepreneurship. In 1970, only 16 offered such programs—today that number is over 400.

> •
> WHAT PRODUCTS OR SERVICES THAT YOU HAVE MIGHT BE FRAN-CHISED?
> •

The share of women-owned businesses will increase into the 2000s; most will be classified as small businesses. Expect more government guaranteed loan programs for minority and women entrepreneurs.

TREND

THE AGE OF CLONES

The following trend presents an ever more popular option for countries that find an innovation deficiency after a "reevaluation of resources."

In the next decade, we will live in a global environment in which all boundaries to the receipt of goods and services from all over the globe will start to decline.

Increased travel and global communications will draw consumers of industrialized nations together, making them more alike and allowing more products to have export potential.

IMPLICATIONS

The United States will generate a disproportionately large share of the world's radical product inventions. Our rivals are good at making incremental improvements; in other words, we're better at the research and they're better at the development. Racing to market will require less-innovative countries to copy products and services from other countries and adapt them to local market conditions.

One paramount proponent of the use of competitive intelligence (CI) and integrative capability (which are politically correct ways of saying *copying*) is Japan, which manages to apply a lot of the world's information that it had no hand in generating. Nikon, for example, absorbed shutter technologies developed in the United States and a single lens reflex mechanism developed by the Germans.

PREDICTIONS

Expect more U.S. companies to get more involved in CI as fax machines, computer networks, a broader usage of the English language and a proliferation of data bases will streamline global intelligence gathering.

To cash in on good business concepts developed by others, more people will buy franchises. The number of U.S. franchises will triple by the end of the decade.

To compete globally, more countries will follow this four-step formula: (1) Foreign technologies are identified and secured; (2) Basic research is co-sponsored and shared; (3) National cartels are formed; (4) Enormous long-term capital subsides are provided for marketing approaches to reach fast-growing market segments.

Legal and political pressure will increase to prevent unauthorized cloning of products and services.

Nationalism in cultural and sporting events will grow as business continues to erode national borders.

TREND

THEY'RE ALL SO SMUG
(SMART, MOBILE, UPWARD, GLOBAL)

Contributor—Dr. Ken Colmen, vice president, SRI International

---

I've known and worked with Ken Colmen for almost three decades, including the 10 years we worked together at SRI International. I value the real-world insights he's developed working as a management consultant and corporate executive. Once again, Ken shows us that the revaluing of knowledge as a strategic but abundant resource and sophisticated competition are truly global megathemes.

All over the developing world, there's a new generation of young, educated, sophisticated, well-traveled and ambitious businesspeople I call *SMUGs* (smart, mobile, upward, global people). A serious problem is developing: dressed for the party with no place to go, SMUGs are blocked in government and industry as they try to move quickly up the organization ladder. They're stuck behind a prior generation of senior managers with little education or knowledge of all of the tools to use to succeed in an ever more complex world.

IMPLICATIONS

With so much underused SMUG talent, countries in the developing world are making new demands. For example, if an economically developed country wants to build a factory, it has to provide the developing country with something in return. The developing countries want companies such as IBM to give them opportunities to move their economies along. Governments are going to ask for technology that will have a lasting impact rather than jobs.

Companies will find it more difficult just going in search of cheap labor. The supply of basic labor could be affected if anyone who has any smarts at all wants to become a college graduate. Colmen asks, "If manufacturing moves out and keeps looking for the cheapest qualified labor source, what happens to the SMUGs?"

The change from an almost primitive business environment to a professional management class is a two-generation change. Colmen, for example, met people in Africa who have studied for their Ph.D.s in Cambridge, yet when they go home, they're still involved in tribal rituals. The next generation will be a little further from that, and so on. That doesn't mean that they're not smart; it just means that you don't let go of your traditions until the rest of the world has changed for you.

PREDICTIONS

Global competitiveness is going to increase, not only in the manufacturing environment, but also in the knowledge-worker competition. *There is no monopoly on brains and there is going to be a bigger brain pool around the world.* That could mean an overall increase in the standard of living of the world but perhaps a decrease in the standard of living in the Organization for Economic Cooperation and Development (OECD) countries. The United States will lose share of the "knowledge-work" market that it feels is its key strength.

There will be areas of specialization around the world, for example, India. When Colmen runs an ad in a U.S. paper for consultants with information technology (IT) backgrounds, he can predict that at least 50 percent will be from Indian extraction because IT is such a strong skill base in India, an area strength. The same is true for Eastern Europe where the basic educational level is high. People will be able to exploit their talents and their skills by coming to the United States; or if things develop in their home countries, they could become competitors in knowledge-based industries. The market for knowledge also will tighten with the communications explosion because knowledge-work can be done in any part of the world. As businesses become so interrelated, barriers such as wanting to live with your own kind will break down and become less important over time. The trend to be more mobile will have global political implications.

People will be overqualified for positions and will have to look for niches to ply their trade. For example, the police departments are getting a lot more college graduates. They didn't need college graduates in the past, and perhaps they don't need them now.

More people in countries like the United States will question the value of a mediocre education. When Colmen got out of school, you went into an entry-level professional job—everyone did, even the lowest member of the class. You did your job and moved up the corporate ladder. Those opportunities don't exist anymore, and I really don't know if they will again. Now, the product of the massive college factory stream needs work of any type.

Another reason excellence will be required to succeed is that even in high-technology areas, restructuring has created unemployment. As businesses mature, they don't need as many people. A workforce needing full-time work to support itself will find only part-time openings available. The lack of other opportunities allows companies like United Parcel Service to put high demands on its workers because there is no other place for them to go.

TREND

ENERGY IS POWER

Revaluing resources, rich-poor and forward-backward are the energy megathemes found throughout this executive summary of global energy trends.

Low prices and high technology have made most people feel pretty relaxed about energy. The prices have created the impression of plenty and the belief that there will always be an answer to any problem that pops up. But there will be an increasing energy focus brought on by such issues as global warming. Wealthy nations that want to end pollution and poor nations that want to end poverty are poor allies—there will be problems!

IMPLICATIONS

The developed countries now account for almost half the world's energy use. Indeed, the total per capita energy consumption in areas such as South Asia is only 5 percent of that in the United States. Poor nations seeking to get rich will use more energy, and that is very significant when you factor in that more than half the human race lives without any commercial supply of electricity. By 2020 when the world's population is expected to top 8 billion (compared with 5.5 billion today), 85 percent of mankind will live in what are now poor countries. Either billions of people will continue to live without even the most basic comforts or the demand for energy will grow prodigiously.

If economic growth is rapid, the Third World could consume three times as much energy as the OECD countries by 2020. Investments in most countries' energy capacity have usually accounted for 15 percent to 20 percent of total investment or 3 percent to 4 percent of GDP. Roughly $30 trillion in new investment can be expected over the next 30 years, and most of this will occur in poor countries. Hence, the overall global mix of supply and demand will be shaped by the attitudes of the Third World.

PREDICTIONS

We will continue to rely on fossil fuels—especially coal, which is plentiful in China and India, the planet's two most populous countries. Since most poor countries care far more about the wealth of their citizens than they do about global warming, there is little chance for the acceptance of renewable forms of energy such as solar power that cannot as yet pay their own way. Therefore, coal and oil demand will continue well beyond the first decade of the twenty-first century.

The former Soviet Union possesses 20 percent of the world's discovered energy reserves and accounts for 21 percent of world energy production. However, the annual environmental damage by Soviet energy producers is estimated at over 10 billion rubles. The former Soviet Union has a vast energy-saving potential, amounting to almost one-third of its current energy consumption. Energy saving and improved energy efficiency programs up to 2010 can cover 55 percent of their energy requirements during the 1990s and 75 percent in the following decade.

In China, total petroleum resources are estimated to be huge. The oil-production target for China in the year 2000 is four million barrels per day. The producing fields onshore in North China may afford opportunities for equipment sales, but bureaucratic resistance to foreign involvement in these fields remains strong. The North China Basin could become China's largest oil-producing region during 1995–2005, and the Tonkin Gulf has been brought into trial production by France's Total Chine. However, the only large discovery in the South China Sea lies in natural gas, which is very hard to sell in an area far from potential markets.

Three structural elements must be considered in analyzing Japan's energy situation: (1) Energy consumption in Japan is expected to grow continuously in the future; (2) Limitations of resources will become manifest; (3) A response to the problems of the global environment will become inevitable. Japan's industries and society have succeeded in drastically reducing energy requirements per unit GNP, and its present per capita energy requirement is relatively low compared with other major industrial countries. Japan is a leading nation in energy-utilizing technologies and pollution prevention. Efficiency in the use of energy will continue with greatly improved energy efficiency built into the design of products, particularly those employing "micro machine" research that can dramatically reduce product size.

By the end of 2010, Japan will need facilities for the commercial generation of 720 billion KW—to reach this target, expect the percentage of nuclear power to be raised further. Existing worldwide deposits of uranium are expected to be insufficient to meet demand by 2010. It is therefore imperative for Japan to establish a technological system to utilize plutonium, a substance that can fully exploit what uranium resources offer.

By 2010, European gas demand is expected to rise by 50 percent, so imports will need to rise in step. In Europe, natural gas is viewed as a clean fuel, driving demand faster than European producers can supply it. West European natural gas demand is expected to increase at an average of 2.9 percent per year. European gas production is expected to increase on the strength of North Sea gas flow. However, less than two-thirds of the gas consumed in Western Europe is produced there. Major contributors to European production will continue to be the Netherlands, United Kingdom and Norway, which together account for three-quarters of today's gas flow. The Middle East is a potential long-term major supplier of gas, with more than 30 percent of the world's gas reserves.

In 2010, total U.S. energy expenditures will be approximately 20 percent lower, reflecting the lack of upward pressure from fixed costs or fuel prices. Residential energy bills will decline as will commercial sector energy costs. The cost of energy purchased by industrial customers will decline. Computer-management systems will become a common way to monitor and control energy use in both the public and private sectors. Moreover, U.S. industry will be able to save 240 billion KW hours annually by replacing standard efficiency motors and drives with those that are only 2 percent to 6 percent more efficient. Today, only about 15 percent of the motors sold nationwide are energy efficient.

TREND

WATCH HOW THEY PLAY—THE NEW ENERGY PARTNERSHIP

Contributor—Dr. Anthony J. Finizza, chief economist, ARCO Corporation

---

The togetherness that Dr. Finizza alerts us to is a dramatic change— whether it's sowing the seed of future problems or a way to avoid them is an important unknown.

With the high cost of exploration, uncertainties, low prices and volatility, we will see a different structural organization within the oil business. We will find consumer countries doing more with producing nations and will see more ownership of the consumer structure by the upstream (producing) countries. So we might have ARCO involved in a strategic alliance with Kuwait just as we saw Star, a joint venture between Saudi Arabia and Texaco.

IMPLICATIONS

To minimize the transaction costs and uncertainties about oil supply and oil demand, anyone who wants to export oil will have to take an equity interest in a consumer country, and every consumer country will have to have an equity interest in a producing country. So this consumer-producer dialogue we hear about in the oil business is not going to be just dialogue: It's going to result in joint ventures that derive from the mutual self-interest of oil consumers and oil producers.

PREDICTIONS

Expect to see more private investment in national oil country activities. First, the OPEC nations will welcome such investment, then Mexico will have to get on the bandwagon.

There will be so much vested interest by both the producing and consuming countries that supply disruptions will be less likely. It will be a much less volatile world.

These new alliances will be viewed by government much more like a utility business. The U.S. government will control these new supplier-producer partnerships by taxation rather than by regulation, which has previously been the American choice for controlling the oil business.

Prices will continue to rise as supplier and consumer companies continue to work together more closely. Expect some congressional action to protect consumers.

Chapter 10

THE MOST IMPORTANT
ECONOMIC TRENDS

•

*They were not prepared for the storm today, so they have
all been thrown into great confusion. They do not possess a
compass, for ordinarily when the weather is fine, they follow the old tradition and steer by the stars in the sky, without making serious mistakes regarding their direction. This
is what we call "depending upon heaven for existence."*

*But now they have run into this bad weather, so
they have nothing to rely upon. It is not that they don't
want to do well, only they do not know the direction and
so the further they go the more mistakes they make.*
TRAVELS OF LAO CAN, BY LIU E, BEIJING, CHINA, 1905

•

If you still need to verify that there are no workable crystal balls on this
planet, just look at the dismal failure of forecasters to predict the weather
or the economy. But even with the complexity of predicting the weather,
it is possible to do better than guess. A striking example of dependable
forecasting is shared by Melvin Cetron in his book *Encounters with the
Future.* While Cetron was growing up not far from the chocolate factory in Hershey, Pennsylvania, his next-door neighbor would forecast
the weather before the neighborhood kids went to school. If he told
them to bring their boots, 9 out of 10 times it would snow. The local
radio station never batted better than 500.

When asked how he did it, he used to say he could feel it in his bones. Years later his secret came out, and it had nothing to do with his bones. He would wait until 8 A.M. to make his forecast—when the morning train from Pittsburgh passed on its way to Philadelphia. If the train's cars were wet, he'd predict snow. Since the train always beat the prevailing winds blowing the weather eastward from Pittsburgh, this man wasn't taking too many chances with his forecast. The trends in this chapter will change our economic climate in the 2000s. They suggest partly sunny times, but I suggest you bring your umbrella when you go to work.

TREND

STEADY AHEAD FOR THE U.S. ECONOMY AND DEFENSE SECTOR

Contributor—Bernard Schwartz, CEO, Loral Corporation

I've watched Loral Corp grow under the leadership of Bernard Schwartz from a small operation in Bronx, New York, where I consulted almost 30 years ago, to one of the largest defense contractors in the world. Schwartz understands the need to shift focus in the defense business.

The United States will experience steady and consistent growth as compared with our international trading partners and competitors. American business has done a lot over the last few years to discipline itself. It has got costs under control through retrenchment, has better quality control, is doing more effective marketing and has restored its balance sheets. American banking is also much stronger than it was five to seven years ago. We are experiencing rising prospects and additional resources. All this change is coming at a time when the opposite is happening in Japan. Therefore, the U.S. dollar will also get stronger. The impact of the confluence of low inflation and low interest plus the above circumstances makes me feel bullish.

IMPLICATIONS

However, I (Bernard Schwartz) don't think there's enough demand worldwide or in the United States to give us the growth above 3 percent to 3.5 percent, which would allow our unemployment rolls to go down, and that's going to be a serious problem. The benefits of improved prosperity in the United States will positively impact two-thirds of our society. The other third will continue to move toward an underclass situation. The disparity between the bottom third and the top two-thirds (if that's the right number) is going to become more pronounced and will cause significant social problems over the next 10–15 years.

From a business point of view, I believe we are improving our position for identifying new opportunities and for America to take advantage of them. The communications revolution, which we are in the middle of, will continue to drive technologies and new applications. There will be more upbeat manufacturing opportunities in the United States than there have been over the last 10 years: NAFTA will have a good effect; China will represent significant market opportunities for American industry; auto and machine tools segments will be stronger than in the recent past, though they won't become the robust leaders of the economy they once were.

The most important factor to the success of the defense industries is the budget. It will be somewhat weaker than it is now, but we're coming to the dollar bottom of where that might be—in other words, about $250 billion to $260 billion of annual budget expenditures for defense. That in itself means there will be something of an inflationary decrease in real units, but the industry can manage that. There will be continued budgetary pressures on the defense industry, particularly on internal research and development (IR&D). The procurement accounts will level off in the $70 billion to $90 billion range but will still be a very important source of revenue generation for a large segment of American industries. Companies that will do well are those that are on the leading technology edges and have leadership positions.

PREDICTIONS

I find the Bernie Schwartz projection for the U.S. economy too optimistic and would instead project that annual growth in real GNP from 1990 to 2005 will be less than 2 percent. This figure compares with an annual growth rate of 2.9 percent from 1975 to 1990. Thus, the projections show a pronounced slowing in the rate of growth. The slowdown in growth of real GNP is a function of the expected slowdown in the growth of the labor force during the next decade and a half.

Intermediate-sized companies will find it increasingly more difficult to grow or even to sustain their market position. This will lead in turn to the consolidation that started several years ago. Expect more merger and acquisition (M&A) activity not only because of the economic climate, but also because public companies will buy or sell parts of the business rather than try to grow it themselves to continue to show growth for their stockholders. "Do the best you can for your stockholders, get the best value you can and join others who have a leadership position" will be the prevailing business philosophy.

M&A activity will be supported by the government. The government will be an advocate for consolidation, not picking winners or losers but supporting industry attempts to consolidate, where as before it was neutral or antagonistic, as a general rule. They will support constructive development to preserve the industrial base that will support the DOD's position. *Therefore, over the next five to seven years, there will be fewer players in the industry, but those that do well will have a larger piece of the market.* (The recent merger of McDonald Douglas and Lockheed suggests that Schwartz is on the right track.)

TREND

THE GLOBE TILTS TOWARD ASIA

The shift in focus is toward Asia.

By 2000, Asians are expected to account for 3.5 billion of the world's 6.2 billion people. Conservatively, fully 1 billion of those Asians will be living in households with some consumer spending power. The rocket-like growth and absolute size of Asia's middle class should create some of the biggest business and financial opportunities in history, and far-sighted Western firms and their workers stand to profit immensely from this trend.

IMPLICATIONS

By the turn of the century, Asia will be the locomotive to drive the world's economy.

If Asia, with its strong growth and high demand for capital goods and services, opens its markets wide to the rest of the world, the trade flow that follows will be dramatic. In fact, American trade with Asia is now double that of its trade with Europe. In 1992, the region bought U.S. $4.1 billion worth of American business, professional and technical services, about U.S. $50 million more than Europe.

While most of the Asian economic euphoria is currently focused on China, Japan, with its U.S. $4 trillion economy, of which only 3 percent to 4 percent is manufactured imports (compared with 10 percent for most G-7 countries) is still a tremendous economic engine. But Japan's economy is in crisis, and the only way out is to import and lower the trade surplus. As long as the surplus keeps rising (it currently stands around U.S. $150 billion annually), the yen will keep getting stronger, bludgeoning Japanese business to death.

The region's economic strength will start translating into political power and influence.

Japan, which has traditionally avoided any kind of global leadership role, will assume the same leadership role in trade that the United States played in the postwar period as it opens its market to the growing economies of Asia. For Global Asia to become an economic reality, stronger and more effective and often less democratic leadership similar to Singapore and Malaysia will be needed in Japan and other Asian countries.

PREDICTIONS

Asia will supplant the United States as the world's number one market before 2020.

The United States will lose political clout as Japan opens its markets.

Merger and acquisition deals in Asia will account for more than one-third of all such global transactions before 2000.

Australia and New Zealand will have very strong economic links with Asia—where many Australians will work.

Parts and components being made in different places require free trade to allow such assembly systems to work. By siting factories and

> ARE YOU OR YOUR COMPANY TAKING STEPS TO BE INCLUDED IN THE ASIAN MARKET?

other operations around Asia, MNCs will help free trade to win out over protectionism.

U.S. auto companies will finally make headway in the Japanese market.

The Asian Pacific trading organization (APEC) will serve as a check for the European Union's protectionist trends.

TREND

THE GLOBAL TRADE WEB

Together-fragmented and shifting focus sum up the megathemes in the next trend.

Once countries become part of the global economy, they can't escape its influence. The global economy can raise a nation's living standards by providing new technologies, advanced products and solid competition for domestic firms. But short of a global calamity, how well or how poorly a country does is primarily its own affair.

World trade denotes specialization: Countries do more of what they do best. When countries trade, they benefit from one another's strengths, but this outside stimulus can only do so much. Ultimately, every nation has its own unique economic system. What counts is the quality of its businesses, workers, government policies, social customs, values and management styles.

IMPLICATIONS

The 24 full-member countries of the Organization for Economic Co-operation and Development (OECD), known as the "rich men's club," encompasses the developed industrial nations that operate a market economy. The OECD exports one-fifth of its GDP. In strict arithmetic terms, a 5 percent decrease in a country's exports would translate into only a 1 percent drop in GDP—significant, but not devastating. The biggest influence on the economy remains the domestic market. This makes sense because, in most advanced countries, services (everything from health care to restaurants) provide 6 out of every 10 jobs. The same logic applies to many developing countries, where up to two-thirds of the labor force continues in agriculture.

National policies need to reflect global trade objectives such as market access, availability and low cost of capital to attract trade. Since trade now follows investment, nations with unattractive investment policies are at risk in the global trading world. Disaggregation of manufacturing allows modules to be apportioned to countries competitively—assembly operations can be moved rapidly to more favorable competitive and regulatory environments. Government policies that encourage investments in infrastructure, education and environmental assistance will increase a country's opportunities in the global trading environment. But government efforts to shield vulnerable industries with protective measures, though understandable, are often ineffectual.

Trading agreements created in or around Asia will be seminal in creating a new world trade order since Asia accounts for 25 percent of world trade. Singapore, for example exports roughly 200 percent of its GDP. How can it be? How can a country export twice what it produces? The answer is that Singapore imports raw materials and semifinished products and reexports them after additional processing and also serves as a transshipment location for other countries' exports. Singapore flourishes when trade booms and is susceptible to a downturn.

But most Asian countries are not in this extreme situation. Vietnam, for example, with abundant natural resources, such as oil, bauxite, coal, and huge pool of cheap labor, will experience rapid economic progress and rising foreign investment. Privatization of agriculture and the lifting of price controls have enabled the nation to become self-sufficient in food—and the world's third largest rice producer. Malaysia, meanwhile, is poised to become Asia's next economic tiger. But it can sustain its economic expansion only by stepping up the industrial ladder. To do this, the country must deal with the pressure of rapid growth— especially with its overstressed infrastructure and labor shortages.

PREDICTIONS

The global economy will be much more volatile in the foreseeable future. As trade and competition increase globally, it's not possible to insulate a country's economy from the economic decisions and performance of the major trading nations of the world. For example, interest rates and exchange rates in the United States are influenced by decisions made in other countries—the interest rates in Germany or the optimism in Japan. Certain issues will have to be dealt with on a global level such as the oceans and the atmosphere.

It remains to be seen how competitive regional trade blocs will become. However, there will be an international cooperation toward common global standards in each regional agreement, including the use of international accounting standards and mutual recognition of professional credentials. Standards are needed—there is significant over- and underinvoicing of international trade.

TREND

THE DECLINE AND TRANSFORMATION OF THE MODERN WORLD

Contributor—Dr. Willis Harman, futurist and CEO, Noetic Institute

Willis Harman sees that dramatic change and togetherness are needed to stop the world from sowing the seeds of future problems.

The decline and transformation of the modern world is a highly significant economic trend. A sense that the modern world no longer works—not even for those who have achieved some measure of success in it, much less for the underclass or for future generations—is increasingly prevalent. Those who are most deeply involved with this situation see it as a decline of one system and its replacement with something else.

IMPLICATIONS

These changes are so profound that they challenge two of the basic myths of the modern world: First, science gives us an adequate picture of the world to live by; and second, it is perfectly reasonable for a global society to be dominated by its economic institutions and economic logic. Parts of both these belief systems are being challenged.

The cultural shifts taking place in the modern world will consist of the three following elements:

Instead of viewing things separately in a great diversity of ways, we will view them holistically. For example, in health care, we're beginning to understand that diseases are not caused entirely by bacteria or viruses but by a whole context of complex interactions. Therefore, you have to deal with such areas as agriculture and the environment as a whole.

We're going toward a holistic thrust and moving away from all of the separateness aspects that have characterized the modern world such as believing it's okay to have sociology in one department and mathematics and ecology and so forth in another. In one sense, the modern world is a shattering of the oneness that characterized the medieval world in many ways—man separate from nature, mind separate from matter, organizations separate from one another, nation states separate from one another and ultimate explanations in terms of separate fundamental particles. All of that is shifting back to a wholeness, an "at-onement."

We will see a shift in the focus of authority from external experts and external knowledge to an inner wisdom and inner authority. In other words, I'm the final authority over my life. *Intuitive leadership,* a hot term in the business world right now, would have been unimaginable a decade ago. Who had ever used the word *intuition?* You see this trend not just in the feminist movement, but also in the feminization of business. Not only are women moving into high places, but also the so-called feminine values are changing business.

We will see a shift in the perception of cause from external to inner-directed. Science says if you want to know the cause, study those fields that you can measure. But in the developed world, a shift to the locus of cause to being inner-directed is taking place and, to an extent, is far greater than we could have imagined a couple of generations ago— what goes on in our minds affects our perception of what's out there.

One sign that this shift is real is the frequency that you hear "We create our own reality" or "There are no coincidences." These ideas didn't make any sense at all in the old paradigm. Now we know what they mean, All persons nod their heads when they hear them. Another social indicator that delights me is the sudden rise and long-lasting popularity of the number one best-seller *The Celestine Prophecy* by James Redfield—it also doesn't make any sense in the old paradigm. It's clear that people are resonating with something and that what they're resonating with is a worldview that is not what they learned in science class—not by a long shot. Of course, the Eastern worldview has always said cause is subject, object is effect. I'm not sure this shift is going quite that far, but it is in the general direction.

An example of the cultural shift outlined above can be observed in how we are beginning to view health care and dying. Health is far more a matter of our inner attitudes. It has become apparent that cancers and other life-threatening illnesses, infections, contagious disease, auto-immune diseases and many of the failures of bodily parts all have to do with an immune system that has been weakened by various aspects of modern culture and negative behaviors. We will have a totally different attitude toward death than we had in previous generations.

We had gone so far down the materialist track that a fear of death pervaded the whole society, manifesting itself in other fears—fear of loss of control and so on. What is eminently clear from book titles and sales is that our attitude toward death is turning inward, making death more of an adventure, a graduation ceremony, something to be worked toward and to be done right. That leaves us to raise questions about the health care system and the fraction of the cost of the health care that goes to keeping physical bodies alive after it would not make any sense at all in other cultures, and it is making less and less sense in ours.

The cultural shift is going to lead us to a totally different attitude toward health and health care—"Screw the federal government that doesn't know how to run a health care system." We will take care of our own health—just lower the taxes, except for some kind of catastrophic health insurance.

PREDICTIONS

I (Harman) predict that we will have some minor economic catastrophes; they may seem major but they will not be the end of civilization. Because of the growing perception that the system is not working, a sharp economic decline could be triggered by a noneconomic event, perhaps an environmental catastrophe. There are numerous things that can contribute to an environmental catastrophe. A moderate one, like another Chernobyl, could trigger a complete loss of faith in our economic and political systems. The catastrophe would make it so evident that nobody's in control anymore—that we don't know how to manage our countries and our economies.

But more likely, a collapse will be triggered by something economic, like the failure of the monetary system. Joel Kurtzman, the former editor of the *Harvard Business Review,* in his recent book, *The Death of Money,* says that the money system is about to collapse. Why? Because of a political decision made by Richard Nixon in the early 1970s and copied by all the industrial nations around the world to totally divorce all money from any commodity base such as gold or silver. There are plenty of theoretical reasons to say that money is just there on faith, and that faith could disappear very quickly. So the trigger could be the collapse of the monetary system, or it could be the debt situation.

A sense that we're going crazy is growing, if you look at the international money flows—only a very small percentage of the international money flow has anything to do with goods and services in the usual sense. The flow has primarily to do with speculation between the different currencies and so on. It's a matter of opinion about whether you call it all speculation or half speculation. But at any rate, what it amounts to is that the global economy is essentially a gambling casino, and that's a big shift from a half a century ago when the world's cultures believed that gambling was wrong and that gambling rewards the wrong parts of society.

Another problematic cultural shift is that we have gotten used to high rates of return and high interest rates that we used to call usury—profiteering from money lending. Now, the accepted and sought after terms of investment are much higher than what was once called usury. Also, the culture has shifted so that we accept far more debt. Indeed, people look at you somewhat curiously if you're not in debt. It's considered good judgment to "be using your money"—you mortgage your house so that you can speculate on Wall Street.

As you have high interest rates, you have tremendous amounts of debt-servicing splashing around in the economy. Moreover, it moves only in one direction: Everyone is paying it out, only a few are bringing it in. It's a systematic transfer of wealth from the poor to the rich, operating the same way between countries so that you've got a systematic transfer of wealth from the poor countries to the rich ones. It's not that people in corporations in these countries are exploitative or that the governments are—it's that we built it into the system and didn't notice it. It will not be very long before people will become aware and react to the injustice. Just what form that reaction takes is not very clear, but the reaction is another event that could trigger the decline in the system.

I would distinguish long-term trends from possible short-term triggers: Short-term trends last less than 15 years; long-term ones last more than a generation. The next 10 to 15 years is going to be a critical time because of a growing awareness that the events that can cause the system to decline are very real; but there is also the long-term attitude, "Well, it's not going to happen on my watch." Maybe not, but those short-term triggers could cause a loss in faith that could bring about a very rapid decline and the beginning of global economic decline and transformation.

It's very important not to overemphasis the decline, though it's going to be very real, with a lot of hand wringing. There are also a lot of good signs. People are finally taking responsibility for positive global transformation. It's still a minority of people, and if you're looking at the numbers game, you could say that you're looking at just a tiny fraction of the population, but it's a very *influential* part of the population.

TREND

AGE OF RETRENCHMENT—SMALL ISN'T SO BEAUTIFUL

As companies have slimmed down, they have become more efficient and profitable. However, like someone with an incurable disease smiling about finally having achieved his ideal weight, these companies are also sowing the seeds of future problems. The improved corporate profits that are mistakenly seen as a sign of economic recovery and health are nothing more then the results of the deep cuts in jobs—the very heart of the economy.

Retrenchment is sadly wrecking our dreams of two cars in every garage. A major contributor to the growing global army of unemployed is the unprecedented rash of corporate mergers, acquisitions, consolidations and bankruptcies. A significant part of my consulting practice involves identifying acquisition candidates for companies worldwide. The practice has allowed me to get a wide perspective of the rapidly narrowing industrial landscape. Moreover, as Ken Colmen of SRI observes, "There is no sign that global downsizing is going to stop—whether it's the right way to go is another question. What it doesn't do is put enough emphasis on investing in the future."

IMPLICATIONS

Corporate megamergers are occurring in all industry sectors. True, mergers seem necessary and helpful in many industries. For example: With about 8,500 banks in the United States, we have many more banks than we need. It has been argued that we need to consolidate them to compete with foreign megabanks for global markets. Business, government and nonprofit organization consolidation will be a major contributor to future economic decline in the next century. We tend to forget or underestimate the ripple effect of job cuts. In the case of banks, reductions in workforces of those who service banks such as building maintenance, advertising, accounting, law, information systems, restaurant and office supplies are inevitable.

Around the globe, corporations are being restructured and downsized, with many of the tasks they now perform contracted out to smaller supplier firms or done by temporary or part-time employees. A large increase in business reengineering projects will further downsize companies.

PREDICTIONS

The consolidation virus will spread. In the United States, manufacturing segments such as machinery and chemicals production will shrink due to acquisitions, cost cutting and the selling of unproductive assets. The number of large breweries has shrunk from a high of 750 in 1935 to less than 40 today, and by 2000, this number will be less than 30. The predictions of there being fewer and fewer large companies are the same for all other manufacturing and service categories. Indeed, government for the first time employs more people than does manufacturing. So much for our free market system!

> **WHAT CONTINGENCY PLANS HAVE YOU AND YOUR COMPANY MADE TO DEAL WITH THE EFFECTS OF DOWNSIZING?**

The economic troubles of Japan will continue. Hurt by both the European and Japanese recessions, even Japanese consumer electronics companies will fare badly as production and exports continue to decline. The German answer to how to avoid layoffs in a period of downsizing is to cut back on work hours and reduce pay. The German "everyone has a job" approach will become an acceptable option for companies and unions around the globe.

TREND

S'NO JOBS

The ever-decreasing number of jobs around the world is a trend that's often buried under the good news about growing corporate profits. But trust me, unemployment is sowing the seeds of serious future problems.

The future of work will most likely differ from, far more than resemble, the scene the world knows at present. In the next three decades, jobs are likely to be increasingly scarce unless, as is beginning to happen, public policy is used to deliberately expand job availability. The world must choose policy responses based on whether citizens want to legislate programs to create jobs or to ease public dependency on payrolls.

IMPLICATIONS

Employment in the U.S. economy is projected to increase by almost 25 million from 1990 to 2005. But even if this overly optimistic projection by the U.S. Department of Labor proves accurate, this projected average growth rate of 1.2 percent annually is only about half that during 1975–90. One reason for less optimistic projections is that *companies employing fewer than 100 workers accounted for over 90 percent of all job growth since 1988, a dramatic change from the past.*

Most of the increase in nonfarm wage and salary jobs is projected to occur in the services division of the service-producing sector. The two largest industries in this division, health services and business services, will account for 6.1 million of the projected increase in jobs, about one-quarter of the total. For the goods-producing sector, job increases in the construction industry will largely offset job declines in manufacturing and mining. Indeed, construction is the only goods-producing sector with job growth projected for 1990–2005. Construction in the United States is expected to have less than one-half the rate of growth it did in the previous 15 years. Manufacturing, despite some bright spots such as printing, publishing, medical instruments, plastic products and furniture, is projected to continue to decline in employment.

Companies that serve travelers constitute the world's largest generator of jobs. By 2005, travel and tourism are projected to support 350 million jobs around the world.

The travel and tourism industry in 1994 generated direct or indirect employment for more than 200 million people, or one out of every nine workers worldwide.

Real hourly compensation adjusted for inflation stagnated in the past two decades and actually fell for male workers, a development unprecedented in the United States over the past 75 years. Data about women show a mixed picture. They are well represented in the fastest growing occupations (health and treating occupations and personal service), but they are also overrepresented in some of the slow-growing or declining occupations—financial records processing, secretaries and computer equipment operators.

PREDICTIONS

Government is projected to increase its rate of employment growth compared with recent years. This increase reflects heavy demands on state and local governments to provide for the education of a growing population of young people. The need to repair or replace bridges, roads and other components of the transportation infrastructure will also spur the growth of employment in state and local government. Health services will account for almost one in nine jobs and business services almost one in six jobs in 2005.

The new decade will reward people who have broad skills and mental agility. Jobs for computer systems analysts and scientists will increase nearly 80 percent. Less-skilled workers will suffer higher levels of unemployment than better educated ones, though managers, lawyers and engineers will find increasing competition and poor prospects for advancement on the job. Rapid technological change will create a sizable elite of high-technology employees whose job titles will differ radically from most of what are known today—from the sysops that run the Internet to "artisans" operators who use CAD systems.

Nursing will grow in both size and stature. Careers in that field will expand by 44 percent, and starting salaries should rise as nurses take on an expanded role in the health delivery system. Leading the growth will be demand for so-called nurse practitioners, diagnostic specialists who will supplement physicians as frontline medical generalists in HMOs' inner cities and rural areas. Home health aides will be the fastest growing job category of all, nearly doubling to over 500,000. Most health aides provide nutritional care, housekeeping assistance and companionship to the infirm elderly.

In the next decade, the private sector will not have enough jobs. Expect massive government expenditures and experimentation in ways to stimulate job growth. While job growth will be subdued everywhere, medium-sized U.S. cities in the Southeast and Southwest offer the best possibilities. Orlando, Florida, and Las Vegas, Nevada, are among the metro areas with the fastest job growth.

TREND

THE RICH GET RICHER AND THE POOR GET POORER

The disparity between rich and poor is sowing the seeds of future problems.

The wealth gaps between rich and poor nations are staggering. In 1988, the average per capita income of OECD nations was just over $17,000. By contrast, Indonesia's per capita income was $473 and China's $301; in Latin America, the average was $2,100, and of the 38 sub-Saharan African nations, 26 had per capita incomes of less than $500.

IMPLICATIONS

Within most of the cities of the world, we see two economic worlds surrealistically revolving around in close juxtaposition. High-powered executives stride out of gleaming office buildings and expensive restaurants and pass within a few feet of people with no homes who live off handouts and charity.

There is movement toward both income poles, shrinking the middle-class consumer as a percentage of population. This phenomenon, particularly evident in the United States, is a distressing fact for business to contemplate. The proportion of low-wage earners in the global workforce is rising, creating an underclass in a two-tier wage structure. Already, a sizable proportion of U.S. workers are paid markedly less than comparable workers in other advanced countries. However, high-paid U.S. workers still earn more than their counterparts in other nations.

The affluent control the discretionary income (DI) in the United States. Only one-third of U.S. households have DI with the average amount being $12,300. Not surprisingly, the rich have most of the DI—just over one-quarter of U.S. households earn over $40,000 a year; however, they account for about two-thirds of the households in the DI group and control almost 90 percent of the nation's DI. This trend will turn us into an increasingly polarized nation by the end of the decade.

PREDICTIONS

The outlook for the poor and middle class is bleak. The world has done very little to reduce the poor population and there's nothing on the horizon that will pull any significant percentage of them into the middle-class ranks.

The future economic reform is uncertain all over the world. Increasingly insolvent, many former communist countries are ill equipped to deal with the poverty and unemployment generated by economic transition. Indeed, while the world praises Poland's remarkable transition to a market economy, Poland's voters made it clear that economic reform is not enough. The reformists won less than 12 percent of the vote with the former communists winning over 20 percent. In the short term, a system of safety nets to protect vulnerable and needy groups will have to be developed.

Mass scale public works programs employing up to 30 percent of a countries workforce will be required in the former Eastern Bloc countries. Government funded but independently operated social funds will also be set up. These funds will not be used design or administer projects but rather to fund proposals from community organizations and local governments who would then subcontract projects to local nongovernmental organizations or the local construction sector.

TREND

THE UNDERGROUND ECONOMY SURFACES

Since the underground economy will limit government tax revenue, it may or may not be sowing the seeds of future problems.

The curve of cash on hand, under the mattress, behind the bricks or stuffed in a drawer has risen to hundreds of billions of dollars. The underground economy is perhaps the most interesting aspect of the rise in cash hoarding. Economic activity done off the books to avoid government taxes and regulations is the way of doing business in many parts of the Third World as well as the more developed countries.

IMPLICATIONS

In Europe working off the books is called "working black or gray"; in French, Italian and German: "travail au noir," "lavoro nero," "schwartzarbeit"; the English wax far more poetic: "fiddling." It covers the need to hold down a second job, preferably unreported and untaxed, which permits a family to live at a level otherwise impossible. Underground income occurs in jobs primarily paid with cash or in jobs where payment is by barter: You handle my lawsuit and I'll paint your house, as a sample.

Smuggling is another facet of the underground economy. In Canada, for example, tobacco smuggled primarily from the United States is sold for roughly half the legal price. The government was forced to cut taxes to reduce the smuggling in tobacco. The smugglers then switched to other lucrative underground markets that are fueled by excessive taxation. Illegal cash from drug trafficking and other criminal enterprises has shown up as excess cash at Federal Reserve bank districts in Texas and California. There is a noticeable increase in the numbers of $50 and $100 bills in circulation.

New York City estimates over $1 billion a year in lost revenue and California estimates at least $1.8 billion in unreported revenue. California has more than half the nation's illegal immigrants, and they cannot open bank accounts or get credit and are often paid off the books in cash. The state's weak economy gets some blame—when the economy is down, a lot of legal transactions don't get reported to avoid taxes. Another likely source is money flowing in from Pacific Rim countries. The return of Hong Kong to China in 1997, the tension between North Korea and South Korea and increased trade with the United States may be prompting Asians to move their dollars to California for investment or safekeeping.

A vast source of material for the gray market is pilfered goods that are resold on the streets. Indeed, urban merchants reporting pilferage losses from 5 percent to 10 percent have recounted seeing items reappear on the streets for sale in front of their stores.

By their participation in gray markets, millions of honest people have withdrawn their consent to be governed by a processes they no longer respect. The underground economy is actually a useful built-in restraint to the fiscal appetites of power hungry governments, but such widespread public cheating can spread to other fields and further erode business ethics. It is a very short step from the underground economy to white-collar crime.

PREDICTIONS

Tax revenues will remain stagnant as the underground economy will grow for many reasons, including the increasing number of illegal aliens who don't use checking accounts; inflation; high taxation; growing disenchantment with governments everywhere; drugs; organized crime; increasing regulation; increasing immigration from countries like Russia, where the "informal economy" is the only hope for large segments of the population. Moreover, a rising divorce rate may persuade parties of both sexes that a less obvious asset profile is a good thing.

TREND

JAPAN SUNSETS

Sophisticated global competition will erode Japan's market leadership in many industry segments.

Japan's global edge will continue to erode despite their fierce competitive drive. As domestic markets continue to soften they will need to increase exports even higher to offset declines at home. But investors feeling the aftershocks of the recent recession have put on the brakes on the consistently optimistic free-spending capital investments, business deals and new product proliferation that put dread in the hearts of competitors around the globe.

IMPLICATIONS

Changing attitudes toward work are also shaking the foundations of lifetime employment. The workaholic older generation is being replaced by middle-aged corporate mercenaries who are no longer blindly loyal to their firms. They, in turn, are being followed by younger workers who seem more interested in leisure than what's happening at the office. So-called salarymen are the cogs that have long driven Japan's phenomenal economic machine. The new-breed salarymen grew up with abundance all around and rarely had to compete for anything. Few seem to demonstrate the drive or resourcefulness of their hungrier predecessors.

Indeed, the bulk of Japanese workers have never had any long-term job security. In theory, those who quit before retirement age do so by their own choice. In reality, a growing portion of these retirements are coerced. Japanese companies will go to extremes to force employees to hand in their own resignations. Voluntary retirement saves the company's prestige because many of these people are older, long-term management employees. People in management are not members of the union and are therefore without anyone to protect them. The Japanese company union has usually supported management; but as more people are forced out, unions will become less cooperative or won't survive.

Another area of peaceful coexistence that is beginning to break down is the relationship between the political and bureaucratic realms. The recent firings of bureaucrats who over decades have built a protective wall around themselves sent shock waves though the heart of Kasumigaseki, Tokyo's bureaucratic village.

PREDICTIONS

Future governments will try to release the economy from the manacles of excessive regulation and to end the heavy concentration of power in central government. Expect more responsibility to be given to the private sector with less government intervention than in the past.

Other predictions: Japan's global acquisition drive will slow; as industry consumers spend less on goods, services and capital equipment, some small suppliers will go under or consolidate, but the Keiretsu structure of supplier relationships will survive the tough times; the Ministry of Trade and Industry will try to force restructuring to new business areas with greater strategic and profit potential through the use of R&D subsidies and bureaucratic guidance; the free-wheeling spending by the Japanese consumer will also slow, hurting the domestic market as well as brand-name products worldwide.

TREND

INDIA IS UP AND AROUND

India begins to move forward from a backward economic path.

India will experience a boom in exports. New companies will spring up in India's south and west. Towns like Tiruppur are already contributing to the U.S. $22 billion in exports.

IMPLICATIONS

The Tirupper success in the world cotton knit trade exemplifies what's happening around India, where cheap, highly available manpower, combined with high-tech machinery, is creating a profusion of small- to medium-scale manufacturing and service operations.

The town, which was a cotton growing village in the 1960s, expects to surpass $1 billion in exports by 1995.

Problems, however, will continue to plague India, especially public squalor, including open sewers, polluted water, traffic jams, strike-prone harbors, overused, antiquated phone systems and a corrupt, ineffective government bureaucracy. These problems lower life expectancy in India to 58, compared with about 75 in industrial countries.

PREDICTIONS

Business growth will be spotty in India. Expect that success in the south and west, political instability, a severe AIDS epidemic in Marxist-ruled Calcutta and the adverse problems of Sikh separatist insurgency in the Punjab will keep buyers away from those areas.

India will become a looser federation: The states will have far more autonomy, and the division between Hindus and Muslims will remain sharp and will detract from stability and growth.

Chapter 11

HOW POLITICAL TRENDS WILL IMPACT BUSINESS

.

If we open a quarrel between the past and present, we shall find that we lost the future.

WINSTON CHURCHILL

Politicians are scurvy fellows who make deals which are without purpose or honor involving large seegars and smoke-filled rooms.

PRE-FEDERALIST "CAESAR PAPERS"

In the future, authoritarian governments may be unavoidable, even necessary . . . to provide for a people who will need, over and above a solution of their difficulties, a mitigation of their anxieties.

ROBERT HEILBRONER

.

The tendency is to see politics as having a life of its own, charging down roads that are ill-defined or venally chosen by politicians acting from a sense of their own divine right or perhaps sensing a path of special interest. By and large, I think this is totally untrue. Politics tends to be an expression of the prime drivers activating a particular grouping of people, whether village or nation. Politics is the public's coherent expression of the sum of drives that are perceived as covering their interests. Thus, it often becomes a very mixed basket of fish. Yet when you check the individual elements, their origin and place of spawning usually become quite clear.

A political leader doesn't originate directions, save in rare instances. The individual reads the economic, social and demographic tea leaves and tries to put together a brew that finds enough consensus so that all concerned will drink it with varying degrees of happiness. Whether they are in democratic or autocratic systems, politicians are thus opinion makers, opinion blenders and opinion wielders aiming at achieving specific purposes.

The present political backdrop is indeed a coat of many colors. It may be better described as a patchwork quilt in which contradictory and violently opposing forces may well rend it into a rag bag. In this chapter, we will cover some of the elements of contention in the political spectrum as well as some of the basic trends that drive them. Above all, it should be remembered that what is presented here is a series of snapshots of a highly dynamic process that is going to continue throughout the next decade. We will identify political trends and directions, not who will be ahead at any given point.

TREND

THE PIVOTAL POLITICALS

A shift in power requires a shift in focus.

Peace is a global trend that requires a major shift in our thinking about the future.

Global politics is undergoing a huge shift of power. The great postwar superpowers are losing their power, but it's not clear how much other countries or institutions will gain. The danger is that power vacuums will arise, leading to new economic, political or military conflicts. Many basic truths of the past 20 years won't survive the next 20. We cannot be sure that the mechanisms that gave us economic stability and an uneasy peace will continue to do so.

With the breakup of the Soviet Union we ended one of the greatest transition periods in world politics. The United States has become the world leader. The United States is viewed with envy, hatred and a certain amount of amusement as being politically naive in many quarters of the world—the United States likes to be loved; therein lies the rub. China and Japan, current contenders for the leadership throne, are loved in far fewer quarters of the world. They are, however, respected and seen as politically more effective.

IMPLICATIONS

In recent years, Japan was in the position to become a world political leader but developed neither the taste nor the political awareness that would have permitted it to grow into the role it tried to assume during World War II. The country is too busy following its business nose to take long-range positions with regard to world leadership.

The isolationism that has been so much a part of U.S. history stemmed from its size and the challenge of the rest of the world. Similarly, it is isolation and current concern with short-term economic gains that have probably kept China from delineating action that might have longer range political consequences. Historically, China likes to keep to itself and has an overriding distaste for the rest of the world. Of course, the Japanese and other East Asian countries are pleased that China has more than enough growth problems to keep global ambitions under international control for many years.

PREDICTIONS

All nations will cede power in one form or another to wider global forces—be they economic, environmental or demographic. The interdependence of nations is irreversible. But will nations survive this process or resort to force? A study found a striking inverse correlation between war expectations and savings and implied that human productivity around the globe could expand monumentally if peace becomes the common reality.

America will act to balance and maintain stability and security in Pacific Asia. The relationship between China and Japan will be crucial for stability and growth. Japan cautiously will expand trade with China, reassured by the U.S. and Japan security alliances.

The United States will become stretched financially and will encourage an expansion of the United Nations's security role from peace-keeping to peace making and law enforcement. America's desire to see all peoples become liberal democracies will cool. The old civilizations around the world are not easily converted. However, because of satellites and telecomputers, the basic values of human rights will become universal.

TREND

IS POLITICAL CORRECTNESS CORRECT?

Political Correctness has gotten out of hand and requires a shift in focus.

While everyone is working and happy, diversity and political correctness is just another management development program. But in these times of downsizing and restructuring, having jobs earmarked for female and minority candidates is making white men very angry. At the heart of the issue is the question of merit and government attempts to pressure employers to diversify the workplace.

IMPLICATIONS

American white men are losing out to less-qualified workers. It isn't an issue of promoting or hiring women or minorities, it's who is the best-qualified person for the job. On the other hand, even when candidates are equally qualified and the company selects a woman or minority, cries of reverse discrimination will be heard from white men.

In a growing number of companies—especially those aggressively pushing diversity programs—white men are feeling frustrated, resentful and afraid.

PREDICTIONS

White men will form business support groups similar to those available to blacks, Asians and women. There will be more women in the workforce, and they will become more politically active in the workplace. Issues such as sexual harassment and comparable worth will increase in importance. The growing number of minorities and immigrants will create new demands for specialized public services and more bilingual public employees.

Public policy will exceedingly bend to the whims of vocal minorities. This trend is behind the Clinton administration foreign policy excursions into areas that have no strategic importance to the United States (Somalia, Rwanda, Haiti and South Africa).

Corporations and the media will increasingly be coerced into providing employment as well as funding for minority-sponsored projects by threats of boycotts and lawsuits by minorities seeking to promote their own agenda. Expect a conservative backlash to unseat constituents who are seen as pro-immigration, pro-welfare or soft on crime. Politicians with the courage to stand up and say "enough is enough" will be popular with white and Asian voters.

Expect pressure to reduce the funding for so-called minority study programs on public campuses. These programs often serve as bully pulpits on which radical minorities blame historical racism for all current minority problems. The United States is fast becoming a nation that is afraid to speak about such issues as the inherent wrong and wasteful cost in affirmative action programs, reverse discrimination, frivolous lawsuits about political correctness in the workplace or when government-supported minority advantages are to be phased out.

TREND

REGULATING REGULATORS

Overregulation is sowing the seeds of future problems.

Business regulation is gaining appeal. A regulator, as Fred Allen observed, is "a man who comes in at 9 A.M., finds a molehill on his desk and has until 5 P.M. to make a mountain out of it."

IMPLICATIONS

The U.S. savings and loan crises brought the banking industry laws requiring a massive amount of paperwork and reporting. It is estimated that it costs the industry roughly $10 billion a year to keep up with the paperwork.

The hamburger—an innocent object named for a famous German city and devoured throughout the world—is, believe it or not, in the United States, the subject of 41,000 regulations, involving 200 laws and 111,000 precedent-setting court cases and quasi-judicial decisions from administrative bodies. To give you a sample of how closely your favorite burger is watched, note the following regulations:

An enriched bun must have at least 1.8 milligrams of thiamine, 1.1 milligrams of riboflavin and at least 8 but not more than 12.5 milligrams of iron. The ketchup, to be considered Grade A Fancy, must flow no more than 9 centimeters in 30 seconds at 69 degrees Fahrenheit (it couldn't be 70?). The mayonnaise can be seasoned or flavored so long as it is not colored to look like an egg yolk. Lettuce must be fresh and show no more than one "rib" per half inch. The pickle slices must be between one-eighth and three-eighths inches thick. The cheese must contain at least 50 percent milk fat and if made from nonpasteurized milk, must be cured for 60 days or more at a temperature of at least 35 degrees Fahrenheit. The meat itself can be no more than 30 percent fat content; inspected no less than six times; the pesticides must have no more than 5 parts DDT per million parts of fat—and that's just for starters!

PREDICTIONS

Regulation will exist at differing levels in various countries, depending on where they find themselves on the curve of economic maturity. MNCs will find less regulation from former zealots in both the developed and developing world who will become considerably more cautious about the effectiveness of regulation and, therefore, will see it as a limiting rather than an ordering device. In other words, companies will be told the limits of what they can be expected to do or achieve and than be left to their own devices about how to function within these limits.

In the United States, reregulation will gain momentum, particularly in health care and environmental areas. System operators in the cable television industry will also face revenue constraints imposed by reregulation.

TREND

GROWING FEDERAL AND LOCAL TENSIONS

State and local governments will be like David, using their slingshots to shift the focus of Goliath-sized federal government revenues.

Expect increased federal and state tensions over dividing the economic pie and providing needed services. "It's different in our state and we know how to do it best" attitudes will lead to increasing state to state and federal policy inconsistencies.

IMPLICATIONS

State and local governments are getting more obligations from the federal governments but no additional revenues. Therefore, it will require more innovation at local levels to make the system work. Budget deficits at the state and local level will force many program cutbacks, spotlighting the fragility as well as the need for innovative job and economic development programs that can demonstrate significant short-term results. State-sponsored nonprofit corporations funded by off-budget mechanisms such as privatization opportunities using government-private partnerships will increasingly be used at all levels of government. They will provide a means of stabilizing the economic development efforts against constantly changing political winds. But economic reform will continue to be predominantly the responsibility of state and local government.

PREDICTIONS

Decentralization will continue globally as "federal governments" delegate more responsibilities to the local level. The pressure on local governments in China to do more with less will be particularly great. Responsibilities will continue to shift from the federal and state governments to the cities, leaving cities to solve their own problems. The mismatch between revenue and problems will cause cities with low tax bases to resort to further service reductions.

New federal grants will be limited to those programs that help achieve national goals, particularly in retraining workers for a high-tech future. These programs will not be cost effective or successful despite propaganda numbers coming out of Washington to the contrary. Indeed, as propaganda and politics take over from facts and common sense, we will have to view numbers coming out of government with suspicion. Taxpayers will seriously question statistics on health care, job creation, the value of costly social engineering projects such as the carpool lane or the benefits to the economy from a swelling immigrant population.

TREND

PRIVATE—COME IN

A dramatic change is taking place in the ownership of formerly state-run enterprises. All over the world there is a trend to privatize loss-plagued, state-owned enterprises. Money from privitization sales will be used to pay off debt and shore up budgets, and some of the inflows will be plowed back into companies.

IMPLICATIONS

Privatization is under way on a mammoth scale across Europe. Investors will be asked to pony up more than $150 billion by the year 2000. Up for grabs are numerous prime properties, ranging from automakers and leading banks to giant oil and telecommunications companies. Though most privatizations have gone smoothly, there is concern that investors are becoming satiated by the massive scale of privatized offerings, causing governments to cut prices or table deals.

At the same time the Japanese move to less government partnering with business, the U.S. government will get more involved with the private sector by greasing what Adam Smith referred to as the power of the "invisible hand" with some government largesse. The White House has lined up with private industry to launch initiatives in new building materials and methods, "clean" cars, advanced semiconductors, electronic packaging and flat panel displays. The policy seems to be for industry to pick the next-generation technology and for the U.S. government to help develop it.

PREDICTIONS

The sale of publicly owned corporations will continue as conservative governments maintain their rule in Europe. Labor opposition to auto, telecommunications and other privatizations will become a major concern.

In India, U.S. telecomm companies will invest hundreds of millions of dollars for regional telecomm networks, using fixed wireless loops and fiber optics. To make investments pay, U.S. carriers would need a share of overseas traffic, currently monopolized by India's Department of Telecommunications. To stave off privatization, telecomm authorities are promising to add additional lines and fiber-optic links. They don't want regional business centers to get state-of-the-art communications ahead of political bosses in Delhi.

The government is also protecting loss-plagued state carrier Indian Airlines. Under a new policy, it clipped the wings of recently legitimized private operators by requiring them to fly a quota of uneconomical routes to remote areas and, to protect Indian Airlines crews, require pilots to receive their employer's consent to switch airlines. These protectionist attempts will fail, and the government will completely deregulate the Indian economy, allowing more foreign investment to sustain predicted economic growth of 2 percent annually for the next decade.

TREND

REVOLT AGAINST THE POLITICAL STATUS QUO

Around the world, voters are insisting on dramatic change in the way governments are run.

"Throw the bums out" is the common theme being sounded around the world. A growing movement to bury the political establishment and resurrect a new order that is half nightmare and half utopian dream is particularly evident in Europe, where mainstream political institutions have prevailed since the end of World War II. The world has become weary of corruption and recession.

IMPLICATIONS

In Britain, the conservative party has a historically low approval rating. The Netherlands and Italy have removed centrist Christian Democratic parties that have ruled for decades and have given big gains to parties on the right.

The nation-state as we know it is being undermined from above by the globalized economies. Transnational institutions such as the European Union have deeply eroded the states' monopoly on power as have recession and soaring unemployment. Economic policies of the left, right, center and free market have failed to turn the economies of many countries around, producing widespread doubts that the nation-states with their aging cast of leaders, some of which had governed for a generation or more, remain an effective instrument for managing tomorrow's global economic complexity.

Other explanations cited for the demise of centrist parties include widespread government corruption and the rise of a universal mass culture. In Italy, a corruption scandal has tainted nearly every government institution and led to indictments and investigations of more than 600 government and business leaders, causing a centrist collapse.

Fed by television, which has relegated much traditional national culture to museums and history books, feelings of powerlessness and alienation from the mainstream as well as voter apathy and pessimism abound throughout the world. During the national elections in Poland last fall, fewer than a dozen active supporters of the Solidarity Party were working at its headquarters in Gdansk, the home base of President Lech Walesa. Three years earlier, the organization had been swamped with volunteers and boasted millions of active members. The movement that led to the overthrow of communism and controlled 98 percent of the seats in Poland's first democratic election in 1989 took less than 5 percent of the vote.

In the 12-member European Union, unemployment is more than 11 percent. In the East, antiestablishment feeling flows from disappointment that the arrival of democracy and capitalism did not mean the rapid arrival of prosperity. Indeed, real income has plummeted 20 percent to 30 percent in Poland and Hungary since the collapse of the Soviet Union and more than 50 percent in most of the former Soviet republics.

PREDICTIONS

Many of the world's countries will not exist in their present form in the next century. Society will continue to fragment from the solid monoliths they once were. The nation-state will look more like a fractured mosaic of "mininationals," defined by ever smaller tribal, ethnic and interest group identities.

Change in economic development, public attitudes, social expectations will be coming from the bottom up not from the nation-state down. By the next decade, Europe will operate as 60 major cities, interacting with each other rather than a Europe of states; the United Kingdom will break up; Northern Ireland will go its own way; Wales and Scotland will have their demands for separate parliaments met.

In the United States, sharper focus on Congress will continue along with increasing interest in election campaign reform. While many special-interest groups typically pursue their own narrow goals, such groups will increasingly form coalitions around major community issues of mutual interest. More minority group involvement, including immigrants in the political arena, will be a hallmark of the next decade. A growing number of seniors will also become politically more active because of their available time.

Many political issues brought about by limited revenues such as the pros and cons of reducing services or increasing user fees—will elicit no clear response from citizens. Citizens will demand more services but will also insist that taxes are not increased, making it more difficult for public officials to set program priorities and balance their budgets. Congress will likely phase out virtually all writeoffs for upper-income taxpayers by 2005. Taxpayers, while averse to new taxes, will increasingly acknowledge that it is the legitimate role of government to provide "safety net" services to the truly needy.

With federal and state financial support dwindling, the middle class fleeing prohibitive taxes and high crime and businesses leaving for cheaper quarters, strong efforts to downsize government spending will be pursued. Limited government revenues will be earmarked for public programs with the highest political payoffs. The public will continue to advocate limited growth of government; however, though government has grown even larger than the manufacturing sector in the United States, some special interests will fight further reduction of government programs and payrolls.

In the developed countries, we will see more battles with the ailing bureaucracies to create more entrepreneurial, responsive governments. Business concepts such as total quality management, workforce reengineering and competition will transform how big government works. Solving the megaproblems that will be caused by urban woes will require strong, sometimes totalitarian government. Witness Hong Kong and Singapore, where decisive policy making has contained what might have been an urban nightmare. Observe the flipside, Thailand, where successive governments' mishandling of key transport projects in the capital has jammed traffic, heightened bankers' fears of political risk, and threatened the much needed tide of dollars into the country's infrastructure.

TREND

EXTERNAL MENACE, INTERNAL EXPLOSIONS

Dramatic change is a key global megatheme.

Practically all countries of the world, developed or undeveloped, see themselves involved in some combination of external and internal tumult. It is a rare country that finds itself totally unoccupied with internal problems and facing no external concerns whatsoever. The external menace may be economic trade incursions or population encroachments or directly military.

Internal explosions may vary from masses of hungry people to angry labor unions to right wing organizations looking to seize power. They may come from religious zealots seeking to change the culture, wrongly convinced that a jihad or holy war is an expression of the will of Allah.

IMPLICATIONS

The world is in the midst of a constant wave of discontinuities. For example, the sleeping giant, China, is not following its past pattern of behavior nor are countries like Russia, which is restructuring its economy.

This external-internal balance is a prime driver in world politics today. Governments of various countries and even such international bodies as the United Nations and the International Monetary Fund (IMF) find themselves at times approaching rigor mortis because of their inability to resolve numerous conflicting interests.

Historically, this conflict is nothing particularly new. In every era, countries find themselves in this situation. The point is that looking through the research, it's hard to come up with a period when all the powers, major and minor, were in so similar a situation. Further, because of the changes in transport and communications, the strains and interest struggles are easily exportable on a worldwide basis.

Over the next 20 years, it's the countries that best resolve this dilemma that are going to end up as centers of political strength. Those who fail may, in the extreme, seek the most violent political solution of all—looping the internal explosion back to the external menace and war.

PREDICTIONS

Willis Harman believes the tensions between the North (economically developed world) and the South (economically developing world) will increase as the South grows wary of providing raw materials and markets for the North. The awakening of the Third World is going to increase radicalization. As radicalization increases, we're going to have to be a lot more concerned with terrorism than before. A general war is not probable, but a very good chance exists for several regional ones.

TREND

SMALL WARS

Contributor: Tom Mandel, futurist, SRI International

Tom Mandel, a futurist colleague who is still at SRI International, believes, like Willis Harman, that limited war will be an unwanted "peace dividend" of the ending of the cold war.

The idea that the age of revolution or conflict is over is not true; there are serious factors that could lead to wars around the globe: We have left the stable, bipolar two great power world that we lived in up to a few years ago, and we're still unwinding from nineteenth- and twentieth-century colonialism, where maps were drawn by European powers. Also, there is no sign that the Third World is going to become prosperous, though there will be large pockets of prosperity. Population pressures will produce large numbers of unemployed young men, making it harder to resist the temptation to go to war.

IMPLICATIONS

As arms suppliers, the United States and the Soviet Union often encouraged conflict, but their huge military presence sometimes prevented wars. As the superpowers cut their arsenals, their restraining influence may be lost. Individual countries may feel more impelled to provide for their own security needs by whatever means necessary.

The military power of some Third World nations is already impressive: By manpower, China has the second largest armed forces, India the fourth largest.

Ironically, the reduction in tension between military superpowers has led to fragmentation and ethnic rivalries in Eastern Europe, Africa and Asia. We will witness more conflict as countries try to balance the two countertrends—globalization and maintaining cultural identity.

The biggest challenge to a global Asia is security. The gradual withdrawal of U.S. military presence is inevitable. After the U.S. withdrawal from Vietnam in 1975, the United States had 157,000 troops in Asia now it just has 93,000. If the United States packs up, all the ancient suspicions and animosities between Japan and China, Japan and Korea, and Korea and China will shift the focus from positive economic gains to defense and security, which is a zero-sum game. Signals from Beijing are mixed, and there is concern throughout the region about China's role and intentions as a military power. Though China has reportedly cut defense spending from 10.5 percent of GDP in 1979 to 3.5 percent last year, the official military budget does not even include sums spent on weapons procurement or research and development. Yet however misleading the official figure is, it leaped 98 percent between 1988 and 1993 to $7.5 billion.

In reality, China has been using its economic boom to finance a far reaching military buildup. China has used the money to bolster its ability to project power beyond its borders, buying fighter jets, missiles and an aircraft carrier.

Arms sales to the Middle East are reaching the saturation point, and sales will slow considerably. Western European nations, particularly the United Kingdom and France, continue to maintain a significant share. However, the United States has become the dominant supplier to the region, selling $25 billion of equipment to Saudi Arabia alone following Desert Storm.

PREDICTIONS

Businesses will have to be very careful when cutting deals in the unstable Third World countries. The tendency will be to avoid long-term deals and to invest where you can get your money out sooner.

The Middle East and Africa will remain unstable. Iran will continue to use its oil money to export global trouble and terror, and the Palestinians will choose violence rather than try to make an economic go of it.

Southeast Asia will be relatively stabilized, and the threat from China diminished due to its preoccupation with economic development. However, the most likely site for a war is the South China Sea, which China claims as its own 1,000-mile pond. Parts of the area are also claimed by Vietnam, Malaysia, Brunei, Taiwan and the Philippines. China and Vietnam fought naval battles in the area in 1974 and 1988. The danger of renewed conflict may be growing because some experts believe that extensive oil and natural gas deposits exist in the area. China last year awarded exploration rights to an American oil company in an area that Vietnam insists is part of its continental shelf.

TREND

COMMUNICATION REVOLUTION OVERTHROWS THE REPUBLIC FORM OF GOVERNMENT (WILD CARD)

Contributor—Dr. Anthony J. Finizza, chief economist, ARCO

Again, Tony Finizza expands our thinking by demonstrating that technology and politics make strange bedfellows that can give birth to dramatic changes.

We started the representative form of government in the eighteenth century. Because of the length of time required for communication, no true democracy was possible—it took three months to tally the votes for president in the first election—the first census took three years. But now, with the speed of data and communication, C-Span will be the next form of government, not Congress.

IMPLICATION

There will be on-line instantaneous voting as well as on-line political discussions that will change the political framework. Congress will no longer be able to debate thorny issues privately. We gave them that power because we didn't think lawmaking was something that everyone should be engaged in.

This increased democratization has negatives as well as positives. For example: Would we all get to vote to go to war immediately without hearing the whole news? Furthermore, democratization may not allow for sober judgments about regulations; and it may make it more difficult for business to get its view across, while small groups, who are very adept at technological communications, have a larger say. Increased democratization takes the elite out of lawmaking, and we get this new populism. But if bad economic conditions lead to very radical political solutions, a tyrant could usurp power even quicker than in the past.

PREDICTIONS

A congressperson will not represent a district but will be the gofer for the district. If there is an issue I'm interested in, I will let my congressperson know how I feel about it instantaneously through the new technology. The representative will become an order taker who tallies constituents' responses—if 8,000 people say go to war and 6,000 say no, the representative will vote for war even though the individual's morality at one point might have dictated "let me think about this" or "let me filibuster."

The modern structural corporation may actually weaken. Business has never been politically adept, quick or active; therefore, it will be left out of this democratized system. There's no way I'll come home and make a call to my congressperson on behalf of my company, but I'll do it for myself. We will see our political system moving toward consensus building and electronic voting.

Enhanced interactive communications will make some government agencies unnecessary, and they will go out of business.

This trend is more likely to happen at the local level as "federal governments" delegate more responsibilities to the local level.

TREND

INTERNET—THE TECHNO-POLITICAL WEAPON OF CHOICE

Contributor—Patricia Singer, international management consultant

Patricia Singer, a Stanford MBA who has been closely watching the evolution of the "net," sees it bringing the fragmented world together.

The Internet (net) will change the way people think and, therefore, behave.

All over the world, people will use computers and phone lines to communicate with each other through the net. Net talk is already the center of discussions among the technically literate globally—dozens of net books are displayed on bookstore tables, and everyone wants to get on the net—or says they do. Indeed, the net is growing rapidly in the United States and around the world.

IMPLICATIONS

On the Internet you can say anything because it's assumed that people have large band-widths not limited or controlled by government rules—it's up to the people to decide what they want to respond to by installing their own magnets and filters. There is no hierarchy among net users. Exchanges allow people with disparate backgrounds and lives to talk to each other on a close basis about personal, professional, political or other shared interests. Communication on the net is based on common interests and the depth of ideas, not age, gender, status, wealth or some other bit of irrelevancy.

The Internet is ultimately democratic, which is a big threat to political organizations worldwide. No political organization wants pure democracy. They are afraid of runaway citizenry, what they call anarchy—anything that does not obey their hierarchical rules. The "net" effect will mean more grassroots activity.

The Internet is currently a hobbyists' system that will allow "knowledge navigators" who communicate through the cold dispassionate light of the terminal to see the issues encapsulated in proposed bills and laws—no longer distracted by flowery speeches, arm waving and the rest of the show.

PREDICTIONS

As lawyer-politicians develop ever more complex bills and laws written in small print, text extraction programs will allow net users to find issues of particular interest. States have made money publishing laws and bills in machine-readable form on behalf of corporations and research firms. By 1997, legal codes in states like California will be on-line to casual users who can call with their own search algorithms, extract and find out what is going on for little or no cost. As governments continually feel threatened by the Internet, they will try to control and censor it in the next decade. But the genie is out of the bottle, and the Internet will prove virtually impossible to regulate.

TREND

Capitalism and Western Democracy Is Not for Everyone

The countries of the world are shifting their focus and searching for economic and political systems to help them survive the dramatic changes the next century will bring.

The "do your own thing" nature of capitalism and our preoccupation with short-range profit has encouraged the free-market countries to avoid long-term considerations, not just about economics, but also about society as a whole. "Free-market" solutions are failing to solve the problems of the former Soviet Bloc countries because the social costs are too great and similar, but less overt dissatisfaction is a trend even in the developed countries.

IMPLICATIONS

Despite the rhetoric, there are many social costs associated with the Reaganomic type of capitalism of the 1980s. Expect that the wholly uninhibited and self-sufficing capitalist entrepreneur as well as the sacrament of central planning are, in the words of John Kenneth Galbraith, "destined for that famed dustbin of historical obsolescence."

There are competing models of capitalism: Japanese capitalism, which is a very strong partnership between very large corporations and government bureaucracies (Keiretsu); the Singapore model, where a small powerful group controls the industrial direction as if the country was a single corporation; and the Chinese model, which makes use of large, extended families and the military to promote business. All these approaches are opposed to the mythical American "free-market" model that says government should keep its hands off the private sector.

Indeed, today's American "free market" now provides tens of billions of dollars in annual protectionist support to agriculture and the steel and automotive industries. In my own state of California, prime stomping ground of the free-market entrepreneur, our giant agriculture industry meets under government sponsorship to control the sale of their major produce through market boards.

There will be a lot of disagreement about what type of mixed systems (central-planned versus free markets) to design or approach, particularly in Central and Eastern Europe. Russia, of course, could not go back to what it was before but could become an autocratic country with more of a demand economy. I don't think there's any going back to a socialist economy.

Asia could be in a position to offer the West and Eastern Europe an example of how to marry economic change to social stability and to reconcile individual freedom with order. The problem with Western democracy is that it is an inefficient vehicle for delivering the services that ordinary people want from government. The inherent need of democracy for equity has become an instrument for helping strong lobbies and minority interests pick the taxpayer's pockets.

A mixed economy is often good for business because the economy provides stability, allows businesses to deal directly with government and with fewer people and avoids competition in an open marketplace. Moreover, business does better in a stable political environment, where the players are clear.

PREDICTIONS

Singapore may be a model for the future. The state is involved in planning and in directing the economy, and it is a peaceful and stable society. Americans might not find Singapore a place they want to live in with its strict autocratic rules, but it's a model that could work well in large parts of the world.

Expect continued economic problems in Mexico, Russia and other parts of the former Soviet Union. Moreover, the Chinese economic growth rate is quite disruptive, and because the government doesn't want to lose control, expect some counterreaction to the free-market reforms.

AN AFTERWORD

•

I returned, and saw under the sun, that the race is not to the swift, nor the battle to the strong, neither yet bread to the wise, nor riches to men of understanding, nor yet favor to men of skill; but time and chance happeneth to them all.

ECCLESIASTES

•

The world doesn't lend itself to summaries; thus, this book is without one. The hundreds of pages in this volume are merely a nosh of what the 2000s are likely to serve. My goal has been to coherently weave together the trends that the successful person and organization should be aware of, with less emphasis on particular businesses or industries.

Obviously, no company or individual will be affected by all the trends, but I'm confident that these 100 driving trends will forge the shape of the future. The need to change the cultural climate to prepare for the future is urgent. Global business success will more likely happen to those who earn it, not to those who fall into it. Muddling through will constitute an invitation to sink in the puddle. Do-it-yourself won't be just a hobby, it will be a way of life for international business.

The time to act is now! Future generations depend on us as individuals and groups to correctly perceive and react to the threats and opportunities our scan of the future presents. Solving complex global problems will require a sprinting start if we're to make some real headway as we pass through the shadow of the new millineum and hopefully into the light.

My sincerest wish is that the future in sight is bright for all who inhabit the earth.

Cheers!

ABOUT THE AUTHOR

Barry Minkin is a futurist, author, and professional speaker. In his 25 years of experience as a global management consultant, including ten years with Stanford Research Institute (now SRI International), he has consulted with scores of Fortune 500 and small-growth companies across most industry sectors as well as government and various trade associations. His insights into the company-specific factors that determine success in the real world have allowed him to accurately develop market forecasts and strategies for his clients.

As his global reputation for accurate forecasting grew, Barry was asked to publish his forecasts in the *Corporate Times* in Silicon Valley. His regular monthly column, "Future In Sight," contained dozens of specific predictions. He has received numerous awards, including the American Society for Training and Development Achievement Award and a Presidential Citation for Innovative Employment Strategies.

For additional services—contact Minkin Affiliates, 115 Alvarado Road, Berkeley CA 94705. Fax (510)644-0101.

INDEX